SOPHOCLES PAPAS

SOPHOCLES PAPAS

THE GUITAR, HIS LIFE

ELISABETH PAPAS SMITH

COLUMBIA MUSIC COMPANY   CHAPEL HILL

OTHER BOOKS

Cartas e Crônicas by Elisabeth P. Smith and Philip H. Smith, Jr.

Library of Congress Cataloging-in-Publication Data
Smith, Elisabeth Papas, 1928-
    Sophocles Papas: the guitar, his life / Elisabeth Papas Smith.
        p. cm.
    Includes bibliographic references (p. 249) and index.
    ISBN 0-9658954-0-8
    1. Papas, Sophocles, 1893-1986. 2. Guitar teachers—United
    States-Biography. I. Title.
ML423.P19S65 1998
787.87'092—dc21
[B]

98-72195
CIP
MN

To my father

SOPHOCLES PAPAS

1893–1986

CONTENTS

A section of photographs follows page *115.*

PERMISSIONS

Courtesy Yale University Collection of Musical Instruments, 15 Hillhouse Avenue, Yale Station, New Haven, Connecticut 06520; for permission to photograph the Papas collection.

Courtesy Gregory d'Alessio, author of *Old Troubadour: Carl Sandburg with his Guitar Friends*, New York, Walker & Co., 1987; for permission to quote from his book.

Courtesy Carl Sandburg Collection, University of Illinois Library, Urbana-Champaign, Illinois 61801; for permission to quote from letters in the collection.

Courtesy Rosenbaum & Colin on behalf of the Carl Sandburg Family Trust, 575 Madison Avenue, New York, New York 10022; for permission to quote the poem "The Guitar" by Carl Sandburg.

Permission to quote from Penelope Niven, *Carl Sandburg: A Biography* (Charles Scribner's Sons, 1991; distributed by University of Illinois Press, 1994ff.), granted by Penelope Niven.

Courtesy Carl Sandburg Tape Recordings Collection, Tape #45, Archives of Labor and Urban Affairs, Wayne State University, Detroit, Michigan 48202; for permission to quote from one of the tapes in the collection, a tape of a party Carl Sandburg attended at the home of Sophocles Papas, 27 October 1961.

Courtesy © 1930 *The Etude Music Magazine*, Reprinted by permission of the publisher, Theodore Presser Company, Bryn Mawr, Pennsylvania 19010; for permission to quote the entire article "The Romance of the Guitar."

Permission to reprint *Mastertone* article courtesy of Gibson Musical Instruments, Nashville, Tennessee.

Every effort has been made to trace all copyright holders, but if any has been inadvertently overlooked, the author and publishers will be pleased to make the necessary arrangement at the first opportunity.

It was a typical July day in Washington—very hot and very humid— and I had been walking, first downtown and in Georgetown, then from Wisconsin Avenue to Georgetown University. The memorial program for my father was about to start in Gaston Hall, an auditorium in the Healy building. But first I needed to find someplace to wash my face and change to better shoes. Before I could do so, I found myself confronted with a horde of strangers blocking my way. I could hardly find room to climb the curving stairwell to the rest room. The queue wound up and up from the first floor. Who were all these people and what were they doing here?

"All these people" turned out to be guitarists, and they were going to my father's memorial service. I was moved to tears later when I saw how they filled Gaston Hall for the first performance of the Washington Guitar Quintet, newly formed for this occasion. Charlie Byrd, John Marlow, Jeffrey Meyerreicks, Myrna Sislen, and Larry Snitzler, together and in various combinations, put on a fine program. I spoke very briefly, to express my own feelings and on behalf of my two half-brothers, Ted and David (only Ted was able to attend), and thanked everyone for coming.

If you and I live to be 92, the chances are that almost none of our friends will be around to attend our funerals. But when my father, Sophocles Papas, died at that age on 26 February 1986, a few hundred people attended his funeral in March and several hundred people attended his memorial program in July. They recognized that he had devoted his life to promoting and teaching the classical guitar, to giving this instrument artistic prestige never before realized.

I wrote this book to tell the story of the development and fulfillment of the life of Sophocles Papas as best I can, but there are gaps: many statements have been hard to verify, and many of the clippings in his scrapbook have no date, although in general it appears to be in chronological order. I have contacted as many people as I could.

I had never thought of writing my father's biography, but at his funeral someone asked me if his life had ever been written up. I thought about it a moment, then said, "No, but I might do it." And that was the stimulus for this book.

I have always wondered how, when, where my father learned to play the fretted instruments, and I expected to find the answer during the course of doing research for this book. But except for his father's teaching, some piano lessons in Cairo, and a very few lessons with some early guitar teachers in the United States, he appears to have learned by himself in approximately three years. Exactly how he developed his love for the instrument and how he learned to play remain unknown.

When I was writing the first draft of this book and discussing it with some friends, they asked me about my childhood. I gave them some details, and they asked if I was putting this information in the book. I said that I didn't think it appropriate, but they thought it was interesting and should be part of it. They can be found in appendix G.

ACKNOWLEDGEMENTS

I wish to thank The D'Addario Foundation for the Performing Arts for their generous gift; Paul and Sachiko Berry; R. E. Bruné; Jo and Frank Carpenter; Maria Costaki; Martha K. Cox at Theodore Presser Co.; Jerry Dallman; Dorothy de Goede; Erica Eisdorfer; Gruhn Guitars; Bonnie Hedges of the Historical Society of Washington; Prof. George Hendrick of the Department of English at the University of Illinois at Urbana-Champaign; Seth Himmelhoch; Dr. John Hoffmann of the Illinois Historical Survey at the University of Illinois Library; Marcelle Jones; Leo Orso; Ron Purcell; Margaret Sandburg; Peter Segal; Chantal Shafroth; Billy Stewart; Jack Smith; the Yale University Collection of Musical Instruments; librarians at the University of North Carolina, College of William and Mary, University of Southern California, Sonoma State University, Philadelphia Free Library, Library of Congress, Historical Society of Washington (in the old Christian Heurich Mansion), Matthew Gilmore, Washingtoniana Division of Martin Luther King Library, the Arthur Friedheim Library of the Peabody Institute, George Mason University Special Collections (which houses the Sophocles Papas Archives), the Walter P. Reuther Library at Wayne State University, and the New York Public Libraries, especially at the Lincoln Center for the Performing Arts. In addition I want to thank all those who contributed by telling me their recollections, by writing to me, by translating and deciphering Greek handwriting and an article in Japanese, and by helping me with translations from French and Spanish. A special thank you to my daughter Thea who has carefully edited the manuscript and shown me what we now call the "Thea computer search"; I hope this technological advance has kept me from repeating myself too often. And of course this book would not have been possible without the support, both technical and personal, of my husband, Philip H. Smith, Jr.

Because my father taught in Washington, D.C., for nearly sixty years, I asked *Washington Post Bookworld* to publish a letter in which I asked for recollections, photographs, or other memorabilia. The letter appeared on 12 January 1992, and I received about twenty replies. Some of them were of what I call the dipsydoodle variety—they told more about the writer than about my father. (Two were from incarcerated convicts evidently looking for female pen pals.) One letter led me to the Walter Reuther Collection at Wayne State University which has a copy of a cassette tape on which Daddy played the guitar at a party he gave for Carl Sandburg. Otherwise the letters were not very helpful.

1: BEGINNINGS

Sophocles Papas was born in 1893[1] in Sopiki, his mother's birthplace, in an area of Greece which was then under Turkish rule but became part of Albania in 1913. Although the date of birth was 18 December, because that part of the world was still using the Old Style or Julian calendar, the recorded date is 6 December.[2] Sopiki was a village with a population of about 1,000 Greeks whose social life revolved primarily around two large churches, presumably Greek Orthodox. Although under Turkish rule, the Greeks remained Greeks: they did not learn Turkish, and they kept their own customs, schools, and community.

Sophocles' family came originally from the village of Vouliarates, which had a population of about 1,500. The family name was Botis, but his grandfather changed the last name of his two sons Thomas (Sophocles' father) and Michael to Papadopoulos because they were children of a priest: in Greek 'papa' means 'priest, teacher.'

My father told me that his village was so small that in the morning those people who owned sheep let them out to follow the village shepherd, who took them to graze. In the evening as he walked back through the village, the sheep returned to their proper owners. Daddy once said that his earliest memory was of eating quinces on New Year's Day in 1897; he also remembered eating ripe figs fresh from the tree.

Sophocles' mother, Konstantina Harispapa, was not musical and probably had no education. His father Thomas, however, was well read and had a degree from the Zografia Teachers College in the village of Kestorati in Northern Epirus. He was a chanter at one of the local churches as well as a teacher of voice in the public school. He played the violin, although not very well, and had studied Byzantine music. These musical activities exposed my father to classical music. An article in the *Washington Star* of 5 June 1927 reports that Sophocles "learned the elements of music and theory from his father, a well-known musician of Greece." In my father's own words, his father, as chanter and violinist, was the most important musical influence on him until he met Segovia. In addition to music, my father studied French, and his language proficiency was to prove highly important in his life.

Sophocles had three brothers, Telemachos,[3] Miltiades,[4] and Christophoros,[5] and two sisters, Demetroula and Anastasia.[6] My cousins in Ioannina told me in 1991 that Christophoros died of tuberculosis in Athens in 1933, and that Telemachos went to Egypt when he was a young man, worked in a bakery, lost his job, and disappeared. Demetroula, Anastasia, and Miltiades lived in Ioannina until their deaths in the 1980s.[7]

Papas lived in Sopiki until he was 12 or 13, when his father sent him to Cairo. There he lived with an uncle, went to school for about five years, worked in a bakery, and took piano lessons. When he heard the mandolin in Cairo, he began to study the instrument with a Mr. Mancini, and he also took up the guitar. Sophocles Papas's lifetime interest in the fretted instruments had begun.

In addition to Arabic, people in Cairo spoke French, Italian, and Greek. Papas had an interest in languages, so while in Cairo he began to study Italian and Arabic and continued his study of French. In 1907 he began to study English from a Berlitz book. Later my father said that his study of French and Italian had helped him to learn English, in part because, unlike Greek, they use the same alphabet as English. Although by this time Egypt was a British protectorate, Sophocles did not have much contact with English speakers. But he was good at learning languages and eventually had, in addition to his native Greek, fluent and idiomatic if heavily accented English, good French, some degrees of proficiency in Italian and Arabic, and a good understanding of Spanish. He was always interested in etymology; some of my earliest memories are of talking with him about etymologies while riding in his black Ford. (He owned black Fords all through the late 20s, 30s, and 40s until he bought a dark green 1950 Olds 88 four-door sedan.) A letter from one of his admirers mentions "the manuscript of an etymological quarterly he [Papas] planned to publish"; however, no evidence of this proposed publication remains.

Although during the time he was in Cairo there were a few guitarists in Egypt, most of them were playing in groups with mandolin players. At that time the guitar was nearly inaudible as a solo instrument because the strings were plucked with the flesh of the finger but not backed up by the fingernail. The pick was introduced about this time, and is still used today by some folk and rock guitarists and lutenists.

In 1912 Sophocles returned to Greece with the idea of going to the United States. But the Balkan Wars began between the Greeks and Turks. Populated by many Greeks, Epirus was Turkish territory, and in 1912 the conquered people overthrew their conquerors and returned the area to Greek rule. For a time Papas fought as an Albanian guerilla against the Turks, but after the Greeks invaded the Albanian territory, he joined the Greek army and fought for nine months in some of the Graeco-Turkish wars. A bullet from one of these battles left a small scar on his right cheek. As a child he had used a gun for hunting. During his time in the army he worked with guns and gained more experience, which would later play an important role in his life. When my father was 77 he told me his memories of the time when the Greeks liberated their town and looted the bodies of the Turks; he still felt ashamed of his role in this.

Probably in 1914, before World War I broke out, my father came to America to study agriculture. The vineyards in his region of Greece were blighted with phylloxera, a plant disease that dries up grapes and makes them useless. His plan was to go to Massachusetts Agricultural College[8] and then to return to Greece.

However, his arrival in America, presumably by ship, did not coincide with the beginning of the school year, so he went to visit Greek friends from Sopiki who were living in Clinton, Massachusetts, near Worcester. At that time an immigrant had to have a sponsor to remain in the United States; his friends offered to sponsor him. Sophocles' idea was to work in the daytime and go to school at night.[9]

When Sophocles went for his first job interview at a gun factory in Worcester, he dressed in the manner he thought appropriate for a job interview and wore collar and tie. The employer asked him if he had any work experience, he said no, and he didn't get a job. His friends advised him to go again without collar and tie, so the second time he went wearing workclothes. This time when they asked if he had any experience, he said yes. His small experience working with guns in the Greek army served him well now, and he was hired to test-fire Harrington and Richardson pistols. He was always good with his hands and became quite skilled at such work as taking a gun apart and putting it back together in record time.

At the outbreak of World I, his love and enthusiasm for his adopted country caused him to alter his plans and try to enlist. At this time there was a general manpower registration in the United States, whether one was a citizen or not. Sophocles wanted to join the navy to travel and see the world, but when he went to Worcester to enlist, the navy asked him his occupation. In an interview with the *Washington Post* of Thursday, 7 September 1972, he recalled, "I had worked in a gun factory, so I thought maybe I was a gunsmith. The man told me the army needed gunsmiths and asked me if I would join the army. I said yes. Of course, they found out quickly I wasn't a gunsmith."

The army learned that he knew French and made plans to send him to France as an interpreter. He was inducted on 1 June 1918 and sent to Camp Hancock in Augusta, Georgia, where he had to fill out a number of forms, which included questions about his languages. They tested his French by having him converse in French with an officer. He passed the test, and he was told he would go to France, but there were endless delays. Eventually he found out that, because his father had left teaching and taken a government post in Greece, and because Greek King Constantine was the brother-in-law of the Kaiser, the army now had to investigate his father for security reasons. So Sophocles signed up for the Ordnance. He was sent to school where he became quite skilled as an aircraft machine-gun specialist. He was to be sent to Dayton, Ohio, to synchronize aircraft guns, but just then the army organized its air corps, which rejected anyone trained in the army; so he was sent to Metuchen, New Jersey, where he worked on French 75s, motorcycles, autos, and other vehicles in a mobile repair unit. His group was ready to be shipped to the war zone, but the Armistice was signed and all the plans collapsed. They were told that they could stay in the service or leave; Sophocles chose to leave.

Up to this time he was still using his full name, Sophocles Papadopoulos. In accordance with Greek custom, he had no middle name. Eventually he took "T" for Thomas[10] for the sake of convention. Later on he shortened his name to Papas "for obvious reasons," as he always said. But in fact during World War I it was not only convenient to Americanize one's name, it was considered "morally better."[11] A copy of "Sophocles T. Papas's Enlistment Record" reports a grade of Private; no horsemanship, no battles, engagements, or skirmishes; no wounds; excellent character; and "Service honest and faithful, no AWOL, no absence under [illegible GQ number]; entitled to travel allowance of two-cent fare from Metuchen, N.J., to Worcester, Mass. Approved for Victory Medal."

Sophocles T. Papas became a United States citizen on 24 July 1918 at Augusta, Georgia, while residing at Camp Hancock, Georgia. He received an honorable discharge from the United States Army on 30 June 1919, at Raritan Arsenal, New Jersey, "by reason of convenience of the Government" (no doubt because of the Armistice), and he was awarded one bronze victory button. In addition, he was "paid in full" the sum of $20 and given the fare from Metuchen to Worcester.

During his time in the service Papas had continued to improve his English. He also played the mandolin and guitar. As he saw how much pleasure people found by listening to him, he began to contemplate music as a career. After the war he became totally absorbed by music, gave up the idea of studying agriculture or etymology, and began his life's work in music.

Between 1919 and 1920 Sophocles visited friends and Greek connections and travelled in Connecticut and Massachusetts. He went to Washington in 1920 because his Greek friends in Massachusetts had Greek friends there. In these early days in Washington Papas met George Vournas, a Greek law student, who was already clerking for a law firm, and Pete (a Greek nickname for Panagiotis) Constantinople, who in 1923 was an intern at the Washington Asylum and Jail at 19th and C Streets, S.E.[12] Although they occasionally lost touch, the three were to remain friends for the rest of their lives. In 1925 or 1926, Sophocles and his friends Constantinople and Vournas[13] caught up with one another again and roomed together in an apartment building called Le Marquis at 2308 Ashmead Place, N.W.[14] Constantinople later became an ear-nose-throat specialist.[15]

Daddy had a polyglot friend named Arson Kendros whom he had met on a trip to New York City. His plan was to visit him in New York and then go to see an uncle[16] in Richmond, Virginia. He never made it to Richmond. Instead, he and Kendros took an apartment together in Washington and formed a musical duo. At first they both played mandolins, but one day Kendros suggested that Sophocles get a guitar: "Two mandolins are not as interesting as a guitar and mandolin. So get a guitar, and we can make a better ensemble."[17] When Kendros left Washington, Sophocles met two other mandolinists, Tony Delvecchio and Pasquale Romano, both of whom were barbers. They formed a trio, Papas again playing the guitar. All three members of this popular trio could read music, which was unusual in those days. They played mostly polkas, waltzes, and Italian songs, music arranged for this combination and published in New York. The trio usually played for fun, not for money—"for Italian parties, Greek parties, weddings...One night we wanted to serenade a girl—Athenian style or Roman style—and we were chased by the police. It's a good thing we escaped—otherwise we'd have had a record! You can do that [kind of thing] in Europe but not in Washington."[18] Soon the banjo, which remained very popular into the late 30s, was added to these ensembles of mandolins and guitars.

Papas was 25 years old, rather old to begin serious study of the guitar. He studied from the Carcassi method book published by Theodore Presser. After about three years of music study, he felt ready to play and teach the fretted instruments. Although he had some instruction, it appears that my father was for the most part self-taught. But then, Segovia himself was self-taught. "I don't know why I waited so long," he once said, "I liked words and languages, so I thought I was going to work in etymology."

For all his popularity, Sophocles was not yet able to rely on music for his livelihood. Boyd's *District of Columbia Directory* gives this cryptic report for 1923: "Pappas, Sophacles [*sic*] [occupation] waiter r[oom] 1125 Fairmont nw."[19] [20]

One of Papas's first guitars was a gut-strung Martin 045, made by the C.F. Martin Company. He was attracted to the sound of this kind of instrument, and also to the fact that one could play classical music on it rather than wire-and-pick music. In his early days of teaching he wrote the Martin Company to ask to sell guitars directly, to become a dealer, but Martin said no. However, he had bought a Martin mandolin, one of the best available, which had sat unsold for years in a music store, and was able to convince Martin that he should be licensed to sell Martin guitars even without a proper shop.

During this time Walter Holt had a studio at 18th Street and Columbia Road, N.W., where he taught fretted instruments. He played on a wire-strung guitar with his fingers, not a pick, which was unusual. He was a good musician and conductor and wrote good arrangements of symphonic works such as Beethoven's Fifth Symphony, Schubert's Symphony No. 8 in B Minor ("Unfinished"), and Von Suppé overtures for his banjo-mandolin-guitar orchestras. Papas sometimes played in one of Holt's groups and made himself useful as a good sightreader who could play mandolin, guitar, mandola, and mandocello. Papas later said that it really was Walter Holt who inspired him to open a music studio.

Papas was used to this kind of group of fretted instruments, known in Greece as a "mandolinata," and popular in Greece in the late nineteenth and early twentieth centuries. The Museum of Greek Popular Musical Instruments in Athens has a number of pictures of such groups, which include guitars and all the variants of the mandolin.

Papas recalled the kind of reception guitarists were given in the 20s: "When I first arrived in Washington in the early twenties I discovered that there were no classical guitarists. As a matter of fact, people considered the guitar an instrument for accompanying the voice. When I said I played the guitar people said, 'Oh, you sing!' A local mandolin teacher [Holt] had a mandolin and guitar orchestra, but his guitarists had wire strings on their instruments. Most people were used to hearing the Nick Lucas 'Tiptoe through the Tulips' style of guitar playing and knew nothing about the gut-strung classical guitar.[21] When people heard the gut-strung guitar, they were eager for more, but still, for many people the guitar was considered "just for gypsies and caballeros.[22]

"One day I was looking at guitars in Droops music store (later Campbells and now defunct) at 13th and G Streets, N.W., and a young man heard me play. He said, 'My father [Robert Lawrence] has a radio program. Would you like to play for that program?' I said yes, and I did. The audience response was overwhelming. People had never heard a gut-string guitar before and couldn't figure out how I was able to get such 'fine tone.'"[23]

Papas's first radio performance on WJSV[24] received so much response that he was asked to play before an audience at Central High School. In general the sound of the classical guitar was immediately popular: previously people had heard only wire strings, not gut. After that, various other radio stations asked him to play. Many were new stations that did not have regular programming; live performances were just what they were looking for. Papas became known on the radio as a performer. It was at WJSV that Arthur Godfrey met Papas and heard him play, and he became a lifetime friend and fan.[25]

Soon Papas came to the attention of the then-secretary of the Greek Legation, Christos Diamantopoulos, and the military attaché of the Spanish Embassy, Major Vitoriano Casajus, probably through one of Papas's students. Both these men were interested in culture and music, and Casajus had heard his compatriot Andrés Segovia play. Such connections would be extremely valuable in attracting students and spreading knowledge of and interest in this "new" instrument.

The Sophocles Papas scrapbook begins with a newspaper clipping, dated 3 June 1922, in which he is thanked for playing in a minstrel show on 18 April. People wanted to hear all kinds of music on the classical and Hawaiian guitars. Such pieces as "Mother Machree" and "Song of India" were always special requests.

His interest in teaching began to increase. In 1922 he began to teach actively and opened a studio near Droop's music store, above a Greek restaurant at the intersection of 15th and G Streets near New York Avenue. Because he was so close to Droop's they sent him many pupils. Pupils also came to him after hearing his radio performances. Many were from the Greek community, as well as from the diplomatic corps.

During the early 20s Sophocles taught banjo, ukulele, mandolin, Hawaiian guitar, and classical guitar. The classical guitar—with gut strings—was already his favorite, so he gradually began to devote more and more time to it. He continued to learn by teaching himself, as he had in the past. For a very brief period he did study with William Foden,[26] but it bothered him that Foden watched the clock when he was giving a lesson and in general had "a negative personality." Later Papas said that Foden was a technically brilliant guitarist but not a good musician: "He made good transcriptions but of trashy music." Sophocles quickly became bored with Foden's transcriptions and long, boring variations of tunes like "Old Black Joe" and "Listen to the Mockingbird." He quit after three lessons.

Sophocles found a kindred spirit, however, in George C. Krick,[27] one of Foden's pupils. Krick was willing to share his extensive guitar music library (now held at St. Louis University). Papas welcomed this wealth of guitar music previously unknown to him. Krick, a German émigré, put Sophocles in touch with German publishers of guitar music, like Schott and Zimmermann, as well as Spanish publishers. At last Papas had access to a large source of guitar music, including the works of Sor and Giuliani. All of this music was new to him and his pupils.

However, Sophocles found that there was still a shortage of guitar music for use in teaching, so he formed his own company and began to publish under the name Columbia Music Company, Inc. He chose the name "Columbia" because he was located in the District of Columbia. Most of his early publications were his own arrangements of music for study. According to guitarist Carlos Barbosa-Lima, "He began with the easier things, for his students; he also published for banjo and other instruments. Soon he began to publish from the traditional guitar literature, and then, from his experience of teaching, the technical exercises such as the Segovia scales and slurs and chromatic octaves."[28]

During this time the American guitarist Vahdah Olcott-Bickford₁, who had made hundreds of transcriptions for the instrument, toured the United States. Sophocles apparently did not meet her in the early days.[29] Her *Olcott-Bickford Guitar Method* was published in 1921 by Ditson. However, Papas later commented that, with a few notable exceptions, her arrangements were not very musical; they were awkward and showed a lack of training in music theory, an interesting observation because he had not studied theory.[30]

Between 1922 and 1924 Papas began to teach at Robinson's. The 1925 directory listed him thus: "Papas, Sophocles T. music tchr, Robinson Music Store, Inc., 1306–08 G St nw; r[esidence] 1822 Vernon nw."[31] The Vernon Street address was an apartment building called The Colonnade. Robinson's business was thriving and could afford to publish large advertisements.[32]

A clipping in the Papas scrapbook tells of his association with Robinson's, "where his knowledge of different languages will be of value to many people of the city who do not speak English fluently." The article goes on to credit Papas with finding "some interesting music for the fretted instruments, from Germany," including a string quintet (for string quartet and guitar) by Boccherini, as well as "transcriptions for guitar by eminent European guitarists," notably works of Bach and of Schubert, Beethoven sonatas and overtures, and some of the Chopin piano preludes.

By now Papas had become widely known locally as a talented solo guitarist and an enthusiastic leader of group work with fretted instruments. He and his students were much in demand as performers and were received enthusiastically everywhere. The guitar was becoming known and appreciated as an instrument fully capable of holding its own.

About 1925 Papas opened his own studio at 1417 G St., N.W. He was already well known on the radio, and attracting students, but he needed more room for his various ensembles.

His repertoire at this time consisted of pieces such as:[33]

"Peruvian Air";[34]
"Fingal's Cave" by Mertz
"Pastorale" by Mozart
"Berceuse"[35] and "Valse Fantaisie," his own compositions
"Valse des Amoureux"
Pavana by Milan
Minuetto by Sor
Preludio and Danza by Tárrega
"Canción"
Sonatina by Giuliani, Op. 71, No. 3
Caprice, Op. 20, No. 9, by Legnani
"Marmotte" by Blum"
"Serenata española" by Malats
"Romanza" by Albert[36]
Prelude, Op. 28, No. 20 by Chopin (C Minor, which he played in A
    Minor)
"Song without Words" [composer illegible, probably Mendelssohn]
"The Maiden's Wish" by Chopin.
"Let Me Call You Sweetheart"
"By the Waters of Minnetonka"

Of the Chopin prelude Papas said, "I played the C-Minor Prelude of Chopin...To use Segovia's comment, you can play a major work on the guitar—you take the essence. You don't have to play all those massive chords...You have one or two. I don't believe there is a five-string chord in the arrangement that I play. You have three or two notes sometimes, but the essence is there."[37]

At this point Papas realized he loved teaching and was at heart a teacher more than a virtuoso, so he began gradually to devote more and more time to teaching. "Papas liked people," Carlos Barbosa-Lima says, "and liked teaching; from the beginning he knew he was not a composer or performer, but he was good enough to play on the radio, and he played accessible pieces to his own possibility. He was good socially, in relating to people, and this was a great gift because in this way he introduced the guitar to certain areas, to people not before exposed to it; it [took] someone like him with this natural gift of relating to people."[38]

In February 1926 he was teaching at the National Park Seminary,[39] a prestigious girls' school that had decided even at this early date to include guitar, banjo, and mandolin in its curriculum. He still had private pupils, as well as many instrumental groups playing in the area, such as his Columbia Tenor Banjo Club, Columbia Hawaiian Guitar and Ukulele Club, and the Sophocles Papas Banjo Band. Papas's group called Guitar and Mandolin Orchestra had 40 members ranging in age from 10 to 60. He was still giving solo mandolin performances and playing guitar solos such as the Legnani Caprice, Op. 20, No. 9, the Chopin C-Minor Prelude, "Danse des Naiades" by Ferrer, "Song without Words," and his own compositions. A letter dated 1 March 1926 from the Pan American Union thanks him for a concert of "Saturday evening last. We have had most enthusiastic comments thereon." In fact, as soloist or director of one of his groups he had given more than 50 radio concerts in addition to making many public appearances.[40]

During 1926 and 1927 Papas taught at the exclusive Hendley-Kaspar School of Musical Art at 1858 Kalorama Road and 1924 Mintwood Place. A brochure from the school says that he studied with George Bournis of Yannina,[41] Greece, and with Professor Mancini of Cairo, Egypt, and that he completed his fretted-instrument education with William Foden of New York. He was listed as a teacher of mandolin, guitar, tenor banjo, banjo, Hawaiian guitar, and ukulele. Apparently the school wanted some kind of credentials.[42]

During this time, Sophocles Papas met the woman who would become his first wife—and my mother. Although I do not know for certain, I believe my father met Eveline Monico Hurcum at the National Park Seminary, where she was a piano teacher. Her maiden name was Hurcum, but she had taken Monico, her Italian-Swiss grandfather's last name, as her stage name for her brief career as a pianist in Britain. A picture of Papas appears on the cover of the June 1927 issue of *Frets*, and a thick gold wedding band shows clearly on his left hand. An undated newspaper picture of her states, "Radio Debut: Eveline Monico Papas, Pianiste who has played in concert and as symphony soloist in Europe, will make her debut in America to radio audiences from WMAL this evening at 8 o'clock." Papas called her "a gifted pianist with a huge repertoire and a fine sightreader and teacher...a very intelligent woman. I always discussed things with her, and she helped me a great deal. She was one of my best teachers, really, musically. She did all my typing and, as you know, my English isn't bad, but hers was much better."[43] In addition to being a good pianist, she loved to teach, and helped my father to meet other musicians and penetrate higher musical circles, probably at least in part because of her posh English accent!

Born in Cardiff, Wales,[44] Eveline went to London to study and received the diploma Licentiate, Royal Academy of Music, in December 1913. Her performing career in England was brief when she had a serious memory lapse during a performance and became ill. The doctors advised a sea voyage so she went by boat to America to visit her elder sister Jo. She never returned to Britain. I can remember hearing her play. She had a fine technique and a large repertoire and played very expressively.

The Papas scrapbook contains the program from a concert and dance given by the Columbia Banjo, Mandolin and Guitar Clubs under the direction of Sophocles T. Papas at the Play House, 1814 N Street, N.W., on Tuesday, 17 May 1927, "at eight o'clock P.M. Admission 75 Cents." A newspaper picture is captioned "Fair guitarists and ukulele specialists of the Columbia Guitar and Ukulele Club follow the lead of Sophocles Papas, who stands behind them in the picture, and tinkle teasing tunes into the WMAL mike every week or so." Another picture shows a very young Sophocles Papas wearing black tie.

In those days the newspaper listed all the radio programs from sign-on to sign-off, and one WMAL program lists: "7 p.m.—Tenor banjo duets played by Sophocles T. Papas and Raymond Donohue."[45] And later that same evening, "10 p.m.—Musical program by the Columbia Hawaiian Guitar and Ukulele Club, directed by Sophocles Papas. Assisting artists will be Ella Hennig, in ukulele solos, and Sophocles Papas in mandolin solos."

Papas was already considered an authority on the fretted instruments. For instance, Frederic J. Haskin,[46] Director of The Haskin Letter, Haskin Books, and the Haskin Information Service, sent him a question from a correspondent: "In playing a tenor banjo in four-four time are quarter notes to be tremoloed or down strokes. How are the notes in duo and trio style of playing formed?"[47]

Papas was also constantly forming and reforming groups and was always busy writing out the arrangements and parts for them. He would write out the original manuscript with a special kind of purple pencil. Later, when I was only a young child, he instructed me to press the original, face down, in a tray of something like firm gelatin. The ink would be partly transferred to the gelatin and then a few copies could be made by pressing blank paper down in the tray, a sort of Ditto precursor.

The Washington Music Teachers Association once asked him to play the guitar after their annual dinner, which he and and my mother were attending. He played. Through enthusiastic applause the audience requested two encores. The second was the Chopin C-Minor Prelude. At the end there was absolute silence followed by a collective gasp and a burst of applause. No one had ever before heard such a sound, especially not coming from an instrument thought to be the sole property of hillbillies! The guitar was growing in popularity at a steady rate, from an oddity to a household word. Someone said, "The guitar has some personal appeal and it is versatile."[48]

Eveline probably also helped him by editing the articles he wrote for periodicals. She had worked as secretary to Billy Mitchell (the pilot who tried to make the United States recognize the value of air power)[49] and was an excellent typist, fast and accurate. She was member of the Friday Morning Music Club,[50] and both she and Sophocles performed there and at the local Young Women's Christian Association. Sophocles first performed there on 23 March 1928. He met many singers through my mother and found that he could read and play a piano accompaniment on the guitar if it was not too complicated, or he would borrow the music for a week or so and write out a guitar arrangement. To hear classical songs accompanied by the Spanish guitar was a novelty.

For a short time in 1927 Papas's studio was at 1416 Pennsylvania Avenue, N.W., and his letterhead read, "Teacher of mandolin, guitar, banjo, tenor banjo, Hawaiian guitar, and ukulele." By May 1927 Papas made a felicitous move of his studio, about which a news item says:

> New Papas club studio: A new 'up town' studio is that of Sophocles Papas, in the Emile Building, 1221 Connecticut Ave., where this teacher of mandolin, guitar, tenor banjo, Hawaiian guitar, and ukulele is located. Mr. Papas has found it expedient to move into this private school center, the better to conduct both his classes and his club rehearsals. These rehearsals now consist of a banjo club, a mandolin and guitar club and a Hawaiian guitar club. He is now organizing something in the way of a new departure, in a Spanish guitar club, the instrument on which Mr. Papas is best known to radio audiences and which is his special solo instrument.[51]

And an ad in a program of 17 May 1927 gives the 1221 Connecticut address, and the Franklin 600 phone number.

Papas said of his early teaching days that when pupils first came they generally had guitars with wire strings, which they played with picks. He would ask them if they knew how to play anything. If they said no, he would teach them a bit of the rudiments of music and have them play a little, just on the first string, without a pick. "If they [the students] had a flat back guitar, I would file the grooves for gut strings. But I would start them on some exercises on my guitar. Play the open strings, whole note, half notes, and, while teaching them, I would restring their guitar and tighten it."

At times he would engage in a useful subterfuge: "I would take up my guitar and play. They would ask 'Is that what you're going to teach me?' 'Is that what you want?' 'Yes.' 'Well now, let me explain to you, these are gut strings. They are softer and lend themselves better to classical music...' 'Well, can I have them on mine?' Or sometimes I would lend them a guitar because I knew if they couldn't tune their guitar, there was no use in sending them home with a guitar with six new strings."[52] Sometimes a new student might buy or rent a guitar. But they usually wanted to continue to play with gut strings, or they wanted to study Hawaiian guitar, banjo, or mandolin. When they heard Papas play classical music on a gut-strung guitar, about eight out of ten were enchanted and converted. So the progression was: wire strings + pick, wire strings + fingers, gut strings + fingers, and, after World War II, nylon strings + fingers.

He often he began by teaching a new student the two chords (tonic and dominant) with which you can accompany many songs. But he told the student that, if he learned to read music, he would be able to do much more. "I would say, 'Here, I'll show you, [then I would] put my method on the music stand, and most were hooked.'"

Thus did Sophocles convert the sons and daughters of Emile's clients to the subtler ways of the classical guitar. The lessons included an education in the proper new equipment.

A 1926 news clipping says, "Sophocles Papas has re-opened his studio for fretted instruments at 1221 Connecticut Avenue, N.W. Cupid seems to have played the banjo effectively, for during the summer Evelyn [sic] Monico Hurcum, pianist, became Mrs. Papas and will also carry on her work at the studio this winter. She studied at the Matthais School of Piano[53] in London,

England. She is a member of the music faculty at the National Park Seminary of this city. At Sophocles Papas's School of Music at 1221 Connecticut she will teach piano, violin, harmony, counterpoint, and composition."[54]

Another clipping from the same era has a photograph of my mother under the heading "Pianist in Recital" with the caption, "Eveline Monico Papas who will be featured in the studio program given tonight at 9 o'clock in the studio she and her husband Sophocles Papas share at 1221 Connecticut Avenue, northwest." And another clip about her performance in a program of the Friday Morning Music Club at Barker Hall at the YWCA says that "she is a graduate of the Royal Academy of Music of London and one of the few exponents of the Mattay Method in this country. She is former member of the music faculty of the National Park Seminary." My parents gave many musicales and often had such distinguished guests as Army Major Carl Spaatz, later to become a general.

The *Frets* June 1927[55] article featured Papas on the cover and discussed his work in great detail. It reported that Sophocles had by this time given many radio concerts in addition to public performances. Eveline, a fine pianist and musician, probably helped him to decide to dedicate his life to teaching rather than performing.

Papas's brochure from about this date gives his prices for lessons: 10 1/2–hour lessons: $15, i.e., by the term. The brochure also states, "The Columbia guitar, mandolin and banjo clubs which are a special feature of the Sophocles Papas studios are for the benefit and pleasure of those students sufficiently advanced for orchestral work." Also included are some comments, apparently from admirers or students, although they are not signed: "I have difficulty in trying to convince my friends that there is only *one* guitar being played, when you play." "You have the most *wonderful gift*—your music *speaks*." "I cancelled an engagement when I found you were to be on the program." "This is the first time I have heard anything of the kind."

A one-cent postcard announcement from the studio, with the phone Decatur 737, says that the Papas Banjo Band will play on local radio station WMAL, and adds, "Mr. Papas will also play Spanish and Hawaiian guitar solos. This is the first of a series of radio recitals to be given by students of Papas's School of Band, Guitar, Mandolin, Hawaiian Guitar, and Ukulele."

A slightly later brochure, giving the phone as Decatur 0737—Washington was growing—advertises the Sophocles Papas School of Music, and the

brochure is copyrighted by the Columbia Music Company, Inc. The brochure appeals to people to study music:

> There is no better or more pleasurable way to relax your mind than
> with music—music that you make yourself. The simplest melody played
> by yourself gives you a hundred times more pleasure than the most
> beautiful and elaborate composition played by someone else. Too busy to
> learn? No time? Then here is the solution—the *fretted* instruments—
> mandolin, guitar, banjo, Hawaiian guitar and ukulele. Because of the con-
> struction of these instruments and the manner of playing them you can
> become proficient in a short time, and because of this and their friendly,
> intimate character they have become the companions of every American
> home—in winter the instrument of the hearth, in summer, the
> instrument of the heart.

Papas became devoted to Emile Beauvais, a hairdresser and the owner of
the Emile Building at 1221 Connecticut Avenue, N.W., and dedicated a piece
to him, "Calling for You."[56] Emile was in fact still at 1221 Connecticut well
into the 50s,[57] and the building was still there in 1994, although one would
hardly recognize it: the street-level windows were covered with signs saying
"We Buy Gold" or "CLOSED," and some of the decorative plaster facade had
fallen from this formerly elegant four-story building.[58] Coincidentally, it is
directly across the street from the site of the present Guitar Shop, which
Stephen Spellman bought from Papas in late 1967.[59]

Because Papas had two rooms in the back of the top floor of 1221 Connecticut, he put a picture of himself in the downstairs entrance with the
words "Teacher of mandolin and guitar." Emile's was the most exclusive
beauty salon in town, so many wealthy women came to him, including
Consuelo Vanderbilt Morgan Thaw, the older sister of Gloria Vanderbilt,
who ultimately became godmother to Sophocles' son David. One diplomat's
wife wanted her daughter to study the classical guitar with Papas because she
had heard the instrument played in Europe. Women like these saw the sign
and heard the music in the stairwell, and many went up to find out about lessons for themselves or their children.

The years 1926 to 1928 had been eventful for Sophocles Papas: he married,
he had a child, he met Segovia, and he began to write articles for fretted-
instrument periodicals, such as *Crescendo*, *Etude*, and *Frets*, probably aided by

his wife.[60] *Crescendo* was the official organ of the American Guild of Banjoists, Mandolinists, and Guitarists. It was published monthly in Boston and was "devoted to students of mandolin, guitar, and banjo."[61]

From 1917 to 1927 William Foden edited a regular *Crescendo* column entitled "Guitar and Steel Round Table," to which people sent technical questions.[62] Sophocles Papas took over this column from March 1929 until June 1930, succeeding Vahdah Olcott-Bickford. Soon after Papas took over the column, the following appeared in the "Letters from Our Subscribers" section. The writer had ordered a copy of Columbia Music Company's recent publication *The Favorite Collection of Hawaiian Guitar Solos*, enclosed one dollar in payment, and added, "I am most happy to have a musician like you [Papas] on the Guitar Round Table for now I know the steel guitar will receive the just treatment it deserves. The bigotry and prejudice of the late incumbent almost passed belief. Moreover I have heard her play; and her knowledge of her guitar far exceeded her artistry! *Crescendo* is indeed fortunate to have a musician of your caliber on the staff." Another letter commented that "Mr. Papas's reply to the 'Knowall' about the 'Mexican Paganini' was a masterpiece. How well he drew the line between the artist and the artisan."[63]

The *Crescendo* issue of December 1924, vol. 17, no. 6, featured Vahdah Olcott-Bickford and her guitar orchestra, organized in September 1923 as the Los Angeles Guitar Society, which eventually became the American Guitar Society. At this time Bickford played with her right-hand little finger resting or braced on the guitar top. George Krick and William Foden did not do this but all three played with fingers but no nails. The magazine advertised the method of Foden, published by William J. Smith & Co., Inc. Foden had been hailed in the United States as a guitar virtuoso, gave many recitals, and wrote many compositions for the instrument. In this same issue Krick wrote about his three-month-long guitar trip in Europe, where he heard Pujol, Llobet, and Segovia. It is said that Llobet played at the Library of Congress some time after 1928 but did not play very well, in part because he had an arm injury. However, he, along with Fortea and Pujol, was considered *the* guitarist before Segovia.

Subscribers to *Crescendo* wrote to ask about tuning, picking, strings (steel, gut, or silk), picks, availability of music, and about Segovia, who had just made his debut. Papas answered the technical questions in great detail, and also quoted Segovia on such matters as the need to damp unwanted strings (to avoid harmonic clashes).

In a 1929 column, for example, Papas offered this advice:

> Silk and gut are the only strings which should be used for solo work...with gut strings a truly musical tone and volume can be obtained with a little effort and practice. In stringing a guitar with gut strings care should be taken to have the bridge and the nut adjusted for the purpose, and a good quality string should be used. For the guitarist who has been using wire strings it takes a little time for him to become adjusted to gut, especially the first couple of days while the strings are stretching. We strongly advise all guitarists to use silk and gut strings if they wish to impress the public with the fact that they are playing an instrument capable of great beauty of tone and nuance.

Crescendo also presented reviews of guitar performances. The April 1928 issue contained George Krick's review of the Schubert quartet performance in which Papas played the guitar part:

SHUBERT [sic] QUARTET—FIRST TIME IN AMERICA
by George C. Krick

The Schubert Centennial Festival, in the form of Three Aprés-Midi Intimes, dedicated to three German Composers, was given by the Elena de Sayn String Quartet and assisting artists, beginning March 12 in Washington, D.C. The first of these series, which concerns us most, included a quartet by Franz Schubert, composed for flute, guitar, viola and 'cello. The guitar part was played by Sophocles T. Papas prominent in the advancement of guitar music in America, and renowned for his teaching ability and musical activities in Washington.

The Schubert Quartet was written in Vienna in 1811, when Schubert was eighteen years of age, and proves that he was not only a fine guitarist, but used, in this composition, all the resources of the instrument. Next to the flute, the guitar has the most important part, and this should undoubtedly help to bring the guitar to the notice of those that still think it is limited as a means of musical expression.

At first, this quartet was evidently written as a trio, as the manuscript showed the word, "Terzett" at the top, which was crossed out, and later changed to "Quartette," by adding the 'cello. The quartet consists of five parts, Moderato, Menuetto, Lento e Patetico, Zingara and Tema con Variazioni.

It is beautifully melodious, and withal, most extremely difficult to execute...and now it is played for the first time in America with Sophocles T. Papas as guitarist.

A Papas performance is also mentioned in the July 1928 *Crescendo*, accompanied by a picture of a very young and slender Sophocles Papas: "The second artist to appear on the evening's program was Mr. Sophocles T. Papas, of considerable prominence in guitar circles. He chose as his selections Sonatina, Op. 71, No. 3 by Giuliani, 'Pastorale' by Mozart and one of his own compositions 'Valse Fantaisie.' Under the fingers of Mr. Papas the guitar ceased to be an 'instrument,' and became as its player willed the voice of a grave and noble loveliness. His virtuosity was companioned by the sensitiveness of his musicianship."

Papas's reputation as a teacher and performer was spreading rapidly. He continued to perform and in early 1928 even played again in a minstrel show, this time with three other guitarists, including his lifetime friend Dr. Peter S. Constantinople, at Ye Jouste of Le Bal Boheme at the prestigious Willard Hotel.[64] He was by this time a popular figure in Washington, both as a teacher and as a performer. And his marriage to a pianist had enhanced his reputation. He was extremely busy, and he had given sixty concerts over the radio in three years—this in addition to teaching and publishing and giving other performances.[65] Many of Papas's performances in the 20s and 30s included a variety of instruments and ensembles, such as a guitar solo, a mandolin solo, then a group of songs for voice and guitar, a few pieces played by a mandolin-and-guitar group, and often only a single movement of a large work.

Papas began to receive recognition for awakening Washington to the potential of the guitar, part of a larger cultural awakening in the nation's capital. There was even a move on to introduce the fretted instruments into the public-school curriculum, but this never happened.

In the summer of 1928 Papas and his wife were "rejoicing over the birth of a daughter. Mrs. P declares that the baby is going to be a pianist and live up to the reputation of her famous mother. However, Mr. P says while that may be right, nowadays she spends most of her time 'fretting.'" His first child, the only one from this marriage, Elisabeth Constantina Papas, must have been a fussy baby.

By the end of 1929 the Depression was beginning, although previously Washington had been considered more or less depression proof. Papas was lucky: he had about 25 pupils, most of whom were wealthy and were able to continue to take lessons during the these lean times. There was some decline in the number of pupils but not in the amount of interest in the instruments. Still, the economic situation made times tough for all, even a successful young guitar teacher and his pianist wife. Papas recalled that in the early 30s he wanted to buy an upholstered chair, but the price was $15 and he couldn't imagine ever having that amount. Also he was able to give Eveline only fifty cents to a dollar a day for food.[66] My own recollection of my youngest years includes the relatively sumptuous treat of lamb patties that came wrapped in a strip of bacon.

However, the music-teaching business in Washington came to a temporary although abrupt halt when in March 1933 President Roosevelt announced a 15–percent salary cut for all government employees.[67] Although this had more of a psychological than real economic effect on people, many of Papas's pupils panicked and stopped taking lessons, and he was no longer making a living. Emile Beauvais, his landlord, let him stay on in the studio even though he was unable to pay the rent, saying, "No one else is going to be able to pay the rent either." When the panic subsided, his wealthy pupils returned, followed by more students. During this time Papas was even able to buy my mother a 1926 Knabe grand piano, style B, from Kitt's music store on G Street. When Papas fell behind in the payments on the instrument, he talked to Mr. Kitt, who said that they would not know what to do with it if they reclaimed it. Thus Sophocles was able to keep it, and he paid a bit as often as he could.[68] In this same way Papas paid off the printing bill for his first Columbia Music Company publications: *American Fantasy, A Medley for Tenor Banjo Solo* (1928), *Compositions and Arrangements for the Guitar* (1929), *Twelve Graded Solos for Tenor Banjo* (1930), and *Twelve Easy Duets for Tenor Banjo* (1930).

During this dry spell Papas gave a "musical tea" in his new studio on Connecticut Avenue, at which he brought together a number of distinguished members of the Washington diplomatic corps and many of the city's music lovers. Among them was Alice Eversman (1890–1974), *Washington Star* music critic from 1932 to 1953 and that rare thing, a critic much loved because her reviews held no venom.[69] [70] When she received an honorary Doctor of Music degree at the commencement ceremonies of the Washington College of Music, then at 1741 K Street, N.W., she spoke on "The meaning of music in the present world upheaval."[71]

The *Star* writeup of Miss Eversman's retirement luncheon held on 11 February 1954 states that "Miss Elena de Sayn, who was Miss Eversman's associate[72] and on the *Star* staff for 17 years, also was honored." Miss de Sayn had been Miss Eversman's "personal representative," and a violinist herself as well. De Sayn had her own string quartet and had joined forces to perform with Papas several times. On 14 April 1927 Papas played the guitar part of the Boccherini Quintet No. 3 with de Sayn's string quartet. For this program Sophocles wrote a short waltz for guitar, which he described as "an innocent composition,"[73] and made an arrangement for guitar and string quartet of one of Mendelssohn's "Songs without Words." A reviewer said, "The guitar dominated...it was very well received."

One of three concerts given in honor of the Schubert Centennial (1928) was the premiere performance of the quartet for flute, guitar, violin, and cello, given on 12 March 1928. The flute part was played on the violin by Elena de Sayn, the guitar by Papas. A review comments about the lento in which the theme is played first by the violin and then by the cello, and the beautifully played guitar accompaniment.[74] (It was apparently at this concert that Papas met Eversman through de Sayn.)

Miss de Sayn, the wife of a Russian who had fled because of the Revolution, was a violinist but not a very good one. She ultimately became an impresario, and Papas eventually would persuade her to bring Segovia to Washington for the first time. He said, "I had to work to persuade her, but then she managed three of his Washington concerts."

Eversman became a significant figure in Papas's musical life, and a few years later acknowledged Papas's contributions to the acceptance of the guitar as a classical instrument. She wrote of one of Papas's 1928 performances, "His overtones, his singing inner voices in his chords give to his playing a wealth of tone that made his unusual arrangement of two Chopin preludes highly interesting."[75] And later she wrote, "The guitar may return after many decades of neglect."[76] This was stimulated by Segovia's New York debut in 1928 and his return in 1933, by Sophocles Papas's teaching and guitar orchestra, and by Miss Eversman's recognition that, compared to the violin and piano, for example, it was easy to develop some proficiency on the guitar rather quickly.[77]

As for the cultural awakening Washington, D.C., was enjoying, the following unsigned letter to the "Musical Editor," *Evening Star*, appeared on 1 October 1926:

> "Musical Washington"! This expression is becoming very familiar to us, and we are feeling gratified that the development of music in this city, especially during the past three years, makes the term highly appropriate. This statement is not based on vague impressions, but on tangible facts which are, in themselves, sufficient evidence. For instance, a few years ago, there was little evidence of music being regarded as a serious art in the city. There was no proper concert hall; a symphony orchestra was still a dream unrealized; a Washington musical magazine was not in existence, and, last but not least, we had no opera!...We have good reason to believe that the further development and establishment of the art in Washington will be rapid.

The writer goes on to say that he finds "a very discouraging attitude toward local effort" but that "Rome was not built in a day." However, he wanted to see "more whole-hearted support of local effort in the world of music."

In 1927 *Crescendo* observed that "Through the untiring efforts of Mister Papas the fretted instruments are taking an active part in musical Washington and are reaching a standard of perfection hardly thought possible a few years ago."[78]

In December 1929 the magazine *School Band and Orchestra Musician* ran its regular column called "The American Fretted League, A Special Department for Fret Players." This issue contained an article about "the talkies," the new movies with sound tracks, which, it was felt, were putting musicians out of work.[79] There was in fact much criticism of talkies, and musicians even organized a boycott. But the writer had a different view: he felt that the talkies would bring good music to the American people and whet the American appetite for more good music. This tied in generally with the interest in getting

music into the public schools and specifically with the cultural renaissance
beginning in Washington, D.C.

The United States debut of Andrés Segovia in 1928 was a significant event for the whole musical world. This event would also shape the rest of the life of Sophocles Papas. The *Washington Sunday Star* of 16 October 1927 announced that Segovia was coming to give his New York debut on Sunday, 8 January 1928 in Town Hall at 123 W. 43rd Street. At the urging of Fritz Kreisler, he had been brought to the United States by a well-known impresario, Francis C. Coppicus of the Metropolitan Music Bureau.[1] Sophocles Papas was in the audience. Many other professional musicians also came to this first concert, intending to ridicule. And the critics came to scoff. But all were amazed, and astonished, and Papas later marveled that in an attempt to do Segovia justice, the critics quoted from poets like Longfellow and Shelley.[2] But the audience was amazed and humbled to see this striking figure of a man seated alone on the stage with only a footstool and his guitar.

Segovia had some reputation in Europe and South America, and his name was familiar to Papas because some of Papas's pupils were children of Latin American diplomats such as Ambassador Sevilla-Sacasa of Nicaragua, dean of the diplomatic corps. Papas also knew of Segovia's immediate predecessors, guitarists Emilio Pujol and Miguel Llobet, and through his connection with Major Vitoriano Casajus, the military attaché of the Spanish Embassy, he met Llobet when he played at the Library of Congress.[3]

Papas tells of Segovia's debut in a short article he wrote entitled "Segovia and I." Papas had been given a letter of recommendation from the military attaché of the Spanish Embassy, who was unable to attend the concert, and Papas presented the letter to Segovia when the concert ended.

> When I realized Segovia did not know English, I spoke to him in French, and he invited me to have coffee with him the next morning at his hotel. Naturally I told him that I was a guitar teacher, and that I was performing on the radio. He seemed glad to know someone who could help his career, especially someone Major Casajus had recommended.
>
> Eventually I was responsible for Segovia giving three concerts in Washington in the early 30s under the auspices of Elena de Sayn.... She was

familiar with the Russian guitar with its fandango tuning GBDGBD, similar to baroque guitar tuning. I persuaded her to bring him to play under the sponsorship of her Washington Performing Arts Society.[4] I also urged colleagues in other cities to sponsor Segovia concerts. The ones I remember off hand were given in Detroit, Niagara Falls, and Philadelphia.

We met again in Detroit and Philadelphia, thanks to my reliable old Ford, and I never missed one of his New York programs....I learned about the cultivation of right-hand fingernails, which weren't used then.[5]

At that time, Segovia played guitars made by Ramírez, the father. He later said that they were not as good as guitars are today, but they were the best available. Hermann Hauser, of Munich, made guitars with wonderful tone, and Segovia obtained one of these. Segovia also made suggestions to Hauser for the construction of instruments, and Hauser was willing to listen to Segovia and incorporate his ideas.

After the debut, Segovia invited Papas to come to New York on Saturdays as often as he could, to sit and listen while he practiced from 3 to 6 p.m. Segovia even encouraged him to interrupt to ask questions, and he called Papas "The Detective" because of his detailed observations and questions, especially about new music for the instrument. Papas asked Segovia questions such as why he omitted some of the chords at the end of the Sonata by Castelnuovo-Tedesco.[6] Segovia said he left them out because they were "not necessary, too many, too long."[7]

Papas later recalled some of the music Segovia played in his early programs. "He started with a slow Giuliani piece...he usually began with a slow number. The first time he played practically all the Bach pieces that he transcribed...about six or eight pieces...from manuscripts. He played the 'Tremolo Study' ['Recuerdos de la Alhambra' by Tárrega] and then the Torroba Sonatina. I remember as if it were the other day."[8]

After Papas had sat in on Segovia's practice time Segovia usually invited Papas to dinner, and sometimes they spent Sundays together as well. "I was in New York every Saturday that he was there—both Saturday and Sunday if he didn't have any social engagements, and he didn't have very many in the beginning. [Then] I would be with him all the time."[9] From the beginning Sophocles Papas was truly awed by Segovia. The relationship between the two was based on Papas's eagerness to learn and Segovia's ability and interest in teaching. In addition to the New York concerts, Papas went as often as he could to his performances in other cities. Segovia was a wonderful teacher, but Papas did not play for him in these early days. He was terribly impressed with Segovia's variety of tone colors and effects, and with technique, especially his use of the fingernails: he had heard a few other players using nails, but most players did not cultivate them for the guitar. Papas soon adopted this technique in his own playing.

Papas was quite aware of the privilege of friendship with Segovia. Others were not so fortunate—for example, his former teacher, George Krick. Papas had not considered Krick a warm person; on the contrary, he thought him rather aloof and haughty and felt he could have been more successful if he had taken advantage of opportunities to become known. Nor was Segovia impressed with Krick. One day my father encountered Krick while driving Segovia from the Spanish Embassy to his studio. Krick had a sister in Washington, whom he used to visit occasionally. "We were driving down Connecticut Avenue just south of Q Street, and there was Krick. We said 'Hello, hello, hello.' That's all, and we went on. He [Krick] later said, 'I thought I'd open a studio in Washington, but I changed my mind. That's why I came there [to Washington].'" Papas later surmised that, when Krick saw him together with Segovia and saw that Segovia didn't respond to him, he changed his mind. Krick went back to New York and later moved to St. Louis.[10]

When Segovia played in Philadelphia he was sponsored by the Penn Club, a prestigious social club headed by James Francis Cooke, president of Theodore Presser Company and editor of *Etude Music Magazine*. At that time Papas was teaching a Chilean woman, wife of a U.S. diplomat in the Philadelphia area, so he asked her about getting tickets. She wrote to her sister-in-law, who was the children's editor of *Etude* magazine, Elizabeth A. Gest.[11] When Gest heard that Segovia was coming to play in Philadelphia, she asked for two tickets for my father; two for the Secretary of the Greek Legation, a Mr. Lely (or Lilis); and two for herself. The *Etude* editor asked to whom to mail the tickets, and the Chilean said to send them to Sophocles Papas, 1221 Connecticut Avenue in Washington. But when they arrived, they were addressed to "Sophocles Papas, Ambassador of Greece at 1221 Connecticut." He quickly phoned Lely so that the newspapers would not state that Greek Ambassador Sophocles Papas was coming to hear Segovia!

Papas then wrote to Cooke, saying: "Since you are about to hear the guitar for the first time, I'm enclosing a short article that I wrote a few months ago for the magazine that was published by the Gibson Company then."[12] When he heard from Papas, Cooke wired back and sent Papas the notes he had taken during a pre-concert interview with Segovia, and said, "After reading your article in *Mastertone* magazine, I think you are better qualified to write this article on Segovia than I am, so here are my notes, and you go ahead, and we can publish it in two months hence."

Papas later recalled, "I thanked him [Mr. Cooke] and then—I had never written anything that extensive on the guitar before, and when I started to think about it—well I couldn't do this in two months. So I wrote back, and I told him, 'This will need quite a bit of research, and I won't be able to have it ready to be published in two months.' He said, 'All right. Take your time.' So I went and did a lot of research." The result was the much longer article "The Romance of the Guitar," in appendix E. Apparently Papas wrote a longer article than Cooke had anticipated, certainly more than just information about Segovia, but the article was a great hit.

On another occasion when Segovia was in Washington, Papas drove him back to New York, even though it had snowed heavily. The trip took nine hours. When they finally arrived in the city, Papas could not find a place to park, so Segovia went into a store and bought candy and coffee. When Papas's friends heard about the long trip, they said "How awful for you!" but he countered that it had been a privilege to talk with Segovia for nine hours, and that they had even spoken of God: "Do you believe in God?" Papas inquired. "Of course," Segovia replied, "how could one not! For example, look at the human body and how it functions."[13]

Segovia's repertoire at this time included works by Giuliani, the "Tremolo Study,"[14] the Torroba Sonatina in A Major, and almost all the Bach transcriptions including the Chaconne. Segovia believed that, even if the guitar could not play all the notes of a work such as a piano piece, one could play the essence of a work on the guitar; in this particular instance he was referring to the Chopin C-minor Prelude.[15]

Although Segovia later was known to be anti-Semitic, he was a close friend of Jascha Heifetz and played with him and other musicians. In early days he played at the Young Men's Hebrew Association in New York, where he received a standing ovation, an honor not given so automatically as nowadays.

The audience demanded, and received, the difficult Bach Chaconne as an encore.

In a letter of July 1938 Segovia mentions his "nationalist" (pro-Franco) sentiments, refers to "the noble Spanish cause," and reproaches the Mexican government for sending arms and munitions to Valencia, then headquarters of the Republican government of Spain.[16] It has been said elsewhere that Segovia detested Franco and fled from the revolution in Spain with only his guitar. In any case, in 1937 he exiled himself from Spain and lived abroad for many years. When visiting Segovia Papas met many Spanish exiles from Franco. Ultimately Segovia's concerts were picketed because he was Spanish and did not declare himself for the Leftist republic, so he went to live in Montevideo. His political loyalties remain ambiguous.

Despite or because of his loyalties, Segovia spent much of his time in the 40s as a guest of the Spanish Embassy in Washington, which always put on huge receptions in his honor. At one of these receptions during World War II Segovia was talking to a British General Lindenmann who had some connection with the Dupont company. The general knew Segovia by his European reputation. During their conversation Segovia told him he was worried because he had been using Pirastro gut strings made in Germany; because of the war his supply, especially of the first three strings, was running low, and he was afraid he would not be able to get any more.[17] The officer said he would see if Dupont could make some of nylon, but he wondered who could distribute them. Segovia suggested Albert Augustine, a New York guitarmaker.

Augustine was himself desperate for strings because he certainly could not sell guitars without strings. He had already experimented by buying some war-surplus spools of rough nylon, refining it, and making strings. At some point Dupont and Augustine got together, and the first three (top) strings were extruded from a die with different sizes of holes, cut in great lengths, and sent to Augustine, a dedicated man, who cut and packaged them himself. Mrs. Augustine personally tested the first package of nylon strings to be sure that Segovia got true ones, and he subsequently praised both Augustine's work and the strings unstintingly. At first the price was $12 for a set but it soon came down.[18]

Segovia had high regard for some of the younger guitarists such of the time as Ida Presti, Alexandre Lagoya, and Julian Bream. After listening to a Bream recording of Britten's "Nocturnal," he told Papas, "He is a great musician." At one time Bream wanted to work with Segovia on this piece, but Segovia had to leave the London area immediately by train for his next destination, Birmingham, in the north of England. Bream boarded the train with Segovia and worked on the music with him on the train, using solfège[19] but no guitar.

Segovia also had high regard for Papas. In an article for the October 1946 *Segovia Society Bulletin* in Washington he wrote, "Among the Charter members of the Segovia Society there is one name that stands out—that of Sophocles Papas, prime mover in the organization. We all deeply appreciate his continuing and selfless efforts to instill an interest and lay the ground work for a true appreciation of the guitar."

To honor Segovia the Washington Classical Guitar Society changed its name to the the Segovia Society about 1940, but would eventually drop the Segovia name at Segovia's request in the middle 50s. The reason is obscure: was it modesty or did he no longer wish to be associated with the organization? The society met regularly, and its members were aficionados, some amateur, some professional. Occasionally they would be honored with Segovia's presence at a meeting.

When Segovia was in Washington, Papas always visited him in his hotel room, and Segovia always had at least a meal at the Papas house. If there were no other guests, Segovia dressed in casual clothes, not his usual velvet vest and flowing tie. But he loved to have company, so Papas often invited people he thought Segovia would enjoy meeting. Once, in the early 50s, Papas and Mercia, Papas's second wife, gave a brunch for Segovia in their house at 29th and Military Road, and the former premier of France, Camille Chautemps, and his wife, a fine pianist, attended. When Segovia's wife was traveling with him, they both came for dinner. During one of the last visits, about 1970, the two of them ate Mercia's French chicken dinner while watching nature shows on the television set in the family room.

Papas was a good friend to Segovia even when the great guitarist was ill. He wrote in a letter on 11 April 1967, "Last Wednesday evening, Andrés was taken suddenly ill with a kidney stone during an after-the-concert supper in Baltimore. He was rushed to the hospital and was at Johns Hopkins for a day and a half. On Friday I drove him to New York....The whole trip to New York was miserable, as he was in constant pain. He must have improved on Saturday."[20] Apparently he was able to perform that day or the next.

One day Papas's secretary called him on the intercom and said, "There's a character on the phone who claims he's Andrés Segovia; do you want to talk to him?" But it really was Segovia. Later, Papas told Segovia this story, who thought it quite funny.

Once, while visiting Washington in the 70s, my husband, Philip Smith, attended a Segovia reception with my father and Mercia. When he was going through the receiving line, the wife of the Indonesian ambassador shook Phil's hand warmly and said, "It's so good to see you again." Phil thought, "You old faker: you've never seen me before in your life." Later while grazing at the enormous buffet tables, he overheard one woman say to another, "Do you know, I think she recognized me—she said, 'It's so good to see you again.'"

On another occasion when Phil was visiting my family, my father and Phil drove Segovia from his hotel to the concert hall. Phil was telling me about this, and I asked, "And did you get to carry the guitar?" Phil answered, "No, your father carried the guitar; but I got to carry the footstool!"

Segovia was a generous person and compassionate teacher; he was genuinely surprised to receive royalties for the publication of his technical works. His scales make up the most popular book the Columbia Music Company ever published; even today they are seen and used everywhere—the work of Segovia but encouraged and published by Papas. Segovia had not published any of his own music until Papas published the scales, and in 1975 Columbia Music Company was selling about 10,000 copies of the scales a year.

Papas once said, "Andrés Segovia is erudite, intelligent, polite, sensitive— a Renaissance man; he is so artistic that everything has to be beautiful for him, even women." But the admiration between the two men was mutual, so that Segovia considered Papas the teacher in the United States most thoroughly acquainted with his [Segovia's] school and his technique.[21]

In 1984 Allan Kozinn, longtime *New York Times* music critic, wrote that in 1930 Segovia was considered "a brilliant interpreter on an instrument not worth cultivating" and said that it had been difficult to book guitarists until the 1950s.[22] However, even before then the classical guitar had been gaining its advocates. The *Etude* issue of September 1939 included an article "The Guitar and Modern Music" by George C. Krick, in which he said: "Some people advocate using the plectrum guitar for popular music, but the advantage of the classical guitar is its versatility: one can play simple melodies, accompany the voice, or take part in chamber music." G. Jean Aubrey, the French critic, said after a Segovia recital that the [classical] guitar can be "sonorous but not noisy...people can listen to it for a longer time than to almost any other instrument played alone. It is an instrument of the present, which succeeds in preserving the sonority belonging to ancient works, without, however, erecting a barrier of several centuries between the listener and the music."[23]

Sol Hurok[24] had become Segovia's New York manager in 1943, but he still had many cancellations in his early days.[25] In fact, Papas had to work hard to convince Washington impresario Patrick Hayes to sponsor Segovia. When Hayes agreed to have him play, he had the choice of paying him a flat fee of $500 or giving Segovia what was left after expenses. Hayes chose the latter. Papas took a large quantity of tickets to sell for Segovia's first Washington concert, and apparently Hayes was nervous about collecting his money, because he came to Papas the very morning after the concert to collect. But Papas (or, more likely, Mercia) had kept his records meticulously and up-to-the-minute and had the ticket count and check ready. And as it turned out, for his first concert Segovia ended up receiving $1,200, close to the average man's annual income. Later in life Hayes told this as a joke on himself; he had been surprised to find that Washington had a large guitar audience and began to book other guitarists annually.[26]

Under Hayes's auspices, Segovia first played at Lisner Auditorium in 1956, and he continued to play there annually through 1968. He played at Constitution Hall in 1969 and 1970, and then moved to the Kennedy Center from 1972 until his last Washington concert in 1986.[27]

The guitar made *Newsweek* a few times between 1935 and 1986. A guitarist new on the scene, Julio Martínez Oyanguren, disagreed with Segovia's Bach interpretation and was in 1935 about to play in the U.S. for the first time.[28] Segovia's reputation for being upset by anyone making any kind of noise during his concerts was noted in "Music: Not for Coughers": Segovia stopped playing in a Town Hall concert because a man coughed, but not for a man who fainted quietly.[29] And a 1959 article again emphasized the audience's rapt quiet during an Andrés Segovia concert. It also mentioned that he was self-taught, and that previously the guitar had been "associated with wine, women, and very low places."[30]

An article in *Time* of 2 October 1950 announced that Segovia was beginning his 41st year of concertizing at age 57.[31] "The guitar is no longer just for gypsies and caballeros. And Segovia says of himself, "The teacher is satisfied with his pupil!"

An article "The Guitar in All Its Glory" stated that "The guitar has only recently come to be taken seriously as a concert instrument. In 1948 American avant-garde composer Milton Babbitt wanted to include a guitar in a piece he was working on. 'It was a very simple part,...but I couldn't find a guitarist who could read music or follow a conductor.' He had to rewrite the part for harp." The writer said that much new music was being written for the guitar, and that nails were no longer a problem with the use of Krazy Glue and slices of Ping-Pong balls. It also mentions the relationship between John Williams and Segovia: in 1958 Segovia dubbed Williams "a prince of the guitar." Later they fell apart a bit, said Williams, "because Segovia didn't approve of crossover; all part of guitarists moving out of Segovia's shadow."[32]

At a guitar competition in Buffalo, New York, in October 1993, Jim Smith[33] asked me for recollections of Segovia, especially his visits to the house. Jim also showed a video of Segovia playing on the Ed Sullivan television show some time in 1954. First Sullivan woodenly introduced Segovia as "the great American artist." Then the piece ended with three chords, but the audience began to clap during the first chord, so Segovia didn't even play the other two: he just waved his hand in disgust.

Although the standards for guitar performance have changed in many ways, Segovia was the first to bring the instrument to the world stage, and he influenced guitarists and musicians all over the world. He was praised yet again in 1983 when Donal Henahan wrote of his aristocratic austerity. "He continues to convey an air of being from another, more chivalric time. So far, he has not turned up on Bowling for Dollars or Family Feud. He has indeed published memoirs, but they are not even faintly scandalous."[34] Segovia was a classical musician and refused to deviate from the world of classical music. This is no doubt why he and John Williams had a falling out.

Segovia also had a falling out with Carlos Barbosa-Lima[35]: Segovia accused the younger guitarist of plagiarizing some Scarlatti transcriptions. I understand that often a guitarist can almost play Scarlatti's music directly from the keyboard score. Also, Segovia himself states that Barbosa-Lima changed some of the keys and fingering. Although the great man wrote with venom, in the same letter he sent affectionate greetings to Sophocles and Mercia. Segovia died on 3 June 1987 and on 4 June was buried in the chapel of the Academia de Bellas Artes de San Fernando in Madrid. In June 1981, he was made the Marqués de Salobreña by His Majesty Juan Carlos I.

Although no one can doubt Segovia's influence on the development of the classical guitar, he went on performing until very late in his life. His musical memory was not what it had been, and he made sudden shifts from one piece to another. However, I think the audience would have been happy to sit quietly and listen to him play scales and arpeggios. Papas had been a lucky man to meet and know Segovia, and he was to incorporate and teach the classical guitar in the style of Segovia.

Papas was in 1928 a busy teacher, performer, conductor, and writer, as well as husband and father. For example, on 15 May 1928, only three days after I was born, his large fretted-instrument orchestra gave a performance. The program lists all the players: 15 mandolins, 4 guitars, 7 Hawaiian guitars, 4 ukuleles, 20 tenor banjos, 4 banjo mandolins, 2 mandolas, and 2 tenor guitars. On Monday, 25 March 1929, a similar group[1] performed during an Evening of Russian Music for the benefit of St. Alexander's Russian Orthodox Church, given at the Wardman Park Theatre, presumably part of the then Wardman Park Hotel at the intersection of Connecticut Avenue and Calvert Street. Papas also played some of his solo repertoire, including "Légende" by A. Nemerowsky.

On Sunday, 7 April 1929, he played at the Congressional Country Club. The program included the Giuliani Sonatina, Legnani Caprice, Blum "Marmotte," Papas's own "Berceuse," and Malats's "Serenata."[2] He was also active in the Men's City Club program, which sometimes broadcast on WMAL. A news clipping from 1930 gives a picture and writeup of the Sophocles Papas Mandolin Orchestra. "This group is under the direction of Sophocles Papas, the distinguished guitarist and former guitar editor of *Crescendo* magazine....Papas's various orchestras are always conspicuous in the major social events in Washington, and this particular group participated in the Festival of Nations last year and also took part in the Bal Bohème of February, sponsored by the Arts Club of the Willard Hotel."

During the early 30s the Sophocles Papas Hawaiian Orchestra, which must have included some Hawaiian guitars and probably ukuleles, played in costume with a hula dancer for the benefit of Opportunity House.[3] His Hawaiian Ensemble played for the District Federation of Music Clubs banquet. He played guitar solos for a number of diplomats who were putting on musicales. His various mandolin and guitar groups performed at the YWCA, then a center of all kinds of activities, and he accompanied several local singers.

Meanwhile the Depression was taking its toll, and Papas found another way to earn money, by doing translations. A friend of Eveline's who worked at the Veterans Administration told her that they needed a Greek translator, presumably for those Greeks who, like my father, had come to America. The VA did not have enough work to hire a full-time person, so they gave out work on contract, and Sophocles got the contract. He became the official VA translator of Greek and worked on documents about pensions, about Greeks killed or disabled, and on marriage, birth, and death certificates. He always wrote out the translations by hand on lined yellow legal pads; in fact, I was an adult before I stopped calling this "translation paper." He must have done this work for many years because I can remember him sitting at the dining table on Sundays in the apartment at 2000 N Street, N.W. writing out translations; I would have preferred to do something like go to the zoo.

During the early 30s, Sophocles Papas met Eddie Gilmore, a newspaperman. Gilmore, born in Selma, Alabama, in 1907, came to Washington in 1931 and in 1935 became a reporter in the Washington bureau of Associated Press but was soon assigned to London. Ultimately he became Moscow correspondent and won a Pulitzer Prize in 1947 for distinguished telegraphic reporting on international affairs.[4] Eddie later wrote an article about Sophocles Papas's research on the guitar at the Library of Congress, presumably for "The Romance of the Guitar" article, and about Papas's excitement at finding guitar-related references to Noah, David, the god Apollo, and even Chaucer. In retrospect these references were no doubt fanciful, but their appeal to *Etude* readers at the time was undeniable. No one then knew much about the classical guitar.

Eddie, a guitar lover, wrote, "Incidentally, Washington's two leading guitarists live on the same street, Macomb.[5] They are Professor Papas and former Treasury Secretary Woodin. Some day, someone may look that up at the Library of Congress." It is not known whether Papas knew William H. Woodin. Although Eddie lived in London, he and Papas continued to see each other whenever he came to Washington and to correspond until Gilmore's death at age 60 in 1967.[6]

Papas continued to be busy performing through the 1930s. Several newspaper clippings tell of tickets available for the fifth annual concert given by the Columbia Mandolin, Guitar, and Banjo clubs, under the direction of Sophocles Papas, to take place at Barker Hall in the YWCA at 17th and K Sts, N.W.[7] "Among the various groups taking part will be the Columbia Mandolin Orchestra (14 members plus an accompanist), the Columbia Hawaiian

Guitar Orchestra (16 plus accompanist), Papas Spanish Guitar Ensemble (7), Papas Junior Banjo Band (14 plus accompanist), Columbia Banjo Band (14 plus accompanist), and the Royal Hawaiian Dance Quartet (4)." A review of this concert on Wednesday, 18 May 1932, read:

> The music was played with great spirit, vigorous rhythm, and a surprising degree of musicianship....The Hawaiian Guitar Ensemble played with nice tone, but their rhythm somewhat lacked swing....Mr. Papas, well known locally, needs little comment. In hearing him play, one is reminded somewhat of Andrés Segovia, especially as Mr. Papas plays many numbers from Segovia's repertoire, one of which played last night was Albéniz's 'Serenata.'[8] This was given in truly Spanish style, with splendid rhythm and tone coloring."[9]

A 23 June 1933 review of another Papas ensemble program reads: "Sophocles T. Papas has managed to strike a new note in orchestral effect in spite of the many combinations that Ted Lewis,[10] [Rudy] Vallee, et al. have given the public on stage and air. Only in Hartford, Conn., has one such orchestra preceded Mr. Papas[11] in similar combination of instruments... about 16 in the group...well worth hearing."

Papas was still giving some solo guitar performances as well as teaching. On 15 December 1933 a newspaper story announced, "Sophocles Papas, Washington guitar virtuoso, will play at the Pan American Union tonight, when folk lore and music are to be combined at a meeting of the Washington Chapter of the Instituto de las Españas."[12]

Frederic J. Haskin, publisher of a newsletter, consulted Papas when he received queries about fretted instruments. Sophocles Papas's scrapbook contains a letter from Haskin addressed to 1221 Connecticut: "We are taking the liberty of submitting to you the following questions: 'I would like to know all the information pertaining to the third finger in playing Hawaiian guitar. Is it an old method done away with? Do they use the third finger in playing number system as well as the notes? Is it the proper way to use the third finger? Can the notes played by the third finger be played by the first and second thus doing away with the third finger altogether? What difference does it make in the playing if any?'"[13]

While Papas still had his studio at 1221 Connecticut, *Mastertone* mentioned him in an article on the rapid increase in interest in the Hawaiian guitar. The

article, entitled "Don't Overlook the Hawaiian Guitar," said, "Or, if you prefer the classic, you should hear such players as Sophocles T. Papas of
Washington, D.C., who with Mrs. William Place, Jr., favored [the audience]
with several harp and Hawaiian guitar duets at the 1928 convention of the
American Guild."[14]

Papas also was involved at this time in attempts to strengthen the cultural
life of Washington, then a very quiet government town. In 1934 the National
Symphony Orchestra under the direction of Dr. Hans Kindler had begun two
series of Children's Concerts and Students' Concerts. On 13 January Dr.
Kindler presented Sophocles Papas, "internationally known authority on fretted instruments, who will demonstrate all these instruments and tell the
audience of their origin and possibilities; he also will give two guitar solos
(Chopin Prelude, Mertz Fantasy)." The review of this concert read, "The
contrasting moods of the two solos amply demonstrated his virtuosity, which
is both brilliant and artistic. His instruments, perhaps because not included
in those of the orchestra, aroused great interest and were as important to
know about as those presented at other concerts in this series."

But Papas's married life was not going well, probably because of both cultural and educational gaps between him and my mother. Also, my mother
was not well enough to take care of me, so I was sent out to Falls Church to
live with an older couple who took in children. About 1935 Sophocles and
Eveline separated, and from then on I lived the usual dismal life of the child
of separated parents, moving from boarding school to summer camp to my
godmother's to another boarding school. Before the separation my mother
had begun to give me piano lessons and, wherever I lived, I continued to have
lessons with a series of teachers. Eveline and Sophocles were finally divorced
in January 1938.

Also about 1935 Sophocles Papas moved his studio from 1221 Connecticut
to 922 17th St., N.W., above The Nosegay, a flower shop run by a delightful
man, Walter Charron.[15] He became a good family friend, and Papas always
ordered flowers from him.[16] The new studio was at the corner of 17th and K
Streets, facing Farragut Square, and I can remember going to visit my father
there after my parents' separation.

An announcement of the move to 922 17th says. "Instruction in Guitar,
Mandolin, Banjo, Tenor Banjo, Hawaiian Guitar and Ukelele. Instruments
for sale. Orchestra practice. Studio recitals. Mr. Papas is the only exponent of

Andrés Segovia's guitar method in this country (this statement is made with Mr. Segovia's approval and consent). Segovia's music and records available."

Papas continued to use his studio for parties and performances as well as teaching. During 1935 an announcement appears: "An informal preliminary reception will be given to Roy Smeck, Wizard of the Strings, appearing at the Earle Theater starting today, by Sophocles Papas on Saturday night at 10 o'clock at the 922 Seventeenth Street studio.[17] The first monthly social evening of the Columbia Mandolin and Guitar Club will be held next Wednesday evening with Roy Smeck again the guest of honor. Membership in the club is open to nonplayers as associate members; and those who are interested can secure invitations for Wednesday by calling the secretary, Mr. George Vickers, at National 6530." Although Smeck ultimately made his reputation as a banjo player, he was a very good guitarist in the early 20s and 30s.[18]

Over the years Papas and his various instrumental groups gave many benefit concerts for China (after the 1937 Japanese invasion), and one announcement says, "Mandolin and Guitar Orchestra, including modern electrically amplified Instruments, Sophocles Papas director, at Foundry Methodist Church Hall at 16th and P Streets." Papas wrote all the arrangements for his groups. "According to Papas, brass passages are usually assigned to the banjos; woodwinds to the Hawaiian guitars; violins to the mandolins; cellos to the plectrum guitars; and bass parts to the Spanish guitars. Electric amplification will be used to amplify the tone of the Hawaiian guitars." A review says: "Mandolins, mandolas and mandolin-cellos play the parts in symphonic works that usually are allotted to the string choirs; banjos replace brasses; and a small group of wind instruments (clarinets and flutes) fills out the remaining part to give a balanced yet extremely delicate and intriguing tone color."[19]

In 1937 Chart Music Publishing House of Chicago published Papas's two-volume *Favorite Collection of Hawaiian Guitar Solos*, a unique collection of popular pieces with optional second and third Hawaiian guitar parts. A Columbia Music Company ad in *Mastertone* gives the following testimony from a customer: "I tried the solo parts immediately upon receipt of your book and thought they represented the acme of perfection as regards steel guitar music, but it was after playing the numbers as trios that I fully realized just how sublime the arrangements are."[20]

During this period Papas was also busy sponsoring student performances. In 1937 various students of his played Vahdah Olcott-Bickford's March in C for tenor banjo solo, and a guitar student accompanied a singer. On another occasion, the Junior Hawaiian Ensemble, made up of Betty Papas[21] and two other girls, played "Pagan Love Song." A prominent local endocrinologist, Dr. Tomás Cajigas, also sang and played the guitar in some of Papas's groups.

Segovia was a frequent guest in the 30s, and Papas often entertained him at the Madrillon, a restaurant at 1434 New York Avenue. A local newspaper reported, "Mr. Andrés Segovia...was the guest in whose honor Mr. Sophocles Papas entertained at dinner at the Madrillon on Wednesday evening."[22] My father used to take me and, later, Mercia and me there as well. It was a great treat to go out to eat, and I liked the trio that played there—usually piano, cello, and violin—and their repertoire of semi-classical "dinner" music. The restaurant seemed elegant to me, with uniformed, formal waiters, white tablecloths and candles, and first courses such as shrimp cocktail, which I was occasionally allowed to order.[23]

Papas moved again that year to 1508 19th Street, just north of Dupont Circle, where he found combined living and teaching space. At that time his studio, although entered from 19th Street, was over Copenhaver's stationery store, a Washington landmark entered from Connecticut Avenue. A Georgetown University professor of Portuguese, Dr. Coutinho, lived on the floor below and became a close friend. Papas began to live in this studio, and I can still recall the odor of chestnuts roasting as he tried to cook in a makeshift kitchen. I don't know what financial arrangement he made with my mother, although I do recall overhearing arguments about this.

Visiting my father in his 19th Street studio was more difficult. The bus from Falls Church did not stop nearby, so the driver had to put me off the bus at 17th and K. I went to Mr. Charron, the florist and friend below the old studio, and he put me in a taxi "collect" to the new studio. I went up the three flights of stairs to get the money for the taxi driver. Once when I arrived upstairs, my father showed me a lost kitten, and I forgot all about the driver, who finally came up, very irritated, to collect his fare.

Papas remained the local expert on the fretted instruments and lectured on "Music Appreciation," as it was then called, for the Music Department of the University of Maryland in 1934 and 1935 and later at American University. His groups played for the Church of the Covenant, at 18th and N Streets,

N.W.; the Sylvan Theater; the Spanish Embassy; the Fox Theater; private parties; local high schools; the League of American Pen Women; and a number
of area churches. Many of these were benefits for Spanish refugees or China,
and one was for a church organ fund. On 1 January 1937 he played at the
YMCA's New Year's Day open house; his program included Chopin's C-
Minor Prelude, "Fantasy" by Mertz, "Listen to the Mocking Bird" by Haw-
thorne, and "Tango of Roses" arranged by Papas.

In 1936 Sophocles Papas founded the Segovia Society, later known as the
Washington Guitar Society. He named it after Segovia to honor his friend
and mentor, who thanked him for the honor.[24] The members were all aficionados—some were amateur players, some professional, but many were simply fans of guitar music and did not play the guitar. The official goal of the
society was simply to promote the classical guitar. The group had social activities, talked about the instrument, and played Segovia records at the
meetings. Sometimes the society invited a guest performer such as Spanish
cellist Gaspar Cassadò who, after a performance at the Mayflower Hotel,
came to a Segovia Society meeting, gave a speech, and played his cello. The
society, in turn, made him an honorary member.

Carl Sandburg also visited the society at least once and was made an honorary member. Sandburg's old friend Marjorie Braye once wrote him: "I love
attending the meetings [of the Washington Guitar Society]...an exceptionally
fine group of people that I like to be with."[25]

The guitar society in Washington underwent several changes of name. In
1974, for example, there were three groups in the Washington area: one with
Papas's Fairfax address, one called Dupont Circle Consertium [sic], and another on 29th Street (but not at his residence address). More than one group
in a large city was not unusual; in the same year there were also two groups in
Albuquerque and two in Dallas.[26]

Papas entertained many visiting guitarists, most of whom had come to
meet him. A Washington Post review of 24 October 1937 says, "The air was
filled with mellow notes from Roy Smeck's Hawaiian guitar and a mur-
muring of foreign languages as Sophocles Papas greeted guests at his studio
party for this celebrity of stringed instruments who is passing through Washington....Later he and Mr. Smeck had the entire audience roaring with
laughter over a skit about a chiseler coming to take guitar lessons." A January
1938 social column called "Peter Carter Says" reads, "Later [Smeck and the

other guests went] to the studio of Mr. Papas for an impromptu musical with Alvino Rey, that marvelous guitarist with Horace Heidt's Band, [and] the four King sisters...into the wee small hours of the morning."[27]

A letter of 27 November 1937 from the managing editor of the *Washington Daily News* to his counterpart at the *Star* says that "Mr. Sophocles Papas has in mind the organization of a civic string orchestra. He asks about newspaper sponsorship and publicity." The editor answered, "The News would be very glad to go along with such a venture [which] would have greater success if all newspapers [were] to give their support rather than one."

Feeling against the Japanese was very high because of the Chinese invasion in 1937, and as part of a review of a Papas program the writer noted that "Neither Mme. Saito nor the Ambassador [Saito] will attend the fireworks display Monday night that has been substituted for the cherry blossom festival." The cherry blossom festival had been cancelled.

In about 1937 Sophocles Papas met Mercia Lorentz who came to Papas's studio to take guitar lessons and later became his secretary. She is listed as "hostess" in one of his studio brochures of the time, and she was present at a China benefit concert put on by the Hawaiian Guitar Ensemble. On 16 July 1938 Papas and Lorentz were wed at the home of one of his first Greek housemates, Dr. Peter Constantinople. A newspaper article gave the following account of the wedding: "The home of Dr. P. S. Constantinople in Wesley Heights was the scene of the wedding of Miss Mercia Lorentz to Sophocles Papas on Saturday, July 16. Mrs. Luise Rey was the bride's only attendant. Dr. Constantinople was best man. The bride's ancestors were early West Virginia settlers....Pare Lorentz, maker of documentary films such as 'The River,' is her first cousin."[28] Another clipping reported, "After a wedding trip to New York and Atlantic City, Mr. and Mrs. Sophocles Papas are making their home at 2000 N Street." What the papers did not say is that Papas's daughter Elisabeth went along on the honeymoon, as did did Alvino and Luise Rey. Alvino later said, "We all went to New York where I was playing at the Biltmore Hotel with Horace Heidt. [Luise and I] had been married a short time and had a nice apartment and got the Papas's a room above us. Well, after the dance at two in the morning we all went back to the apartment and as usual I started playing and Luise came in and said to S.T. [Papas], 'You are on your honeymoon! Get out of here!'"[29]

A *Washington Star* Capital Chat article[30] reported later, "Last July he took a bride—a pretty young brunette who had come to him for guitar lessons. 'I started courting her,' says Papas, 'and she had no time to practice.'"

Before the wedding trip to New York, Papas abandoned his bachelor quarters and studio on 19th Street and rented a five-room apartment at the corner of 20th and N Streets, N.W. He called it "five rooms above a grocery store," and thought it very nice. He had arranged for it to be completely furnished during their honeymoon. "I went to what is now the big furniture store on Connecticut Avenue—Sloan's. It was Peerless Furniture then. The brother of the owner was a pupil of mine, and I knew his mother who was managing the store with her older son. I told her I was getting married, and I had this place here. 'While I'm away on my honeymoon, will you take care of it?' So I gave her carte blanche and she furnished it, drapes and all that. Very nicely."[31]

Shortly after the wedding, "Miss Anna Wolcott Archibald[32] gave a luncheon at the Hay-Adams House for Mr. and Mrs. Sophocles Papas who were married a week ago; Mr. Papas is a well-known guitarist, ranking with Segovia as one of the great exponents of fretted string instruments."[33]

The 1938 move to 20th and N Streets maintained Papas's pattern of teaching in the Dupont Circle neighborhood.[34] The apartment was in the old "railroad" style, that is, a long hall with each room opening from it. At first Papas rented only one floor for combined living and studio, but eventually the other floor became available so he rented both floors and put the family upstairs and the school downstairs. In the late 30s Papas was feeling financially secure enough to look for a summer cottage in the area. However, he was told that they did not sell to "foreign-born."

Another Capital Chat article gushes about a visit to the studio:

We had never thought the day would come when we would enjoy hearing a Bach fugue played on the guitar. Last week the day came, in a studio on N Street, where we sat beneath a big autographed picture of Anna May Wong and listened to Mr. Sophocles Papas play the guitar....Papas does not like people who spell his name with two p's. It is an old Greek name. By hard work and scholarship he has made it a name known to guitar and mandolin circles throughout America. For these are the distinctions of Mr. Sophocles Papas: (1) He was a pioneer in radio. Graham McNamee used to announce his programs over the now defunct Washington station WCAP, when men boasted of their crystal sets. (2) A personal friend of the great Spanish guitarist Andrés Segovia, he calls himself the only American guitar teacher recommended by Segovia. When Segovia comes to Washington next month Papas will entertain him. (3) He is a scholar who disputes encyclopedists. Information services run to him for data about stringed instruments. He probably knows as much about the history of the guitar as any man alive. (4) He originated and conducts the only orchestra of its kind in the world: an orchestra composed entirely of guitars, banjos, and mandolins, which are trained to sound like cellos, drums, woodwinds, brasses—in fact, like anything except guitars, banjos, and mandolins. It is a slightly surrealist orchestra in which the instruments are not quite what they seem. There are about 50 players in Papas's philharmonic, which played at the Capitol Theater for its first performance, many years before this.[35]

In 1939 Papas stayed busy performing as well as teaching. On 27 April one of his groups gave a concert at the Jewish Community Center of Washington, D.C., at "Sixteenth Street at Que." And on 10 May, at the Annual Banquet of the District of Columbia Federation of Music Clubs, the Papas Hawaiian Ensemble from the Sophocles Papas Studios played, and music critic Alice Eversman of the *Star* praised the "splendid tonal blending of the several fretted instruments." On 2 June at the Madison School Auditorium in Falls Church, Virginia, the Papas Mandolin, Guitar, and Banjo Orchestra program included "Cielito Lindo" and "March Militaire," both arranged by Walter Kaye Bauer.

This same year, Papas apparently opened a short-lived branch studio in Arlington, Virginia. The Marion Venable School of Dance program of 23 June 1939 included this advertisement: "Sophocles Papas, School of Guitar, Mandolin, Banjo, Electric Hawaiian Guitar and Ukulele, specializes in Fretted instruments; modern methods, ensemble training, instruments furnished; Studios: Washington, D.C., 200[0] N Street, N.W., MEtropolitan 1420 and Arlington, Virginia, 1116 N. Hudson Street, CHestnut 4171."[36] My father probably placed this ad in the dance program because I was one of the Birds of Enchantment in the Enchanted Forest ballet, but I could not have been very enchanting—a chubby 11-year-old dressed as a canary with strong eyeglasses perched above a yellow bird-beak. I have no recollection of his

Virginia studio, but I do recall that he tried again later in his career to open a branch studio in Virginia. That, too, was unsuccessful. I think the problem was that he could not be in two places at the same time, and he was never satisfied with the way any assistants ran the studio. He was ever the perfectionist.

Although the Virginia studio would not succeed, it probably benefited to some degree from a lengthy and flattering article in a small local newsletter on 10 June 1939:

> Mr. Papas gave an outdoor concert on the terraces of Colonial Village playgrounds at 1903 Key Blvd. Mr. P is unique in the musical world. He came to this country in 1914 from his native Greece, all primed to study agriculture in Massachusetts. Came the war and agriculture was out. Mr. P enlisted in the U.S. Army. Came the end of the war and agriculture was still out. The boys 'over there' had liked the way he strummed a guitar. They had applauded liberally. And out of this grew an idea. Maybe people would pay to hear such music. Maybe they would pay to learn to play....There were plenty of pupils....He decided to form his own orchestra and the Papas Philharmonic was born. Composed entirely of guitars, banjos and mandolins, the orchestra is trained to make them sound like cellos, drums, woodwinds and brasses....Mr. P himself is a great guitarist. A personal friend of the great Spanish guitarist, Andrés Segovia, he likes to refer to himself as the only American guitar teacher recommended by Segovia....For Wednesday night's concert, Mr. P will bring 26 of his pupils, who are members of his band.[37]

About this time Papas gave a farewell luncheon at Essex House in New York in honor of Andrés Segovia. The Spanish guitarist was sailing for South America immediately afterwards to join Señora Segovia in Montevideo, Uruguay.[38] He was due for a rest after a long tour. Papas would miss Segovia during such interludes, but he kept extremely busy as a teacher and entrepreneur as he built up his number of students and began to sell instruments, accessories, and music.

In the 30s Papas attended the Music Trades Convention in New York and gave a short illustrated talk on the guitar in the Vega exhibit rooms. He also went to "Providence, R.I., to deliver an illustrated lecture on the history of the classical guitar, its masters and its literature from ancient time to the present before the members of the American Guild of Guitarists, Mandolinists and Banjoists, whose annual convention is being held in that city from Wednesday to Sunday inclusive." He played guitar solos during the lecture, but even the members of the guild had never heard the instrument as he played it.[39]

In 1936 he gave one of his last public performances at a meeting of the guild in Minneapolis. This performance was mentioned in *Time*, which described him as "that maestro known to all Hawaiian guitarists, Sophocles Papas."[40] I wonder if my father ever knew that he had made *Time* magazine, although it's hard to believe that a student didn't tell him. However, he never mentioned it.

He usually went alone on these trips to New York, but I remember going with him sometimes.[41] It was a long drive: one went seemingly endlessly out Rhode Island Avenue, N.E.,[42] then up Route 1, past such landmarks as a huge statue of a dog, an advertisement for One Spot Flea Killer. By the time we reached Laurel, Maryland, I would be asking how long before we would get to New York. One time when I went with him to New York, we went to Segovia's hotel. My father sat in one room and asked questions while Segovia practiced; I had a Bolo Bat[43] and stood in another room batting; I counted up to over 1,000 without missing, but then my father said we had to leave to go out to dinner. We went with Segovia to a smorgasbord restaurant. Neither my father nor I had ever been to one before, and we thought the "cold board" was the whole meal. We were already full when the hot meal was brought on.

Like most music teachers, the average student was just that—average. But Papas also had some outstanding players. In 1939 my father and two of his star pupils, Ainnah Bryant and Pauline Blundon, played several times on local radio stations WMAL and WINX, and it was noted that he had been playing on the radio since 1925. Papas's repertoire at this time included a Sarabande by Robert de Visée, a Bach Prelude originally written for lute and transcribed by Andrés Segovia, a Bach Fugue, *Caprice* by Ernest Shand, Theme and Variations by Giuliani for violin and guitar, and Turina's *Fandanguillo*. He also accompanied German Lieder on the guitar.

Papas's travels often blended business with pleasure, and occasionally Mercia and I accompanied him. A social note says that "Mrs. Papas and Miss Betty Papas will spend the weekend as the guests of Mr. and Mrs. Roy Smeck of Sunnyside, Long Island." This was in 1939, and as part of that visit we attended the World's Fair that took place in 1939 and 1940.

Papas became very busy and successful during his years at 2000 N, and the guitar society flourished under his leadership.

By the 40s people were beginning to realize that the guitar was no longer just for gypsies and caballeros.[1] Gradually people found the instrument's advantages: one could learn a few chords in a few minutes, and it was portable. According to a *Time* magazine article reviewing the guitar's history in America, "it looks good on girls and dashing on boys. And best of all, it has a plaintive beauty and warm tone even when played in an elementary fashion."[2] Papas had been at least partly responsible for the wide acceptance of the instrument.

During these years Papas was busy teaching and running the Columbia School of Music as well as the Guitar Shop, where he sold many makes of guitar and all kinds of guitar accessories. The building at 2000 N had ten rooms, all for the music school and business after 1946 when he and Mercia moved to a house. Theodore Thomas was born in 1940, and in 1942 Betty left for boarding school, followed by university. Papas was so busy that he had to hire people to run the shop but usually found them unsatisfactory: he wanted someone as hardworking as himself, someone who would spend any spare time straightening up the shop and the waiting room, not trying out new guitars or lounging against the counter—in other words, people with the same attitudes as the proprietor of the business. But such people were hard to find. Nor were the other guitar teachers he hired always satisfactory.

Just before the war and even during the early part of the war, before gasoline was rationed, Mercia and Sophocles gave a number of huge parties. Sometimes they were catered, sometimes Mercia made huge pans of spaghetti with sauce, served with Chilean Riesling. One party was given in the large garden of a wealthy student who lived in Takoma Park. Uniformed caterers cooked lamb and pork chops on barbecues, and people drank Martinis from which I ate the remaining olives.

At this time Mercia and Sophocles also became close friends with Sally and Carlos Montoya,[3] who often stayed with them in Washington, and all of us stayed occasionally with the Montoyas in their New York City apartment or at their summer home in Wainscott, Long Island. I especially remember staying in Wainscott around 1943 with Mercia and Teddy, a preschooler at this time. Neither my father nor the Montoyas were there. One day we were burning rubbish, as allowed in those days, but the dry grass caught fire. Mercia panicked, and I received much praise later on for calmly connecting the hose, wetting down first the grass between the burning area and the house, and then putting out the fire.

The Montoyas also had an estate near Leesburg, Virginia, and many weekends they drove to Washington and spent the night at our house. Then on Saturday we would all drive down to Leesburg for the rest of the weekend. Papas always invited people to come on Friday nights to meet the Montoyas.

Papas did not play or like flamenco music; he found it boring even when played by an expert like Montoya. But Montoya admired Papas and wrote on a photo of himself: "For my dear friend Mr. Papas with great admiration for his great musical talent and great love of the divine guitar, warmly, your friend, Carlos Montoya."[4] Flamenco music was usually not written down but improvised. Papas worked out some flamenco arrangements, and played them for Montoya as a way of authenticating them. He also put in some notations about flamenco techniques.[5]

My father's students included the wife and daughter of General Omar Bradley, and usually the general was in Europe while the rest of the family stayed in Washington. One weekend Omar happened to be home, so Papas invited the Bradleys to come to meet the Montoyas. But, Papas recalled, Omar wouldn't come because he had only his fatigues to wear.

Papas had great musical talent, for all the fretted instruments. For example, the wife of a diplomat brought in a balalaika and instruction book to him and asked him to teach her daughter to play. He studied the book, found that the instrument should be tuned EEA and strummed like a ukulele, and then gave her a few lessons. He also taught the zither to a few pupils. As with the guitar, the left hand plays on the fretted neck of this instrument, but the right hand plays with a pick. Again, he studied a bit and then taught it, another example of his all-round musicality. The sudden rise of interest in the zither may have been inspired by the film "The Third Man," made in 1949. I can remember sitting around in the office of the Columbia School of Music during the dog days of a Washington summer, tuning a few zithers with old banjo keys, which are hollow like clock keys.

The Hawaiian guitar was still popular, and on 24 October 1941 Papas put on a program entitled "Memories of Hawaii" at the Hotel Roosevelt. And his instrumental groups were still performing. "The concert given by Sophocles Papas's Philharmonic Orchestra of Washington at the Purcellville Library Sunday afternoon was enthusiastically received by an audience which filled the assembly hall. The mandolin orchestra won the hearts of the audience....Mr. Papas' guitar solos by Bach and Mozart were outstanding....Miss Lillian Somoza, daughter of the President of Nicaragua, was charming in her guitar solo."[6]

During World War II Papas was about the only fretted-instrument teacher in Washington; the others, all younger, were drafted. The war gave Papas, his teachers, and pupils many opportunites to perform for such organizations as Greek War Relief. One program, to "feature a program of Greek folk songs headed by Sophocles Papas of the Columbia School of Music," was broadcast on station WINX. Another benefit was arranged by Achilles Catsonis, then-president of the District Branch of National Greek War Relief Societies and one of Papas's Greek friends from early days in Washington. The *Sunday Star* of 23 March 1941 announced another benefit for Greece, in which Papas "will play ancient Greek music for the guitar, and pupils of Mr. Papas will play an arrangement of the Greek national hymn. As part of this effort, Sophocles Papas, director of the Columbia School of Music, will dedicate the school's weekly radio program to the cause of Greek war relief." This program was also broadcast on WINX.

The rest of the United States suffered years of shortages, especially rationing of gasoline, tires, meat, sugar, and shoes during World War II. Washington, however, became a boom town. Thus Papas also benefitted. Harold Ickes, Secretary of the Interior and the man in charge of the draft, had to consider drafting even men who had children, and when covering this issue a local Washington newspaper came up with the headline, "Ickes Says Papas Vital to War Effort." Papas put the headline up on the bulletin board just inside the entrance to Columbia School of Music. Everyone who came in naturally read it as his last name, not as the word for fathers.

In spite of the growth of interest in the classical guitar, people still did not know much about the instrument. Both during and after the war Papas was still invited to give talks on the history of the instrument, some of them in prestigious places. On 26 January 1946, the *Washington Times-Herald* reported: "Sophocles Pappas [*sic*],[7] prominent resident master of the fretted instruments, discussed and illustrated guitar music and the instrument itself, which traces its ancestry to 600 B.C. and ancient Greece at a session of the National Symphony Forum in the Phillips Memorial Gallery."

Papas could be extremely generous with time for his pupils and other musicians. During the war years he auditioned and took on as pupils two talented sisters and their brother—Helen, Doris, and Conrad Bruderer, whose father was a chicken farmer. They took lessons weekly and paid each time by bringing a chicken and two dozen eggs, very nice for us in wartime. The three siblings were very talented and hard-working, and often performed as a string trio. For instance, they played at the prestigious Mayflower Hotel on 3 January 1942.

Papas also hired refugees from the war as teachers: Ivan Servais, a powerful basso, who had sung in operetta in Washington, taught voice at the school beginning in 1941; and Mme. Camille Chautemps, wife of a former premier of France and a fine pianist and pupil of Alfred Cortot, taught piano.

In 1945 the Columbia School of Music was certified to teach music to veterans under the GI Bill, and many changes had to take place quickly. Papas had to hire teachers of many instruments as well as the theoretical subjects and music history for an average of 64 veterans a month who more than filled the ten-room school: I remember finding people perched on the edge of the bathtub, practicing the guitar.

Soon the school was able to offer a certificate and a diploma; and the Guitar Shop had expanded into a "complete music store offering everything pertaining to the guitar," as well as "advice without charge." Papas also became a member of the National Association of Music Merchants. In 1946 Dorothy Perrenoud, certainly one of the most outstanding students of Papas's career, came from California to study with him (see chapter 5).

During the late 40s music issuing from the corner of 20th and N could be heard from a block away, a blend of many different instruments, even a harp. Occasionally a crowd would gather to listen to a pianist practicing with the windows open, or to watch a grand piano being hoisted into one of the top-floor studios: the stairwells were too narrow to accommodate a grand. Thomas Simmons taught theory and composition; Conrad Bernier from Catholic University took the few organ students; Marie Seuel Holst taught some of the many piano students; Beatrice Landheer, harpsichord; Alba Rosa Vietor, violin and viola; Harriet Rose, accordion; Dana Garrett, trumpet; and his brother Paul, clarinet. James Wood, one of Papas's best students, became a fine jazz guitar player and teacher and taught and worked for Papas for many years.

On Papas's birthday, 18 December 1948, the *Washington Times-Herald* published a profile by John White entitled "Did You Happen to See Sophocles Papas." White reported that at the age of 13 Papas went to Cairo to go to a regular school but money troubles sent him to business school instead. He worked in a bakery in Cairo for two years, then returned to Greece. He then "fought with the Greek army against the Turks, came to this country to study insects.[8] Why? Because Greece has always needed knowledge for its fight against plant diseases. But once again he was diverted from his course. He got a job in Worcester, Mass., went to school nights, and kept on with the study of music. In 1917 he joined the American Army. In 1920 he came to Washington, where he has taught music ever since. Now he is president of the Columbia School of Music, specializing in the teaching of Spanish guitar technique, and he has become one of the very best....Sophocles Papas, indeed, has made himself a national reputation."[9]

In the midst of all his professional activities, Papas's home life was also getting busier. Papas's second son, David Stephen Papas, was born on 1 March 1951.

At this time Papas was also interested in the guitar as therapy; he had had several students who claimed that they were better able to relax because they practiced the guitar daily. The *Washington Star* of 22 May 1949 published an article entitled, "Guitars Provide Musical 'Cure' for Ulcers." The article referred indirectly to Papas's student Herrlee Creel, who wrote a long article entitled "Guitar Therapy" in which he claimed that his ulcer had been cured by playing the guitar.

In the boom years after the war, Papas tried hard to have the school accredited to grant the degree of Bachelor of Music. A long and dismal correspondence with the Board of Education of the District of Columbia extends from 1949 to 1953. The Board asked for more and more details of courses, vitas of instructors, statistics on enrollment, and the like, but from the correspondence it appears that the information was not reaching those who had requested it. In 1951, a wealthy student had even made a pledge of $30,000, no inconsiderable sum in those days, as an endowment if the school were approved for the degree. Inspection committees came and went and made recommendations, such as the establishment of an advisory board, and

Papas corresponded with such dignitaries as then-conductor of the National Symphony Howard Mitchell. But it all came to naught.

Despite this great disappointment Papas had some compensations. He was well known now, even in England, where *Guitar News*, a periodical and the official organ of the International Classic Guitar Association, published by Wilfrid M. Appleby in Cheltenham, carried several mentions of Papas. In a 1957 issue there was a notice and review of Columbia Music's publication of the Segovia scales, as well as mention of the activities of the Washington Guitar Society.[10] Another issue featured a picture of Segovia listening to Papas play the guitar. The writeup concerns for the main part Papas as a "'giving' teacher; sparing with praise, lavish with constructive criticism."[11]

In 1959 Papas again appeared on the cover of an issue of *Frets* [12] in which his long article, "The Romance of the Guitar," was reprinted.

As Papas's career headed into the 60s, another issue of *Guitar News* featured a program of the Washington Guitar Society in which Papas played duets with one of his best pupils, Carol Bistyga.[13]

Sophocles Papas wrote educational articles in addition to his teaching in early years. He wrote regularly for *School Band and Orchestra Musician* from October 1929 until June 1930. (This periodical became *School Musician* in 1930.) He wrote a long article in the October 1929 issue, entitled "That Old Guitar of Mine." In this "Story of One of the Most Romantic Instruments in All History" he traced the history of the guitar from Egypt and Apollo through Sor and Carulli. He listed "the most active guitarists in this country at present: William Foden, Johnson Bane, George C. Krick, Vahdah Olcott-Bickford, and William D. Moyer." He also mentioned Tárrega "who died several years ago" (really in 1909) and Heinrich Albert, "a guitar composer in Germany." The article is accompanied by a picture of Papas with a rather leggy trio of women guitarists, Hilda Allen, Ella Hennig, and Margaret Moore.[1]

The issue of November 1929 ran an article about teaching fretted instruments in the public schools. There was quite a lot of interest in this at the time because the guitar was considered easier to learn than other stringed instruments. Intonation was less of a problem than with, for example, the violin, because of the frets. The article focuses more on the banjo, mandolin, and crosses like the cello-banjo and mando-bass than on the guitar. But it encourages the formation of fretted-instrument orchestras, and also advises 50 banjo players to join together to form a banjo band.

During the 40s and 50s, Papas's reputation as a teacher blossomed. He had many students, and among them were some who became important lifelong friends and dedicated musicians. A number of talented students moved to Washington to study with him, often sent by other teachers in the United States and other parts of the world. And Washington society continued to provide Papas with students from all levels of society. He was a remarkably unprejudiced man, an attitude which served me well in my own life. He also had many friends who were not players themselves but who loved the guitar and worked to spread knowledge of and interest in the instrument. They all came to the numerous parties held at the house and the studio.

Dorothy Perrenoud de Goede

In 1946 Dorothy Perrenoud (now de Goede) came from Los Angeles to study with Papas. Raised in Los Angeles, she had begun by studying Hawaiian guitar at the age of nine, first with William Moon, who peddled lessons door-to-door during the Depression. Moon accompanied his students by playing finger-style on an old Martin guitar. Dorothy found the voice of the old Martin far more appealing than the twang of her Hawaiian guitar and asked her teacher to "swap" instruments with her. He passed along his limited knowledge of the classical guitar to Dorothy—and as a bonus taught chess to her entire family! He took her as far as he could, and then, because he recognized her special ability and love for the guitar, turned her over to Vahdah Olcott-Bickford, one of the few guitar teachers to precede Papas (see chapter 1). Although not on good terms with Bickford, he knew that she was the only teacher in Los Angeles who could continue to develop his student.

Vahdah was a devoted teacher and Dorothy progressed rapidly. In the 30s Bickford was using the Aguado-Carcassi method with the little finger of the right hand supported on the sounding board. Also the guitar was held high on the lap in an almost upright position. In 1939 Vahdah introduced her star pupil, now a teenager, to the American Guitar Society, and Dorothy became its mascot and a regular member for a number of years. In 1948 she was described as "the beautiful girl with 'unusual poise' and a 'fine representative of the younger generation of guitar artists' and 'foremost among the younger guitar artists of the fair sex.'"[2] Dorothy has always been extremely pretty.

Dorothy studied with Vahdah until she was in her teens and then stopped. When she was in her 20s, she resumed lessons with Luís Elorriaga, an inspiring and insightful teacher from Mexico. He tried to change Dorothy's right-hand technique because planting the little finger put her in danger of becoming a two-fingered guitarist. Planting means losing the use of the little finger and also inhibits the use of the third finger. The habit was deeply ingrained, so that trying to change was a struggle. Elorriaga even resorted to wrapping rubber bands around her third and fourth fingers![3] He also had her change the position of the guitar by lowering the neck of the instrument and raising her left knee on a footstool. But Dorothy became discouraged and dropped her guitar studies again.

About 1944 Milo Lacey, an amateur Washington guitarist, became aware of Dorothy's talent during a visit to the west. He probably heard about her from other guitarists in California. He told his friend Sophocles Papas about Dorothy Perrenoud and said that she was the best guitarist he had come across on the west coast. Papas wrote her and told her that, if she wanted to resume guitar study, she could come to Washington, study with him, and live with the Papas family. He suggested that she contact Segovia during his next concert tour and play for him, so that he could evaluate her playing. Dorothy kept the letter for a year but didn't act on it. She and Papas continued to correspond, and the next year she wrote that she thought perhaps it was too late for her to begin her studies again. Papas again recommended that she play for Segovia. This time she did phone Segovia, who knew her name from information Papas had sent to him, and played for him. Segovia was warm and encouraging and recommended that she move to Washington to study with Papas. His critique was not all glowing by any means: he said that her technique was incorrect, that she would have to change everything—the position of the guitar, the left hand, and the right hand. In fact, he said that her right-hand position was impossible (with the little finger planted).[4] Segovia also promised to coach her whenever the opportunity arose. (He was living in New York in the 40s but frequently traveled to Washington.)

In 1946 Dorothy finally decided to go to Washington to study the guitar seriously with Sophocles Papas. Papas drove to the airport to pick her up on one of those typical Washington hot and humid July days, and she was barely off the plane when he asked her about George Smith. Smith had been a studio guitarist in Los Angeles; he had come to Washington a few years before to teach jazz at Papas's Columbia School of Music, and he and Papas had decided to collaborate on a course of guitar studies at conservatory level. But he and Papas had had a falling out and Smith had returned to California, very bitter and disappointed. Papas had reason to be concerned: Smith had met with Dorothy before she left for Washington and tried for two hours to convince her not to go. Dorothy found Smith's criticisms of Papas unsettling, but she decided to stick to her plan.

On the way home from the airport, the topic of the hot weather arose. Papas agreed that the day was warm but "not bad." Dorothy was receiving her first lesson from Sophocles: mind over matter; don't let trivial things like the weather distract or bother you.

Lessons began, and both teacher and pupil realized that there was a difficult road ahead. First there was the matter of Dorothy's thumbs: both were double-jointed. Her left thumb, particularly, collapsed into a right angle as it supported the neck of the guitar. This not only looked strange but also placed the fingers at some disadvantage on the fingerboard. Papas wanted the thumb to caress the neck of the guitar and insisted that Dorothy conform to this idea. It became such a point of contention that Papas took Dorothy to his friend Dr. Cajigas, an endocrinologist and guitar buff. Cajigas said that nothing could be done about the thumb and explained that, under the circumstances, it found its strength and control in this unorthodox position, and that it would be better not to waste any more time trying to change it. This convinced Papas. In general he was a man who did not try to fight those things that could not be changed. Dorothy still believes today that this extreme position of the left thumb limits her speed and technique. She had right-hand problems too, because her little-finger technique was so set, but Papas was very helpful to her in overcoming the planting problem.

Whenever Segovia came to Washington, he would check on her progress, coach her, and inspire her to intensify technical studies. In the late 40s Segovia's impact was already inspiring an interest in classical guitar study. But there was no conservatory in the United States where one could study guitar intensively, despite Papas's efforts to establish such an institution in Washington. Whereas today there are more than a thousand colleges and universities teaching the guitar, ranging from a few students to a doctorate in performance, in those days a talented guitarist such as Dorothy Perrenoud was lucky indeed to be able to study with Papas and have Segovia as a coach.

Dorothy considered Papas "a fascinating person" and admired his ability to make his way in the world as a "self-made man." Despite his lack of formal education, he was multi-lingual and fit comfortably into all kinds of company. She noticed that he seemed more at ease with people at high-level jobs than with ordinary folks. "He was their mental equal, no doubt of that," she commented.

Papas was a well-organized teacher, but he did have deficiencies. He could dwell on a detail and keep after a student about problem areas (like Dorothy's left thumb) until he had proof that his method would not help (for instance, when he received Dr. Cajigas's advice). He could be demanding and difficult, and Dorothy fielded her share of problems with him. But on the whole he was kind, generous, and quite positive. His attitude was, if you practice hard, you can do it. Papas had high hopes that Dorothy would be The Student, the one who would go on to be a master of the craft, but she had lost quite a bit of ground by dropping her guitar study in her teens. During her years with Vahdah she had studied the masters (Giuliani, Carcassi, Carulli, Legnani, etc.); but she had not studied the works and transcriptions of the great composers such as Bach, Granados, and Albéniz.

Dorothy lived with the Papas family when she first arrived, first in the apartment on N Street. But when the family moved to Calvert Street that same year, Dorothy stayed on at N Street above the music school, along with Ruth Anderson, a veteran and trumpet student. Betty Papas, now 18 and away at the University of Pennsylvania during the academic year, also lived with Ruth and Dorothy in the summers.[5] However, Dorothy often spent weekends with Mercia and Sophocles and occasionally baby-sat their son, Teddy, when they took trips. This was a very difficult time for Dorothy, who had come from a quiet and peaceful household; whereas her own family never fought, and she had never heard her parents argue, Sophocles and Mercia argued constantly. Dorothy was often forced into the position of taking sides, and she tended to side with Mercia, which made for an awkward situation. In spite of these problems, Dorothy remained lifelong friends with both Sophocles and Mercia.

Toward the end of 1948 Dorothy left Washington to go to New York to study with Segovia, who kept an apartment there above the apartment of Rose and Albert Augustine. But she had a miserable time in New York. First of all, her apartment was robbed. As far as she could see the room had been completely stripped. Heart in mouth, she looked under the bed: there was her Hauser guitar. After the robbery Augustine suggested she leave her guitar at his own apartment whenever she went out. She did. Meanwhile, Segovia's personal life was in chaos during this time because of his romance with a (married) Brazilian woman, Olga Coelho.[6] Coelho was extremely jealous and became infuriated when she saw Dorothy coming and going from the same building where Segovia lived. Coelho found out from Augustine that Dorothy kept her guitar there. No one was supposed to tell Coelho when Dorothy was to have her lessons with Segovia. Once when Dorothy was out walking with Segovia, she noticed that a gallery they were passing was putting on a Rembrandt show, so they went in and immediately ran into Coelho's husband, Gaspar. Segovia accused Dorothy of setting him up. She cut her next lesson. It is amazing that Segovia finally phoned and apologized.

Segovia was Dorothy's idol, but he had human weaknesses. He was a very suspicious man and quick to jump to conclusions. Dorothy was offended by his unkindness to students in master classes; she felt he undermined their ability to do their best. But he could be very generous and often gave so much to his students. And probably because of his enthusiasm for teaching he inspired others, such as John Marlow, Larry Snitzler, Jeffrey Meyerriecks, Clare Callahan—and Dorothy Perrenoud—to become teachers.

But in general life did not go well for Dorothy in New York. She did have some good, long, relaxed lessons with Segovia, and he did give her some close attention, but his concert and recording schedule grew increasingly hectic as his fame increased with each tour. The combination of circumstances helped Dorothy to make the hard decision that she could no longer aspire to a concert career. In 1951 she returned to Los Angeles and married Martin de Goede, her high-school sweetheart. Raising six children cut into her practice time, but she developed a modest career doing duo work with singers and flutists. She later began to play standards and bossa nova and played for many years at various Los Angeles department stores and restaurants.[7]

Marcelle Jones

While living in Beirut from 1964 to 1966, Marcelle Jones, the wife of a tele-communications executive, began to study guitar with a teacher who taught the Segovia method. He "spoke 10 or so languages but [the] worst was English! If you think the guitar can be difficult, try your first lessons in a mélange of French, Arabic and quite imaginative English!!"[8] This teacher, however, had met Sophocles Papas at Santiago de Compostela, where Segovia regularly taught in the summer,[9] and as a result he advised Jones that if she ever went to Washington, D.C., she should study with Papas.

At the time Jones had no idea she would ever live in Washington—Hong Kong, Bangkok, and Dallas intervened. When she finally did come to Washington in 1968, she made inquiries about Papas but felt intimidated by his reputation. However, she went for an interview, during which she was asked, somewhat peremptorily, to "Play something." Her letter continues, "I stumbled through Sor's Etude No. 5, was told I had no technique but was accepted as a student. When I told Sophocles about having helped to form the Dallas Guitar Society, I was of course promptly introduced into the Washington Guitar Society. My experiences as a student in connection with the society remain influential in my life and have affected it in important ways."

Jones studied with Papas for nearly three years, but, in her own words, never became "a decent player," because she had started rather late in life. She was an enthusiastic member of the guitar society and worked to encourage awareness and appreciation of the classic guitar.

Jones became a family friend, especially to Mercia. And she was the one who organized Papas's 80th birthday party. "Mercia was most kind to me. She was unfailingly a charming and gracious hostess to anyone she and Sophocles invited. Their parties after concerts, usually with the artist present, were legendary. One year, Mercia said to me that she would enjoy hearing other instruments so she and I signed up for the next season's subscription series at the Kennedy Center, to hear various artists and instruments. We had a lovely time." Now retired and living in Florida, Jones maintains connections with local guitar teachers and guitarists.

Jim Moran

Jim Moran, amateur guitarist and publicity agent, was a longtime friend of Papas. Between 1938 and 1942 as some of his publicity stunts he took a bull into a china shop, sold an icebox to an Eskimo, and on the corner of Connecticut Avenue and N Street in Washington looked for a needle in haystack.

He traveled a great deal from his base in New York City, but periodically he would turn up at the Papas studio or house from such places as Guadalajara, sometimes with his friend Burl Ives.[10] He wrote Marcelle Jones about his first meeting with Papas when he responded to an invitation to Papas's 80th birthday party.[11]

Dear Miss Jones, Is it really true that Sophocles Papas is turning 80? I can't believe it. I knew him when he was 35 and that seems like yesterday and besides he doesn't look much older.

My first meeting with Sophocles in 1928 was purely accidental.

Or was it?

In any event it certainly changed and enriched my life. Then began a warm and rewarding friendship which has continued throughout the 45 short intervening years.

At the time of our meeting I was 21 and a salesman of radiator covers. One of my customers was the Delman Shoe Co. of New York City which had just leased the street floor of a five-story building on Connecticut Avenue, one block north of the Mayflower Hotel for their soon-to-be-opened Washington store.

On the day of our fateful meeting I visited the store. There was a disorder of chattering decorators, electricians, etc., and the carpenters were banging away. I had come to supervise the installation of the custom-built radiator cabinets which had been ordered previously.

When things quieted down during the lunch hour I heard some celestial music wafting down the stairwell in the hall. I had never heard such beautiful sounds before. I couldn't determine what it was. It was too fragile a sound for a piano. Was it a harp? If it was, I'd never heard a harp like it. It positively was not a guitar because I played a bit of hillbilly folk guitar which I had learned back home on the farm in Virginia.

Then just what the hell was it? I determined to find out. (You must remember that this was prior to Segovia's first concert in this country and no company had yet recorded the classical guitar. This was also before nylon strings, Kleenex, zippers, filter-tips, dial phones, T.V., Tampax, computers, or airlines, to name a few.)

The small elevator in the rear was not working so I started up the stairs. The second and third floors were occupied by Emile's fashionable hairdressing salon. The fourth floor was Emile's private apartment. The music was definitely coming from the fifth floor. I made my way up. Down the hall was an open door. The music was cascading from this room. And what music! I couldn't believe my ears. I approached the door and there was our Sophocles, alone, sitting in a straight-back chair with his left foot on a footstool, playing Tárrega's arrangement of the Thème Varié of Mozart on his guitar.

I was flabbergasted and knew something tremendously important was happening to me. The business downstairs was completely forgotten. After introducing myself I must have talked Sophocles' ears off for several hours. I couldn't get enough of his playing. I guess he recognized my zestful enthusiasm. I probably leaned on him pretty heavily but he was gracious, patient, and kind. I, then and there, enrolled in a course of lessons. He didn't need any salesmanship to sell me the best classical guitar in his studio.

Bless you, Sophocles, for fanning my initial enthusiasm and inspiring me to study and practice. I am still at it.

But most of all bless you for introducing me to the wonders of the classical guitar which, next to woman, has been the single enduring love of my life.

[signed] Jim Moran

And in a letter to me Moran added a note about his first meeting with Sophocles and the guitar: "After a long chat I bought my first Martin guitar for $155.00 payable on time. That was the start of my guitar career—I studied with Sophocles for some time....My life would have been entirely different if I hadn't learned to play the guitar."[12]

In the early 50s, Gregory d'Alessio, Secretary of the New York Society of the Classic Guitar, saw Moran play on Steve Allen's "Tonight" show and invited him to play for the society. In a letter to Steve Allen, d'Alessio described Moran: "This great hulk of a man, hunched over a fragile guitar, playing a dainty Chopin prelude to the lacy obligato of a flute, was one of the high points of all your shows."[13]

Gregory d'Alessio

Gregory d'Alessio, an artist and cartoonist, met my father in the 40s, a time when the New York Guitar Society was flourishing. This society had many prominent people as members and was able to sponsor a number of guitar concerts. During this period Carl Sandburg and d'Alessio became guitar buddies; in fact Sandburg spent many weeks at the d'Alessio home at 8 Henderson Place.[14] Penelope Niven, most recent biographer of Sandburg, says,

In 1950 Sandburg was getting to know other musicians in New York, and enjoying their company immensely. His host and hostess for 'long boxcar evenings' of music, talk, good food and drink were artists Gregory and Terry d'Alessio, whose brownstone on Henderson Place on the Upper East Side of Manhattan was the setting for some of the best private parties Sandburg ever got to be the life of. Sandburg and d'Alessio, a superb classical guitarist and editor of *Guitar Review*, shared a friendship with the master guitarist Andrés Segovia, whom Sandburg had met years earlier in Chicago. Segovia tried in vain to teach Sandburg additional guitar chords and fingerings and occasionally sent him gold guitar strings.[15]

D'Alessio tells more guitar stories in his book *Old Troubadour: Carl Sandburg with his Guitar Friends*. For example, Sandburg had an interesting pair of guitars the family called the Washburn twins.[16]

"As soon as the delighted grandfather noticed that the little kid-fist could grasp the fingerboard of a guitar, one of the pear-shaped pair [of Washburn guitars] became his. 'Buppong gave it to me many years ago,' John Carl [Steichen, Sandburg's grandson, son of Helga] wrote me in March 1968, 'and I used it when I was studying with [Sophocles] Papas in Washington in 1961.' When Sandburg wanted to find a guitar teacher for John Carl, he turned to his friend Segovia for advice. Segovia recommended Sophocles Papas, a distinguished guitarist and teacher whose school for the guitar was located in Washington, D.C. Carl and Sophocles became fast friends, and Carl's appreciation for his teacher-friend never waned."[17]

Maestro Segovia's endorsement was translated into poetic terms by Sandburg in an inscription in *The Sandburg Range*:

Sophocles Papas
a great apostle, great teacher
of the guitar
and a good friend of unfinished,
clumsy fingers
like the undersigned scrivener's
    Carl Sandburg
    1 9 6 0[18]

"The other Washburn went to a young couple in Washington, Dr. Bill and Marjorie Braye."[19] Marjorie was a student of Papas and also designed some of the Columbia publication covers.

In 1959 a guitar-composition competition brought together a number of well-known guitar people of different nationalities. In the winter of 1959, we announced the results of our competition [for the best set of variations for guitar based on an American folk song, "Colorado Trail"]. It was cosmopolitan from start to finish. Judging...was headed by Andrés Segovia of Spain and Vladimir Bobri, a Russian émigré; first prize winner was John W. Duarte of London, England; runner-up was James Yoghourtian of Racine, Wisconsin, son of Armenian immigrants;[20] the prize money was provided through the sale of a flamenco guitar made in Madrid and donated to The Society of the Classic Guitar by the son of a Swedish immigrant [Sandburg]; the purchaser of the guitar was John C. Tanno of Phoenix, Arizona, guitar pedagogue and historian, and first-generation Italian;[21] and Sandburg's wishes were first put into motion by another first-generation ditto [d'Alessio].[22]

D'Alessio told me in 1992 that Papas was like an uncle to him, that he truly loved Papas. He said that he thought of him daily when watching a daily television cooking program that featured Charlie Byrd playing background music, that he thought of my father because of Byrd's connection with Papas. D'Alessio said that Papas was always helpful to him, that he bought some of his paintings himself and sent other people to see his work, including the King Sisters.

Jesús Silva[23]

Jesús Silva, a guitarist from Mexico, taught for many years at the North Carolina School of the Arts and later at Virginia Commonwealth University. For Papas's 80th birthday he wrote:

Dear Mr. Papas, I had the great pleasure of meeting you some time in 1957 at a party for Maestro Segovia after one of his marvelous concerts at Town Hall in New York City. I felt very fortunate because your name was already familiar and meaningful to me.

Shortly after that you were so generous inviting me to give a guitar concert in Washington, sponsored by you and your Guitar Society. You even very kindly invited me to stay in your house. I will never forget it and I will be always grateful.

The review in the paper next day was good but the critics pointed out the need to include in the program some of the most important and formal works from the repertoire of the guitar.

You called Maestro Segovia in New York, and read to him on the telephone the review. I was so overwhelmed by your kindness.

Suddenly, you said to me...with a very friendly but authoritative accent: "Silva, you can be very successful here in North America, but you must work." I realized immediately how much you knew, what you meant, because of your own experience.

You really have worked very hard, Mr. Papas, with much love and patience. You were so aware of the many needs of those who choose the guitar as a medium to express themselves through the beauty of its sounds. So you devoted your life almost entirely to the guitar world. As a teacher, musician of great sensitivity and knowledge; as composer and publisher; as responsible for the many benefits of your shop and with the constant encouragement and help you have given to new talented artists of the guitar.

Not only myself and the guitarists of this time but the world of music give you recognition for your very significant work, full of love.

Mr. Papas, you have become an inspiring symbol for all the people always in need of beauty and peace.

With much affection.

Jesús S.[24]

In 1990 Columbia Music Company began to correspond with Silva about publishing his *Ten Preludes*[25] and in various letters he wrote to me: "Mr. Papas did very much for the development of the classic guitar in this country. I always remember your father, Mr. Papas, how kind and generous he was to everybody. Mr. Papas sponsored a concert I gave in Washington in 1957, when he was the President of the Washington Classic Guitar Society. For that concert Mr. Papas, very kindly, invited me to stay at his house. Also on different occasions he invited me to dinner or lunch at his house in the company of Maestro Segovia."

And in another letter he wrote:

Your father, Mr. Papas, always called me "Jesús." When Maestro Segovia came to Winston-Salem, early in 1966, to give a two-week master class at the School of the Arts, Mr. Papas came to watch those classes and to be with the Maestro....Maestro Segovia was always happy to be with "Sophocles" as he called him. When the School of the Arts gave an honorary Doctor of Fine Arts degree to Maestro Segovia, on Monday, February 3, 1975, there was a very moving ceremony....Mr. Papas was present. Maestro Segovia invited him to come. In the afternoon of that same day, Maestro gave a class on the stage...There were three chairs on one side of the stage. Maestro Segovia was sitting on one, listening to the students. Mr. Papas on the right of the Maestro. I was on the left. It was a remarkable day. I saw the deep affection the two good old friends felt for each other, as I had seen it before many times.

Bill Harris and Charlie Byrd

Jazz guitarist Bill Harris started his career playing a wire-strung guitar with a pick. Then in the late 40s, he studied with Papas and began to apply classical guitar technique to jazz, i.e., he played jazz with his fingers on gut strings. Meanwhile, guitarist Charlie Byrd had been living in Binghamton, New York; he also played jazz guitar with a pick. He heard Bill Harris play in 1950, asked about the new technique, and Harris told him about Papas. Byrd visited Papas several times that summer, and in the fall moved to Washington to study with him. Thus the classical technique of the guitar was introduced into jazz via Charlie Byrd and Bill Harris. Byrd later went a step further and brought Brazilian bossa nova to North America.

In the 50s, Byrd often played duets with Papas—for charity, churches, and the like. The family saw him often socially and at Washington nightclubs. About 1958 Byrd was on a TV show and invited Papas as a featured guest. They played some duets, including a jazz piece for which Byrd had written out Papas's part, and they played with some other musicians Byrd had invited, a violinist and a bass player. My father never liked jazz, but he admired the ability to improvise and said that, for him, improvising was "instant composition." Later Byrd studied in Siena, Italy, with Segovia, to whom Papas had recommended him.

Byrd was unable to attend Papas's 80th birthday party in December 1973, but sent a letter:

Dear Sophocles, I'm so very sorry I can't be with you on this occasion, since I can't think of anyone I would rather honor than the foremost exponent of the guitar in the United States.

Mr. Papas, all American guitarists owe you a great debt of gratitude and I more than most.

Here is wishing you 80 more years as productive as these last.

I am sure that those few months that Segovia is older than you are the only reason that he is more renowned as a guitarist.

Happy Birthday[26]

Byrd would remember Papas fondly after his death: "The guitar was our life, both of us. And that gave us a lot in common. He was also a damned good cook and loved to have parties, and that was enough for a friendship right there."[27]

Byrd is currently playing all over the United States and Europe, after recovery from a serious illness.[28] He played to sold-out houses in Raleigh, North Carolina, in 1996 and 1997.

Solomon Snyder

At the time he studied with Papas, in the 50s, Sol Snyder was a bright young man still attending Calvin Coolidge High School. Although Snyder's parents encouraged him to be a musician, he resisted and chose a career in medicine.[29] The first instrument he studied was not guitar but mandolin. But after taking mandolin lessons from Papas for a couple of years while still in junior high school, Papas told Snyder that, like Latin, the mandolin is rather dead. "I would be well advised either to switch to the violin, whose stringing is like the mandolin, or play the guitar. There was never any question in my mind as I always yearned for the guitar and only played the mandolin because I had inherited one from my grandfather." Snyder was a particularly apt student, who practiced several hours a day in high school and made sufficient progress to be invited to give a solo recital for the guitar society during that time. When he went to college at Georgetown in 1955, he worked in the guitar shop, minding the store and giving lessons on Saturdays.[30] Oddly enough, it was his guitar training that led to his first research job. While in pre-med at Georgetown University, he was teaching the guitar to a scientist from the National Institutes of Health, who hired him as his research technician for the summer. Snyder said he found research "very creative, like composing."[31] He is now a Distinguished Service Professor of Neuroscience, Pharmacology and Psychiatry at Johns Hopkins in Baltimore, director of the Department of Neuroscience,[32] and author of such books as *The Mind and the Brain.*

Snyder and Papas stayed in touch throughout subsequent years. He wrote to Papas in 1982, "I manage to keep up with the guitar. Besides classical music I am learning some of Laurindo Almeida's arrangements of popular songs."[33] Snyder keeps a pair of music stands in his office so that when his octogenarian father drops by, they can play duets—his father on the flute and Snyder on the guitar.[34]

In the late 50s, two of Papas's bright, high-school-age, talented students asked him where one could study music and major in the guitar. But there was no such place.

Then, in 1959, Betty Dove,[1] one of Papas's students, was taking a course at American University. She had a connection with the university because her husband was in the concrete business and had supplied materials used in university construction. She spoke to Dr. Gordon Smith, then-chairman of the Music Department, about the possibility of a degree program in guitar. Dr. Smith was dubious: was there enough guitar literature for such a program? He made a search at the Library of Congress and was amazed by the wealth of material. Thus in 1961 my father began to teach at American in probably the first guitar degree program in North America.[2] Among those who studied in this program are Dave Arnold, Carol Bistyga, Richard Blankenship, Regis Ferruzza, Tom Hartman, John Marlow, John Nottingham, and Gretchen Voitel.

Fretts! announced Papas's appointment to American, noting that it was now possible to major in guitar. And on 12 March 1961 the *Sunday Star* printed an article by Harriet Griffiths, entitled "The Guitar Goes to College." It included a picture of an American University guitar student, Bill Leonhart, playing for Dr. Smith. Griffiths wrote: "Sponsors at American hope that inclusion of the classic guitar in the degree program will help develop virtuosity and topnotch teaching talent. Growing interest in the instrument is creating a demand for teachers." Another picture carries the caption "Instructor Sophocles Papas lends a knowing ear as Carole Bistyga reads through a score." And still another, "Sophocles Papas with a group of guitarists, including John Marlow." Three more pictures show the difference in hand positions for classical and other methods of guitar playing.

The article continues, quoting Dr. Smith:

In addition, there undoubtedly is a wealth of material awaiting today's musicologists through research by college-trained music scholars in old guitar and lute notations, including renaissance and medieval literature.

As instructors, the university engaged two guitarists. One is Sophocles Papas who claims the famed Andrés Segovia as a former teacher and long-time friend. He has been teaching in Washington since 1922, and has published music for the guitar. The well-known Charlie Byrd is among his former pupils. The other teacher is Aaron Shearer, author of two published instruction books and others to come.

Mr. Papas did some spadework toward the present recognition of the guitar as a degree subject at American when he was operating a GI school from 1945 until 1952. The guitar, he reports, claims about one-fourth as many players as the piano, the only instrument which ranks above it in popularity.[3]

In fact, Segovia regarded Papas as "the American teacher most thoroughly acquainted with his method and technique."[4]

The article concludes with a brief description of the difference between classical and other guitars such as plectrum, an explanation apparently needed even in 1961. The article also points out that many classical guitarists began on electric or pick guitar before changing over.[5]

Papas and Shearer certainly had their differences, but they both taught at American. In 1965, Dr. Ultan, new head of the Music Department, told Papas that he would have to retire in December because it was mandatory at age 72. Ultan had wanted Marlow to succeed Papas, because he wanted someone with a degree and because Marlow had graduated under Papas. When Papas suggested Marlow, Ultan said, "I hoped you'd recommend him." Segovia, who it is said could spot a phony a mile away, had great respect for Marlow. And Marlow was faithful to Papas's teaching and methods. Up to this time no one else had been teaching the Segovia style, and Marlow was the next to do so.[6]

During this period Papas's fame continued to grow and, although in his seventies, he remained very active in the guitar community. Paul Hume, the *Washington Post* music critic, said in an article about him entitled "Pioneer Here Can Share Credit in Reviving Respect for Guitar":

It was in 1922 that Sophocles Papas began teaching in Washington. This was six years before Andrés Segovia gave his first recital in the United States and almost an entire generation before Segovia's supreme

musicality would help to restore the guitar to its present prominent position among the world's most distinguished solo instruments.

The fact that the present concert season already includes four major
guitar concerts in Lisner Auditorium must come with particular satis-
faction to a man who has been the instrument's chief proponent in Washington for nearly 40 years. This year's guitar recitals range from the lute
and guitar concert of Julian Bream to the flamenco playing of Carlos
Montoya, as well as the unusual duo of Presti and Lagoya. It will conclude
with what is, for many, the crown of all guitar concerts, that by Segovia.
None of this comes as any surprise to Sophocles Papas, who next year will
celebrate 40 years of preaching and teaching and playing the guitar in
Washington.[7]

A 1966 issue of *Fretts!* wrote up a convention held in late August by the
Fretted Instrument Guild of America,[8] and noted that: "Mr. Sophocles Papas,
the distinguished classical guitarist, teacher and author from Washington,
D.C." gave a classical guitar workshop."[9]

In the 60s Papas wrote a number of articles about the guitar. In 1962 he
wrote a feature article for *Fretts!*, and a John Tanno article later that year
quoted from his "The Romance of the Guitar." Papas wrote on George Krick
following Krick's death on 3 April 1962. He also wrote a lengthy article in *Accordion and Guitar World* "Reflections on the Present State of the Classical
Guitar," in which he points out the need for four things: education, publicity,
more guitar music, and more high-quality, low-priced instruments.[10]

In 1963 A. P. Sharpe included Papas in his book *The Story of the Spanish
Guitar*, one of the early books on the guitar and its proponents. Sharpe also
states: "The Columbia School of Music grew and prospered, offering instruction in nearly all instruments but specialising in the guitar. Today the School
is certified to grant a Bachelor's degree in music—the only school in the U.S.
where a student may work for such a degree with the guitar as the principal
instrument.[11]... Sophocles Papas is founder of the Washington Guitar Society,
and has done much as a publisher in furthering the repertoire of the Spanish
guitar."[12]

As the local guitar specialist, in 1967 Papas was asked to come to the stage
of Constitution Hall to help the engineers set up for a pops concert featuring
guitarist Laurindo Almeida. They wanted to try to reinforce the sound of the

guitar so it would not be drowned out by the orchestra. Laurindo had asked Papas to sit in for him during the tryout, and the press was also invited. While the technicians were busy preparing the equipment, Papas was "constantly interrupted by the photographers, who asked him to stand up, sit down, to play and not to play."[13]

Among my father's papers I found a small pamphlet, dated October 1968, almost all in Japanese, including a program of guitar and fretted-instrument music and a photo of Kyoji Sekizuka, a Japanese guitarist, and Daddy standing in front of the house on Wynford Drive in Fairfax, Virginia.[14]

> Sophocles Papas is a 74-year-old Greek guitar teacher and he owns a guitar shop in Washington, D.C. Since I had an opportunity to meet him when I was on a business trip last September, I'd like to take this opportunity to introduce one of the important people in the American classical guitar world....Currently Papas does not perform due to arthritis in his right thumb. He composes, arranges, and teaches the guitar in the style of Segovia....I went into his guitar shop. There is a guitar-shaped neon sign at the front of the building. He has a great range of guitars, as well as recordings and music scores. As I was playing one of the guitars in the store, a clerk came to tell me that Papas would like to see me and led me to his studio at the back of the store. The studio consisted of a large desk with piles of music and papers and next to it a footstool and music stand....Papas was, unlike what I had expected, a little plump small old gentleman. His hands were big for his size, and his fingers fat and sturdy, like a worker. A girl of about 14 or 15 had just had her lesson. I was very pleased to see a classical guitar fan like her, while the music of students and hippies was dominating the United States.

> The display of unusual music instruments made the room look like a small museum: a mandolin made in Naples 200 years ago, a long-necked Okinawa shamisen, an African harp made of hyde, a Renaissance lute at least 300 years old with shells embedded in the sounding board.[15]

> Although it was the first time I had met him, he welcomed me very cordially. In fact, I was a little embarrassed as he himself made me a cup of coffee. He gave me some guitar magazines and music, and invited me to dinner that evening along with a young American guitarist[16] who happened to be in town. It took us about a half hour to reach his home in Fairfax, Virginia.

Leaving clean and green Washington that looked like a park, we came to a wonderful highway of three lanes in each direction. Wide forests spread on both sides of the highway. Papas talked a lot about the current guitar world as he drove: the unexpected death last year of Ida Presti, which he blamed on lung cancer from excessive smoking.[17] And he said that the reason Segovia does not go to Japan is because he is afraid of his physical safety as the Japanese fans are too passionate.

His house, with woods at the back,[18] is in a nice residential area. The white walls and light brownish bricks contrasted with the fresh green lawn. It looked wonderful, just like a western cake. As soon as we walked in the house, we toasted with bourbon whiskey. Then he led me to his study and showed me his guitar collections, which I really wished to have for myself. The records, music, and papers were displayed beautifully. All I could do was sigh. His collection of musical instruments also was wonderful...He took out and played the sweet-sounding and well-balanced Hauser, and a Ramírez with an amazingly big sound. He played many pieces, including some Japanese music. But according to him all the Japanese music is in minor and the melodies sound the same, and he asked me why.

I played duets with the young American guitarist, and also played with the recorder. I was so involved that I didn't realize it was very late. I was really impressed and thankful for Papas's kindness.

by Kyoji Sekizuka

An article in the *Washington Post* of Sunday, 2 February 1969, bore the headline, "Guitars strum along, but pianos pedal ahead." At this time there were more than 23.5 million amateur pianists in the United States, which still outnumbered the guitar players; but the guitar was being taught in classrooms along with the traditional band and orchestra instruments. The article also said that pianists were "unaffected and unmoved by the guitar fad," but it turned out that the writer was referring only to folk music. Also American University was permitting students to major in the classical guitar.

In 1972 Phil Casey interviewed Papas and wrote a long article for the *Washington Post*, headed "I Did More for the Guitar."[19] A picture of Papas playing the guitar was captioned "In the old days, when guitarist Sophocles Papas played more often, well-known performers would drop into his studio for a little concert." Casey mentioned that Papas's wife had said he would probably never retire fully, although at this time he had only about 20 students. Some of them came out to the house in Virginia for their lessons. And of course he was still busy publishing music.

Awards and Acknowledgements

By the late 1960s the classical guitar had made a huge advance in the world of classical music and Papas began to receive awards for his life work. In 1967 he had been elected a fellow of the Society of the Classical Guitar of New York, and on 2 May 1967 he was presented with a scroll signed by Vladimir Bobri, President, and Martha Nelson, Secretary. *The International Who's Who in Music* also gave him an award for distinguished achievement. He was well known in many circles.

In 1971 Sophocles and Mercia came up to Canada to visit my family and me, so we invited a few friends in to meet them. Always generous about performing for people, my father played a few pieces. Afterwards, one of our guests commented, "Gosh, Mr. Papas, you're almost ready for the *Glenn Campbell Show!*" Fortunately, Daddy had apparently never heard of Glenn Campbell and didn't know that he was a country-music guitarist.

On 1 September 1973, in Santa Barbara, on the occasion of the National Guitar Convention of the American String Teachers Association, the ASTA Guitar Committee awarded its Certificate of Appreciation to Sophocles Papas for a lifetime of dedicated service to the classical guitar in the United States. The certificate is signed by Thomas Heck, Roy Petschauer, and Ronald C. Purcell.

Of this occasion Dorothy de Goede wrote:

I remember traveling to Santa Barbara in '73 with Sophocles Papas and Alvino Rey. Sophocles was on vacation from Washington, D.C., and we were all in a celebrant mood....I must say in all honesty that I harbored some negative feelings about the prospect of a national guitar organization enduring over time....happily I was unduly negative....The young guitarists of today can't imagine how bleak the guitar scene was 60 years ago. It has thrilled me to have watched the guitar develop to its present stature. The magnificent efforts of those who assure the lifeline of the Guitar Foundation of America have my admiration.[20]

The Guitar Foundation of America (GFA) was established in 1973, and a 1993 issue of *Soundboard*, the GFA's quarterly publication, carried an article titled "The GFA at 20: In which we look back over the past two decades and contemplate the future (20th anniv. of founding of GFA)." Thomas Heck wrote on the establishment of an American guitar foundation:

> I had made the acquaintance of Sophocles Papas in the late '60s, and discussed these concerns with him. He made me aware that he had founded something called the American Guitar Foundation many years earlier in Washington, D.C. as a non-profit society; nothing in particular had come of it. He offered to let the younger generation of guitarists expand, redefine, and possibly even relocate the American Guitar Foundation to make it a truly national and perhaps international organization.
>
> Inspired by his gesture, and while still on active duty in the Army, I composed and mailed out a four-page letter....This lengthy and impassioned mailing gave my sad perspective on the fractured state of guitar interests nationally and internationally. I noted that a schism had already occurred in Washington, D.C. between the American Guitar Foundation and the National Guitar Society."[21]

In 1975 Papas was the guest of honor at the first American String Teachers Association convention to include the guitar. Composer Loris Chobanian, director of the guitar division of the conference, spoke of that occasion when I visited him in Berea in 1992. He said that the Cleveland meeting had been a huge success and even made a profit, although they had charged only $37 per person!

In an article entitled "Fifty Years of Classical Guitar" by Jerry Dallman,[22] there are two pictures of Papas, one when he was quite young, one in advanced age. The article, based on Dallman's four interviews of Papas, ends by saying: "When asked if he had considered writing a formal autobiography, he looked at that afternoon's list of students, some music he is currently editing, the manuscript of an etymological quarterly he plans to publish, a stack of unanswered correspondence. 'A man should have most of his accomplishments behind him before he sits down to write his autobiography,' he said. 'I don't think I'm ready yet.'"

Guy Horn, President of the 1977 Carmel Classic Guitar Festival, invited Papas to be a judge, but he was unable to go because he had an obligation to be in Washington on those dates. The festival organizers planned to give both Papas and Vahdah Olcott-Bickford certificates of recognition "for long and fruitful labors on behalf of the classic guitar in America." Papas's award was mailed to him.

On 28 April 1978 the Washington Guitar Society presented a Certificate of Appreciation to Sophocles Papas in recognition of his half century of contributions to music and to the classical guitar. The certificate is signed by Herenia Doerr, President, and I believe she did the calligraphy as well.

Guitar 78, the second international guitar festival, was held in Toronto in June 1978. Ron Butler, President of the Guitar Society of Toronto, presented an award to Papas in acknowledgement of his dedication to raising the standard of performance and in appreciation of his contribution to the classical guitar in America. Ronald C. Purcell, President of the Guitar Foundation of America, spoke at the presentation:

> Now into his fourth year of the octogenarian club, Sophocles Papas was born in the Northwest part of Greece (now known as Albania). His parents were Mother, Konstanto[23] Harispapa, born in Sopiki, Pogoniou; father, Thomas Nikolau Botis, born in Vouliarates, Drynoupoleos, Epiros (he changed his surname to Papadopoulos after Grandfather Nikolaos was ordained a priest). Papas came to the United States in 1914. After a tour of duty with the U.S. Army, Sophocles opened a music store and school in Washington, DC.
>
> [Sophocles Papas is] a very active and popular teacher who can claim many famous people as students, such as Charlie Byrd, Bill Harris, Nancy Ames, Alvino Rey, David Kennedy and John Carl Sandburg—grandson to the poet, Carl Sandburg—who also sought Sophocles' advice on his own guitar technique. An untiring worker, adjudicator and supporter of guitar events (also a member of the Board of Directors of the GFA) Sophocles is still active with teaching and publishing. He is occasionally reminded of his years in the teaching field—like when a new student being interviewed for lessons tells him the name of the person who recommended him—he reflects for a moment, "Oh yes, I taught her 50 years ago." We congratulate you Mr. Papas and wish you the best and continued good health and thank you for your contributions to the world of guitar.

On 29 July 1978 Papas wrote to Purcell about this award: "[I] just want to thank you and the American Guitar Foundation for your part in the presentation to me of that special award for my fifty years of guitar teaching. It is a great honor and the certificate is installed in a prominent place on my studio wall. My guitar teaching has been my life's work as well as my hobby. I still have two students just to keep my hand in.

"It was a pleasure to meet you again in Toronto. I enjoyed the convention very much. I thought it was well organized and well managed, and I hope it will be a regular 3 year occurrence.

"Mercia joins me in sending our best to Mrs. Purcell."

During the 1970s Papas continued to promote his students and colleagues. Entrepreneurs such as Patrick Hayes came to count on him for advice and help. Once when John Williams was to play, he had to cancel at the last minute. Hayes phoned Papas, and Papas told Hayes, "I have Carlos Barbosa-Lima." But Hayes did not yet know that name and countered with a suggestion about an American guitarist. Papas reported that he really was not a good player. Hayes checked on the American's reviews and found they were consistently bad, so Barbosa-Lima played at Lisner Auditorium, in Williams's place. This gave Barbosa-Lima's career a big boost and began many years of annual Barbosa-Lima concerts.

On another occasion Julian Bream found himself snowbound in Connecticut: there was absolutely no way he could get to Washington for his program, and at 1 o'clock on a Sunday afternoon he phoned Hayes to cancel his 8:30-p.m. concert. Again Hayes phoned Papas, who called Dick Phillips, a Peabody graduate and a former student of his. When Hayes announced the substitution that night, he told the audience that Papas had rescued him and asked him to take a bow.

Papas never directly sponsored guitar concerts, but he did provide support for guitar concerts in Washington by selling tickets to pupils, guitar society members, and aficionados of the instrument. Today some of the wealthier guitar societies are able to sponsor concerts by quite well-known players, but the Washington group just never had that kind of money.

On 28 April 1978 Jeffrey Meyerriecks, another of my father's students, gave a program honoring Papas on the fortieth anniversary of his founding of the Washington Classical Guitar Society.[24] The concert was held at the YWCA's

Barker Hall where Papas had given his first concert in 1938.[25] Meyerriecks, a local guitar teacher, played his *Canonic Variations*, written in Papas's honor, as well as his *Four Preludes*.[26]

Papas maintained his contact with guitar students, performers, teachers, and aficionados, some of them famous, throughout his life.

Carl Sandburg

Sometime in the 40s Sophocles Papas met Carl Sandburg through Segovia, probably at the home of Gregory d'Alessio. Sandburg, born in 1878, was already very well known for his poetry, newspaper and union work, books on Lincoln, *American Songbag*, and other writings, and he had won two Pulitzer prizes. Some of the earliest correspondence between Sandburg and Papas concerns the then-forming Segovia Society.[1] The correspondence went on irregularly until Sandburg's death in 1967.[2]

> May 1, 1958
> Brother Papas:
> You will permit me, I hope to stand and give you salutations. Sometimes the word "Teacher" is one of the finest words in the language. In its highest and noblest sense that word goes for you in the work you have done with your pupil Marjorie Braye.[3] Years ago I had a belief that she had aptitudes and instinct about the guitar. And this week I have heard her play that noble instrument. In americanese we can say of her, "she's a natural." I feel gay about you as teacher and her as pupil. So I would pin a rose on you as a great teacher and some nice bashful flower on her as a pupil who has toiled and wrought. I hope to be seeing you in Washington ere the year is out.
> Faithfully yours,
> Carl Sandburg

[6 January 1959]

Dear Mercia Papas:

Comes along from you and Sophocles the extraordinary and beautiful Segovia album.[4] Let me thank you and say, "Hosannah in the highest!" I hope to be seeing you sometime when in Washington. I can never forget the good results that Sophocles got in teaching Marjorie Braye. She naturally loves the guitar but he brought her along. I want to hear you fellows talk about Segovia who is a hero worthy of the love and admiration lavished on him.

Ever good wishes,

Carl Sandburg

Marjorie Braye wrote to Sandburg,[5] "I am very much enthused about my lessons and my practicing. The guitar is so wonderful and the tones and sounds and instruments that you hear in it are almost endless. Papas was so pleased with that nice 'hurrah' you sent him. He is such a fine man and [has] such a nice 'sandburgish' sense of humor. I know you will like him very much....I never cease being grateful to you and Mrs. Sandburg for [your] nice shove into such a nice new musical world....It [the guitar] is the companion, the friend, the solace and the joy that you said it would be a hundred thousand years ago when you gave it to me."[6]

On 9 October 1959, Papas wrote to Sandburg about a Catalan song the writer had arranged. "Marjorie told me that you like the Catalan song I arranged[7] and that you will write words for it. I am delighted with the prospect as I would like to publish it as a song.[8]

August 23, 1960

Dear Carl,

I am taking time out from Marjorie's lesson [Marjorie Braye] to write this brief note. I've been wanting to write you and send you the music and words of the song, "Whiskey Won't Hurt This Baby" which was given to me for you by Mr. Janney of the National Geographic. I will make a clear copy of the words and music over the weekend and mail it to you early next week at the Bel-Air Hotel.[9]

The book that I am sending along with Bill [Braye] is a copy of your "Complete Poems" which I hope you will be kind enough to autograph. I gave the book as a graduation present to the son of Mrs. William O.

Douglas[10] because his mother had told me what a great admirer he is of yours. His name is Michael Davidson. I would be grateful if you could inscribe it for me and I know he will be happy and proud. I am also slipping some clippings in the book for you that I think might interest you.

Your work with the new picture with George Stevens sounds very interesting and I know that when I view it I will see evidence of your fine hand. Mercia joins me in sending you our love.

Affectionately,

Sophocles

Sandburg did autograph the book for the Davidson boy.

November 24, 1960

Dear Carl:

I am writing this letter on Thanksgiving Day. There are so many things I am thankful for—too many to enumerate—but I will mention a few of the most important ones.

I am thankful to God for having given me Mercia, Betty, Teddy and David. I am thankful for our good health. I am thankful to America which gave me the opportunity to enjoy the life I live. I am so very thankful for the friendship of Carl Sandburg, Andrés Segovia, the Brayes, and a host of others. I am thankful for a Democratic President who I am sure will make this country greater, stronger and an even better place to live.

And now I want to thank you personally for the copy of "Playboy" containing your beautiful poems, and for your new book "Wind Song" sent to David. He received it 2 weeks before publication date.

You will be interested to know that the Guitar Shop is now carrying the Sandburg books on its shelves.

I get weekly reports from Marjorie about your activities, and I am particularly happy to learn the good news about you and Helga.[11]

We are all looking forward to seeing you on your next trip to Washington.

Affectionately yours,

Sophocles

Sandburg's grandson, John Carl Steichen, born 3 December 1941, began six months of study with Papas beginning in January 1961. Papas wrote to the poet on 5 January 1961: "I think the best gift I can send you for your birthday is a glowing report about John Carl—and a truly glowing one it is! What a charming young man, so intelligent, besides possessing musical ability. I find his quickness of mind unusual. I am sure you have noticed it too. I enjoy teaching him very much, and am looking forward to making him a fine guitarist."

John Carl Steichen wrote to me in 1993:

> I have most, if not all, of the music I used as a student with your father. Since he dated each lesson, I can see that I was his student between January and July, 1961. The sheets are annotated by him....I was a poor student, not for a lack of will, but for a lack of talent. Your father's patience was great, but my clumsy fingers often pushed him passed [*sic*] his limits and he whacked them with a baton as a sheepherder would on his errant flock. However, I got through better than Paula, my sister,[12] or Helga, my mother,[13] who became so frustrated with their mediocre skills, clearly highlighted by the baton, that they returned from lessons with tears in their eyes.
>
> A few clear memories remain. I can remember the day that I was doing my best in your father's office sitting in the student's chair next to his desk. Segovia knocked and entered the room. You never saw anyone divest himself of anything as fast as I did that guitar. Now, I had been blaming my poor performance on my chubby fingers, but when I saw how large Segovia's hands were, I decided that I had better stop looking for perfection and be happy with the performance I was able to demonstrate because it wasn't my hands, but my neurons which were limiting me.[14]

In March 1961 Sandburg wrote to Papas about his grandson's study of the guitar:

> You have struck some great chords in the personality of John Carl. He has launched out into the world of music beyond the guitar in a very interesting way. One sentence of a letter from him reads, 'Using the guitar has greatly increased my knowledge of symphonies and the converse.' He follows this with a citation that you might read at anytime when you feel somewhat useless. The sentence goes: 'Mr. Papas's teaching is one of the most enlightening experiences I have had and I think he is one of the best and greatest men I know or can hope to meet.' And this boy is seldom given to extravagant speech. He has nothing less than deep adoration and gratitude about you.

Papas was justifiably proud to have Sandburg as his houseguest and to sit and talk about and play the guitar with him. Once when Sandburg arrived to spend the night but had forgotten his toothbrush, Papas took him to a People's Drug Store in a Virginia shopping mall to buy one. As they walked around the store, a customer said to the poet, "You know, you look just like Carl Sandburg," to which Sandburg replied, "I *am* Carl Sandburg." The man was so excited that he ran to the rack of paperbacks, found a book of Sandburg's poetry, and brought it to him for his autograph.

My father was a terrible punster, and apparently so was Sandburg. They must have enjoyed out-punning each other. Papas liked to retell a joke Sandburg had told him: "After the deluge, Noah opened the gates of the Ark. As the pairs of animals made their exit, he blessed them with 'Go forth and multiply.' Presently two snakes came along and when Noah gave his blessing, they hissed at him. When Noah asked why, they replied, 'We are adders.'"[15]

Papas's young son David was apparently impressed by Sandburg during one of the poet's visits to the house. The day after Sandburg had spent the night, David's grade-school teacher held a Show and Tell session. When it was his turn, David said that Carl Sandburg had spent the night at his house. The teacher did not believe him and sent him to the principal's office for lying. A phone call home soon straightened this out.

Sandburg used only a few chords to accompany himself. Segovia once sent him a short progression of chords, written out in manuscript, complete with fingering and first-position indication,[16] but there is no evidence that Sandburg could read manuscript. Segovia once tried to teach him a few chords, probably at d'Alessio's house, but without success.[17] Sandburg wrote to d'Alessio, "Enclosed, under federal insurance is the long delayed lesson in chords from Brother Segovia.[18] You are to learn this lesson and pass it on to me. It was at the Buchbinder apartment in Chicago that I first met Segovia and failed to amaze him with my virtuosity. He had never met anyone so deeply loving of the guitar and nevertheless so faithless in his love.[19]

In 1967 Papas wrote to Herbert Mitgang, "By 'tónico' or I, and 'dominante' or V, he [Segovia] meant that Carl sings his songs with an accompaniment of two chords, although he sings in more than one key depending on the range of the songs.[20]

In writing poetically of Segovia and the guitar, Sandburg revealed his own love for the instrument:

> Segovia holds his guitar as though it is the world's greatest belonging. In his hands it is definitely the world's greatest guitar. In his hands it becomes a testament, a living book of numbers now strange and again familiar to us. As a naive twelve-year-old boy he said to himself, 'I shall become the apostle of the guitar,' and this young hope of his has become a complete reality. To all the continents of earth and to hundreds of cities he has gone with the instrument and whatever the language of the audience he faced, they knew what he was saying. It was an international language. The syllables in which he speaks are measured and coordinated sounds, evoking a living speech known to all peoples no matter what their tongues, dialects or slang. His results are wrought out of intensive practice and infinitely fine calculations that have become instinctive with the micrometric modulations of his themes. His poise is a paradox. His fingers summon from the strings winter storm crash or the blue whisper of a low valley wind, one moment profound contemplation and then bright whims windblown. After hearing him once I imagined him saying, "I have toiled, loved, suffered, laughed and sung. I have been moved the same as trees in either zephyr or hurricane. I have been identified with roses blooming in the sun and with dry roots in the underground darkness. I tell my story as best I can through my guitar and when I have played my final themes, I will await any fate with the calm of a silent guitar." To that polyphonic instrument Segovia has brought a new high name and a tall true dignity. He sheds a flow of light and meaning on the multi-voiced orchestral values possible in guitar music.[21]

Sandburg said of the guitar, "There has been [a guitar] in the house since 1910. The guitar is part of our lives. Sophocles Papas is going to arrange a song for me. You know Sophocles Papas. In Washington? Segovia sleeps there when he comes to town." Helga adds, "[Carl] hunts in a closet and comes out with a lute-shaped guitar. 'That is for you [Paula] and John. One of you might want to fool around with some chords sometime. And there's Sophocles Papas, Segovia's friend and a guitar teacher, who'd give you lessons!'" Helga continues: "Remember the lute-shaped guitar that Buppong gave Paula? She set it in a corner of the apartment on our return to Washington and John eyes it with interest. The case is battered with travel and use, an adhesive-tape patch half-mended hangs on one side. The guitar itself shows signs of having been around, has elaborate scrolled giltwork set into the face. Sophocles Papas' studio is but four blocks from where John works. How lucky that Carl was moved to present this particular instrument at this time! Before long classic guitar chords ring out in the evenings. A check and note have arrived from the grandfather."[22] The note reads:

Dear John Carl,

This enclosure for guitar lessons with Papas. It goes to you near your birthday and Xmas—even tho any day in the year is one wherein there is love of you from

Buppong[23]

Helga quotes a letter in which Sophocles refused payment for John Carl's lessons: "John told me that you sent him the money to pay for the lessons but I refused it. Your friendship pays for everything I may be able to do for the Sandburg clan."

"John writes Carl words that enchant him....The boy gives his grandfather a further report that, "I am finding that my ability to play the guitar attracts people. Tonight, on the way back from my lesson, the cab driver asked me to show him how to tune a guitar. In a short time I was showing him all I knew about the guitar and he was showing me what he knew about the harmonica. I must admit that the people in our apartment house must have strange thoughts when one of the tenants is playing the guitar for a cab driver on the sidewalk. Again, I would like to express my thanks for your giving Paula and myself the means for buying better guitars."[24]

Sandburg died in 1967, and in the summer of 1969 Mercia and my father visited Sandburg's widow Paula, who at that time still lived in Flat Rock, North Carolina. Daddy was especially pleased that he was invited to sleep in Sandburg's bed. An article in the *Washington Star* reported that Papas had gone to Flat Rock to prepare four of Sandburg's guitars to be given to the National Park Service. Sandburg's widow, in her 80s, was giving the home to the National Park Service.[25]

Sandburg wrote more than one poem about the guitar. This one was dedicated to Segovia.[26]

The Guitar
Some definitions by Carl Sandburg

A chattel with a soul often in part owning its owner
    and tantalizing him with his lack of perfection.
An instrument of quaint form and quiet demeanor
    dedicated to the dulcet rather than the diapason.
A box of chosen wood having intimate accessories
    wherefrom sound may be measured and commanded
    to the interest of ears not lost to hammer crash
    or wind whisper.
A portable companion distinguished from the piano
    in that you can take it with you,
    neither horses nor motor truck being involved.
A small friend weighing less than a newborn infant,
    ever responsive to all sincere efforts
    aimed at mutual respect, depth of affection
    or love gone off the deep end.
A device in the realm of harmonic creation
    where six silent strings have the sound potential
    of profound contemplation or happy go lucky whim.
A highly evolved contrivance whereby delicate
    melodic moments mingle with punctuation of silence
    bringing the creative hush.
A vibratory implement under incessant practice
    and skilled cajolery giving out with serene
    maroon meditations, flame dancers in scarlet sashes,
    snow-white acrobats plunging into black midnight pools,
    odd numbers in evening green waltzing
    with even numbers in dawn pink.

But Papas was happiest with Sandburg's endorsement of him personally:

Sophocles Papas

a great apostle, great teacher
of the guitar
and a good friend of unfinished,
clumsy fingers
like the undersigned scrivener's

Carl Sandburg
1 9 6 0[27]

Alice Artzt

Alice Artzt is a guitarist who lives in New York City but also performs in many other cities, often with her international trio. When I interviewed her she said that she is not absolutely sure of the first time she met Papas, but she thought it was probably in the late 50s or early 60s. "I played a little concert for the New York Guitar Society and this was way back when the Guitar Society concerts were *the* Concerts; they were the way you heard the guitar in New York. There wasn't too much else going on. Of course there was the annual Segovia concert. But this was probably before Bream gave his first concert."[28]

Papas drove up from Washington to hear her play. "I was extremely impressed and honored to find out this famous, famous person had come up from D.C. to my concert. Perhaps he came up for another reason, but he gave me to believe that that was the reason he came up. It was winter and snowing, and I thought wow, boy, that's something."

The concert took place at the Society of Illustrators,[29] where many of the Guitar Society meetings were held. Artzt recalled that Rose Augustine, Martha Nelson, Bobri—all the regulars at guitar society meetings—and "all the old guard" attended.

Artzt recalls another program she gave, this time in Washington. "I was playing at some place, possibly the Phillips Gallery or the Smithsonian or another gallery. When I got to the concert here comes Sophocles Papas with a big heavy metal footstool, kind of wrought-iron with a green cushion. He plopped it down in front of my chair and said, 'You have to use this: it is

Segovia's footstool, the one he always uses.'"[30] Artzt was overwhelmed, in more ways than one: "I was a little afraid of it because it was so heavy—it must have weighed about 20 pounds—and it was big too and took up a lot of floor space in front of the chair. And of course with a flowing skirt I couldn't see where my feet were, and I was quite worried that I would trip over it. But I didn't. So that was fun, and that was the major other occasion when I met him."

In 1974 Columbia Music published Artzt's Cimarosa transcriptions,[31] and she recalled that Papas wanted to change the fingering in a particularly tricky spot.

> I think it was a matter of preparing, of sustaining lines. The obvious and easy way to grab the notes was one thing. But if you did a rather awkward thing, then you had your fingers all prepared so that in a very minimal amount of time you could slide to the next thing with a couple of fingers already more or less on the chord. And that was a priority for me. I remember your father wrote me and said, hey, why do you do this crazy thing when you could do nice, reasonable fingering. And I wrote back defending my point. I think he wound up sort of half correcting it, because now that spot has sort of half one thing and half another. It's not a playable thing at all.

Later Artzt's colleague guitarist Liona Boyd told her she too had been playing the piece. Artzt said, "Let me give you the right fingering for that section because it's kind of weird there, sort of half one fingering and half another." "Well," Liona said, "I've been doing what it says on the music!"

Artzt added when speaking of her own transcription of the Bach Chaconne: "My version of the Chaconne is substantially different from Segovia's, although I don't think it's much different as far as difficulty is concerned. But you know that Segovia tended to add things, enormous numbers of things, and I add some, but basically what I do is add them *where they can make an effect*. I think mine is a little more subtle than his. Then the other major change I made is in all the arpeggiation, which is meant to be done violinistically by the violin. Segovia basically took the patterns a violinist would do [Artzt sings the phrase], which aren't particularly suited to the guitar, so I chose other patterns...easier to play, so I would say that the arpeggio section is more guitaristic, that it fits better under the fingers."

Carlos Barbosa-Lima

Carlos Antônio Barbosa-Lima, a Brazilian-trained guitarist, became a close friend of the Papas family and did the fingering on many Columbia Music publications. Seth Himmelhoch, a guitarist in New York City, interviewed him on 27 June 1986. Following are excerpts from the interview.[32] First Seth asked him about Papas.

> I first heard of Papas in Brazil when I was in my teens, from Savio, my teacher, who in turn heard about him through Bonfá. But later I developed a close friendship with the Papas family. I enjoyed his humor, which lasted until nearly the end of his life.
>
> Papas liked people and liked teaching; from the beginning he knew he was not a composer or a performer, but he was good enough to play on the radio; he played accessible pieces to his own possibility [sic]. He was also good socially, in relating to people, a great gift because this way he introduced the guitar in certain areas, to people not before exposed to it. It takes someone like him with this natural gift of relating to people. He also had the advantage of speaking several languages, which left him in a good position in the Depression.[33]
>
> He also knew how to lay the groundwork for promoters and how to open doors for performers. He was interested in anyone who showed any promise as a performer and in different styles of music. He was one of the few people who went beyond boundaries of the guitar. He was accepted in other music circles, and was respected by impresarios, record producers, and producers in New York and so on. He gave lots of parties and introduced people. His wife [Mercia] was a great cook, and she made Greek dishes although she was herself an American.

Barbosa-Lima explains how he first came to know Papas and his generosity.

> I played in the United States first in 1967, under the sponsorship of the Brazilian Minister of Foreign Affairs. Also Ambassador [Vasco Leitão] da Cunha had heard me in Brazil at a party, and he happened to know Papas and connected us through one of my recordings. Then when I came to play in Washington for the first time, the Ambassador phoned Papas. (The

Ambassador happened to speak Greek also, although Papas had excellent English.) Papas called the critics and people to come to the concert. Papas truly made the concert a real event. His reputation was strong so the critics came because they respected Papas.

Papas told me to phone him after my concert and to come to see him. I made an appointment with him, but I never got there because the person driving me had a flat tire. I thought he would think, oh, just another South American with no sense of time. I had to phone him and with a mixture of languages made a new appointment with him; he was very understanding. I didn't speak much English, but we managed with a combination of French, Spanish, Italian, and English.

Papas continued to make connections for me and ultimately introduced me to Segovia. The Ambassador of Brazil helped me to get a scholarship to go to Spain to work with Segovia. Papas encouraged me to go there; in fact, he insisted. And I'm glad I went: I won three prizes.

In 1970 Jack Duarte, the English guitarist and composer, received the following in a letter from Papas: "Antônio Carlos Barbosa-Lima was rechristened Carlos Barbosa by Andrés. He is gifted and the latest of Andrés' protégés. Carlos has just completed two records for Westminster. #1 contains "Nine Scarlatti Sonatas" to be published by CMC and #2 has various pieces including your Prelude."

Duarte also thought highly of Barbosa-Lima and wrote to Papas, "We had Carlos [Barbosa-Lima] here several times and found him a good player, an outstanding sight-reader (in that he gets to the heart of the music as he reads it—and even plays the fingering!), and a lovely person. He even travelled out here on the underground to see us for 15 minutes on his last day—to say thank you for the hospitality. Most unusual."

And even Mrs. Duarte[34] was impressed; she wrote: "Have you seen Carlos lately? He stayed a few days with us in April. We had a reception for him to meet Jack's pupils and had a very good time and a house-full. The pupils were delighted by his playing. We rate him now in the top flight of players, after Segovia, Bream and Williams, both in temperament, musicality, technique—everything that goes to make an outstanding performer. Jack is recommending his name everywhere he can."

Barbosa-Lima continued: "He [Papas] then opened doors for me even in Europe—through his contacts. He introduced me to other guitar people and to important people. He had a European background but became Americanized too, which made a good bridge culturally."[35]

My father took a great interest in the career of Barbosa-Lima who did not come from a wealthy family and needed financial support to build a career in music. Papas included him in the family, and Barbosa-Lima helped him with his publishing company by doing arranging, writing out manuscripts, and so forth. Papas became interested in Brazilian music and produced some successful publications.

Barbosa-Lima continues:

Papas helped me by sending out my recordings. But I didn't study with him and in no way did I adopt his style.[36]

I was kind of shy and in fact spoiled when I came to the U.S., but he gave me support and the confidence to keep going. He helped me in my social and thus career relationships, as well as in my business efforts— going to the right places, for example. He told me that you cannot rush things, that "who rushes, stumbles," and thus helped me build my career.

In 1970 he invited me to stay several months at his home, so I wouldn't have to spend money on a hotel.[37] I built a close friendship with him and he gave me the parental protection I had had from my own family in Brazil. I helped him by copying manuscripts and this saved him money. I found it fun to do and it was helpful; also I learned the editing process. I learned lots about the music business from Papas, which I need to know because you have to edit music for the guitar, even Ginastera's work. Until the year 1972–1973 I was away from Brazil about half of every year. The rate of exchange got worse and worse, so I began teaching at Carnegie-Mellon. This was my first teaching experience, and Papas helped me with the philosophy and psychology of teaching, especially how to get the best from your students. After being on the faculty from 1974–1977, I finally moved to New York in 1980. From the mid-70s I spent lots of time at his house. We took walks and talked philosophically. He had incredible energy and was always creative and still socially active and interested in people. He accepted that his old age was coming. He was a statesman of the guitar. He really was the center of the guitar scene, and not only in Washington.

He lived to be 92. He was a man of great vitality, although he didn't do much exercise — just walked a couple of blocks. But he always had a short nap, like so many Europeans and South Americans. He was privileged to have good health and a healthy attitude to life. He worried just about the necessary things — a good philosophy. He was wise and very young at heart, youthful. At the same time he was very businesslike, therefore successful. He got annoyed with people who didn't behave correctly. He ate anything he wanted. He kept going by his inner being and this collapsed when Mercia died. After Mercia died he was a bit confused but was aware of her death.

Once Charlie Byrd and I made a tribute to him. He was living in the retirement home, but he came to the nightclub and enjoyed it.

In a general sense I think he felt that he had accomplished his mission. He had raised a family: from his first wife he had a daughter, Elisabeth, who is also a musician; her husband is a professor and they live in Canada. From Mercia he had two sons, Theodore and David. Mercia was so generous, dynamic, a remarkable person, and very important in his life. He was a humanitarian. He enjoyed teaching. He made many close friends of his pupils. Many came to take guitar just as a hobby, but wound up being close friends. He had a big bar in his house, he always had fun, people playing, enjoying people and music. The hospitality he and Mercia offered was genuine and generous.

Without his presence I don't think the guitar would have taken off the way it did. The guitar was his vehicle of contribution to mankind.

Himmelhoch ended this interview by saying, "I'm sorry I began [guitar study] so late that I didn't come under his influence."

In May 1976 Barbosa-Lima received an interesting letter from composer Alberto Ginastera concerning the problems of composing for the guitar. Ginastera had met Segovia in Buenos Aires and received proposals from the great guitarist about composing some music for him. Ginastera had always found the guitar difficult to write for, but Segovia told him, 'Just compose like if it was for a left-hand piano,' which hardly clarified anything. Ginastera ended the letter by saying, "If you happen to see Mr. Papas, please give him my cordial regards since I always remember the day when we met, some thirty years ago."38

I well remember Carlos in Washington: he stayed at my parents' house, he gave concerts, we met him at the airport. He is now playing much crossover music, such as his own transcriptions of Scott Joplin and Gershwin.

John Duarte

John W. Duarte, born in 1919, is a prolific British composer of music for guitar and guitar with voice and other instruments. Trained as a chemist, he retired from science to devote his time to the guitar—writing, reviewing, composing, judging, teaching—everything related to the guitar. His compositions numbered nearly 200 in 1995, and Columbia Music has published several of them. Duarte also hosted Segovia, corresponded with him, and wrote music for the great guitarist.

Alice Artzt recalled a party at Papas's house in Washington at which she met Jack Duarte.[39] "Jack told me about his own first meeting with Papas. He had seen lots of pictures of him and thought he was a big tall man. So Papas was coming up to Jack's hotel room, and Jack was standing in front of the elevator looking at a certain height. The door opened and he didn't see anybody. He was looking for a giant to come out of the elevator."[40]

Papas's correspondence with Duarte, in appendix M, began in 1954 and ended in 1979.[41] The reader may find it interesting to relate their letters to the Segovia-Papas correspondence in this book.

Incidentally, Duarte has never found out the fate of his *Three Songs without Words for Carlos Andrés*, composed about 1970.[42] Papas was to publish them, and they had been sent to Segovia for editing and fingering. Daddy was in correspondence with Segovia about this work in 1970 and 1974, but no one, not even Duarte, has a copy of the work. Perhaps a photocopy is languishing in someone's music stack.

Duarte came twice to visit the family at the Wynford Drive house. He later wrote to me, "I had forgotten that Mercia was Sophocles' *second* wife; odd that she should have succumbed to 'a couple of sudden and massive heart-attacks' [he is quoting a letter from me], not too common a female fate. She was such a tower of strength to him that I'm not surprised that Sophocles wasted away when she disappeared...I'm sure that when you get to be 93 or 94 you *need* a strong prop.[43] Funny, too, how little things come back to mind:

when I visited them in Fairfax in 1973 Sophocles asked what I would drink as an aperitif, so, it being a 'Greek' household, I suggested ouzo; after a little search he found a bottle—it had never been opened and had to have the dust blown off it! On the next visit the exercise was repeated; out came the same bottle—untouched since '73, as the liquid level confirmed."[44]

Jack also said, "Many years ago, when I was about to publish my first piece with Columbia, Segovia said to me: 'Be careful with him [Sophocles], he is entirely honest, but he is a very sharp businessman!' As his undoubted honesty was all that concerned me—and was all I ever perceived, I still wonder why he bothered to say it!!!"[45]

Clare Callahan

Clare Callahan's family moved from England to Washington, D.C., when she was a teenager. She had studied guitar in Europe and England and wanted to continue. Her mother asked around, and everyone recommended Sophocles Papas. She did well in her study with him and taught for him in 1974 when he went to Santiago de Compostela. As Papas reported afterward, "She did a fine job."[46] Apparently he had vetted her for teaching in his place, in part by observing her as she helped other students while waiting for a lesson, and also during her lessons by asking her how she would finger a given passage or teach a piece.

In 1972 Clare was invited to start a guitar program at the University of Cincinnati's music conservatory (known as CCM, for College-Conservatory of Music). In 1992 CCM celebrated the twentieth anniversary of its guitar program. Now a tenured professor there, Clare remains an active promoter of the guitar. Her stated goal is to work hard to produce many good guitarists. She would like to see more women in the program at CCM, but she says that most classical guitar students come from the world of popular music in which few women perform. The other face of this is that the students have not listened to the traditional classical repertoire—symphonic music, for example—so they lack much of the background important to style in performance. CCM offers both bachelor's and master's degrees for guitar majors and puts on an active program of guitar workshops and concerts by visiting artists and the large number of guitar students. Callahan also runs a Classical Guitar Workshop at CCM in the summers.[47]

James W. Symington

Papas met Senator Symington (D.-Mo.) in the early 1960s. A note in the *Star* of 22 December 1967 says that "the father of the guitar in Washington is working on a children's teaching program with [Sen.] Symington" for the children of Washington. Apparently this never matured.

In 1993 Senator Symington wrote to me from his Washington law firm:

> Your Dad was one of those rare individuals whose touch on people's lives is never forgotten. When I came to Washington in 1960 to enter law and government, folksinging with guitar was my connection with sanity and serenity. Checking in with the Guitar Shop at that time I met your incomparable father who:
>
> 1. Greatly enhanced my understanding of the instrument, via lessons, discussions and the example of his playing at various informal recitals;
>
> 2. Found me an instrument made by his friend[48] in Florida, which I still treasure; and
>
> 3. Gave his crucial and invaluable support to my project to bring guitars and guitar lessons to the young inmates of Junior Village.[49]
>
> As I was leaving my job as Chief of Protocol to run for Congress, I gave a benefit performance for Junior Village at the Shoreham Hotel. Some 500 attended, and the proceeds ($8,000.00), were invested in guitars and lessons for the Village youngsters, all under the supervision of Washington's prima [*sic*] guitarist, Sophocles Papas.
>
> Everything your Dad did he did with a kind of twinkle and a modesty that belied both his enormous talent and his dedication to the community. Those were golden days for us all, never to be repeated except in the next world when I can once again enjoy your father's glorious skills, and more importantly, his invariably refreshing company.
>
> Sincerely,
>
> James W. Symington

Over the years Papas corresponded with a wide range of people interested in the guitar, and he repaid that interest with enthusiasm.

Alvino Rey, the catalyst who brought the King family and the Papases together, recalled the beginning of his long friendship with Papas: "I heard about him in Toledo—a lady there recommended Papas. She said, 'If you want a real teacher go to Washington and there is a certain Mr. Papas who will really teach you the correct method for the classic guitar.' I was intrigued and I flew down. That was the start of a lifelong association and friendship. That was when I was traveling all over the country, but whenever I had a chance I'd come to Washington for a guitar lesson with him."[50]

On 18 December 1968 Patrick Hayes, Washington entrepreneur, sent a telegram for Papas's 75th birthday: "Have asked mayor and city council to pass special law forbidding you to become 75 years of age this must not happen but if it does warm good wishes for a happy birthday and a long life ahead."

Papas also kept correspondence from Ben Bradlee, Executive Editor of the *Washington Post*; from Melville Grosvenor of the National Geographic Society; from Albert Schweitzer in Lambaréné; from author Oliver La Farge; from *Washington Post* cartoonist Herb Block; from Gregory d'Alessio, author and artist; and from students such as Clare Callahan. And letters of appreciation came from the Director General of the Pan American Union; from Sharon Isbin, who took a number of lessons with him; from Liona Boyd, and others.

An unknown admirer once wrote, "This is simply a thank-you note; it is to thank you for pointing me in the right direction with guitar technique back in 1969 when I was playing [at] a restaurant in Washington."

In 1977 Joseph McLellan, another *Post* music critic, wrote:

> Our town is uncommonly endowed with good classical guitarists (we can thank the benign influence of Sophocles Papas for much of that), but its difference from other towns of similar size is not overwhelming.
>
> Look around the United States, and you may be led to the conclusion that people who play the guitar almost outnumber those who don't; that's a slight exaggeration, but the guitar is certainly the most widely played instrument on the musical scene.
>
> It has taken a bit over a half-century since Segovia began to show the world the instrument's potential, but the golden age of the guitar may be finally upon us.[51]

In 1993 a guitarist in Frosinone, Italy, faxed me: "Your letter reminded me with great pleasure of the outstanding personality of your father Sophocles, a true pioneer of the guitar in America....It has been an honour and a pleasure to hear from you."

8: PAPAS AS TEACHER, PUBLISHER,
JUDGE, COLLECTOR, AND COOK

Papas as Teacher

Sophocles Papas was an extremely busy teacher who rarely took a long vacation.[1] A number of Papas's appointment books are held in the archive at George Mason University, and they provide some interesting information about his students.[2] Recently I looked through a number of them and noticed lessons for Charlie Byrd, Bill Harris, Sol Snyder, Pick Temple, Marjorie Braye, Sandburg's grandson John Carl, John Marlow, Larry Snitzler, George Crile, Myrna Sislen, and Jeff Meyerriecks. He kept weekly tallies of new students and those interrupting or discontinuing lessons. His average number of students per week was about 70, but at times he had as many as 90. In any case, the records show that he taught many more than 40 hours a week. Papas typically would schedule one half hour for his dinner, but by dinnertime he was usually running a bit late, so he would squeeze it into 15 to 20 minutes. Then it was back to teaching, usually until about 10 p.m. Once, when he felt that he would like to cut back a bit on the number of teaching hours, he raised his fees, in the hope that he would scare away some of his workload. Only two students stopped taking lessons. Even on Sundays Papas often taught a few students or did some teaching preparation, and only occasionally did he take time for family. His appointment page for Sunday, 11 May 1952, contains the succinct notation: "B.P.C.U.," which no doubt meant "Betty Papas [in recital at] Catholic University"; and he did attend this, my first solo recital.

Papas did not confine himself to teaching only prodigies. He also had many pupils who made little progress but seemed to derive something so special from the lesson time that they continued for many years. For example, Dr. Benjamin Frank, a criminal psychologist, began taking lessons in 1936 and continued until the mid-60s. Frank often had to cancel lessons when he traveled on business, but he always resumed on his return. He did not make great progress, but he was musical and found the lessons therapeutic in some way; he even bought a Fleta guitar. Another of Papas's longtime students was

Paul Gray, a Washington psychiatrist. Papas had always been interested in psychology, so contacts like this were especially enjoyable for him personally.

A former student wrote: "I never got to be a real guitar player—I had no voice and no talent, but your dear father was such a fine gentleman that he never made me feel uncomfortable although he certainly knew I'd never make it! I still wish at age 71 that I could play my lovely old delicate Martin guitar which is much older than I."[3]

Former student Irene Rosenfeld, now of Chapel Hill, North Carolina, studied with him for about four years beginning in 1949, and remembers his exceptional style of teaching: his patience, his ability to explain, his kindness, his interest in each student as a person.[4]

My association with Sophocles was a combination of intensive guitar lessons, plenty of Turkish coffee (a part of each lesson), and lots of support in case of troubles, personal or otherwise. Members of the Washington Classical Guitar Society would speak about his quality of being so supportive. Some said they didn't come to take the lesson so much as to sit and talk with him because he was such a wonderful human being.

He never pretended to be a shrink, but just spoke out of concern for people and from his own life experience. At the guitar society meetings one always heard people saying 'Isn't he marvelous!,' but they meant him as a person as much as a guitarist and teacher. Many Washington people were far away from home at that time, and needed someone to talk to.

I never saw anyone come to him for a lesson who wasn't enthusiastic and excited to be there. He was always very kind in making corrections, also very constructive; that is, when he criticized, he didn't devastate you. I thought that he should have been teaching only advanced students or master classes, but he had great patience and was so encouraging to beginners.[5]

In 1975 Jerry Dallman wrote: "Rather than play the pedant, Papas likes to direct students to make discoveries for themselves. He realizes that all pupils search for reasons. The fundamental requirements for classical technique are Segovia's scales and slurs, a good series of arpeggio studies, and chromatic octaves. But you must remember that the end product wanted is quality of sound, with maximum volume and speed when required. Individual requirements differ. 'If you can only achieve this while standing on your head,' Papas says, 'I'll teach you to play standing on your head.'"[6]

In addition to Charlie Byrd and Sharon Isbin, Papas had also taught Aaron Shearer. After he heard Segovia in Seattle, Shearer asked Segovia where he could study this guitar style. Segovia recommended he go to Washington to study with Papas, and he was Papas's pupil for about 9 months in 1953.[7] Today, Shearer is a well-known guitar teacher at the North Carolina School of the Arts and author of a series of graded guitar methods.

Arthur Larson, a prominent lawyer who lived in Durham, North Carolina, studied with Papas in 1952. In 1986, Washington guitarists Myrna Sislen, Larry Snitzler, John Marlow, and Jeff Meyerriecks, all Papas students, formed a special quintet with Charlie Byrd to play at Papas's memorial service in tribute to their teacher. They liked playing as a group so they continued and have given a number of programs since then.

Sharon Isbin, winner of first prize at Guitar 74 in Toronto and now head of the guitar department at Juilliard, began to study with Papas when she was 14,[8] and even when studying at Yale she occasionally came down to Washington to take a lesson with him. In 1986 she was quoted in the *Post*:

> As a teacher with a promising student, Papas could be highly exacting. What I learned from him, at a crucial time in my life, was the importance of self-discipline. I began studying with him when I was 14, commuting from Minneapolis, where I lived, to Washington. I was proud of myself because I practiced an hour a day, but he was appalled and insisted that I should do four hours. He gave me scales and exercises, which I had never done, and he gave me a sense of responsibility. From him I learned the importance of preparation and the amount of work it takes to meet my responsibilities as a musician. He was demanding. When he recognized a person's talent, he wanted to develop its full potential, and he would not stand for laziness.[9]

Later, in a Christmas card to me, she said that she had memories "of the very important role he played in my life."

Another performer, Liona Boyd, did not study with my father, but she had great respect for him and often sought his advice.

Many students began taking lessons with Papas with the idea of learning only a few chords so they could accompany songs. And it is true that with only two chords you can play many accompaniments, with only three, many more. But Papas always explained that, if students learned to read music, they would be able to do much more than that. He would put his method[10] on the music stand and begin to explain the principles, and before long most students were beginning to read the notes.

Guitar composer Jim Skinger, who was also a student of Papas's, recalled the following:

> I'll tell you how I came to know Sophocles. As a young student in the late fifties, I would order music from his company and every so often he would send me a complimentary copy of something new he had just published, with a little handwritten note—it was a wonderful personal touch. I still have some of the music.
>
> Some time in the mid-sixties, I called him and arranged to come down for lessons; at the time I was living in Worcester, Massachusetts, and would fly down and back in one day! I loved it—he was so generous with his time and his knowledge. At that time I needed someone who understood real technique and he was one of the very few teachers who understood what was necessary and what had to be done. I still have his own copies of Segovia's left-hand studies which he gave me before they were actually published.[11] Sophocles did offer me a job in his shop so that I could continue to study on a more regular basis with him, but I had just started college and was married, so the idea of uprooting seemed difficult, at the time. Our time together was brief, only a few lessons, but the knowledge I gained has lasted a lifetime.[12]

Because there was so little music available when Papas began teaching, he often had a student play the scales while he copied a new arrangement into the student's manuscript book. This way each student had a new piece to practice. These arrangements included lots of song accompaniments. His students used his method until they were able to move on to the Carl Fischer edition of Carcassi.

Papas emphasized the practice of scales to develop speed in playing. He believed scale practice should occupy a third of total practice time, and that various approaches to scales could be used.[13]

Papas believed that teaching was a real commitment; that it was not work but pleasure; that teaching was creative; that one had to love to teach to transmit knowledge, otherwise the teacher himself would be bored and would transmit boredom to the student. A former pupil wrote him, "What Segovia is in the field of performance you are in the field of guitar pedagogy. It is a shame that those true torch-bearers, the private music masters, are not given a fraction of the credit in the advancement of music that their performing counterparts are given."[14]

As a youth, Jesuit priest Kevin F. Kersten studied with Papas. Twenty years later he wrote this tribute to his teacher on the occasion of Papas's 80th birthday, in which he attributes both character and spiritual development to his guitar training:

> Warmest congratulations as you celebrate this anniversary of your teaching career! Studying the guitar under you as a young boy in the early 1950s touched me deeply and influenced me indelibly. This influence has taken the form of three gifts for which I will always be grateful....They will be with me when I die.
>
> The first gift is a sense of discipline.
>
> The second is a love of music, whose fruit has been growth of the heart and the deepest kind of aesthetic pleasure.
>
> The third is immersion into the mysteries, fun, disciplines, and love of the guitar itself—enabling me to appreciate the work of the masters and enticing me to meet the challenge of this most personal and soul freeing instrument. Thank you for these gifts. I will treasure them always.[15]

After my father died, Kersten wrote to me: "Music is in my bones, and your father along with two or three others in my life are responsible for that. He not only provided me with fundamentals in playing the classical guitar, but in the process taught me, at a very impressionable age, what a good teacher is and what a gentleman is."[16]

Not only students but also colleagues would write to Papas to express gratitude for his help and admiration for his dedication. Lloyd Ultan, a composer and chairman of the music department at American University in Washington, D.C., wrote in 1967: "You have been a very major influence upon me in arousing my interest in the guitar and have always retained my respect for your devotion and dedication to the promotion of this instrument and its literature."[17]

An unknown admirer wrote:

> One happy result of the United States's open-arms immigration policy was the arrival in this country of Sophocles Papas in 1914....To have knowledge of and love for the guitar is one thing—but to be able to pass it on to others is more. This Mr. Papas can do. To the students who bring to the studio only a humble willingness to learn, Mr. Papas gives himself unstintingly. Sparing with praise, lavish with constructive criticism, Mr Papas has inexhaustible patience with the clumsy fingers and uncertain ear of the beginner.
>
> One of the most valuable contributions Mr. Papas makes to his students is a love for the guitar and an insight into its special possibilities. This is a transference, rare enough in modern life, of an ideal beauty from one person who possesses it and whose life is enriched by it, to another whose mind and heart are ready to receive it. If a student gets this and nothing more from his relationship with his teacher, he has a cause for unending gratitude.

Papas's datebooks continue to be quite full until 1971; the books for 1972 and 1973 are missing. By 1974, at age 80, the book contained more medical appointments than lessons. He hardly taught at all after 1975 because his hearing began to deteriorate, and after a flight to Brazil in the summer of 1977 it was so bad that he really could not even tune his guitar. When he and Mercia moved to a retirement home, he took a guitar with him. When family visited he occasionally took it out of the case and tried to play a bit, but he could not hear it. It was touching when he asked me to tune it for him.

Papas as Publisher

Papas began to publish music in the 1920s because so little guitar music was available. At first he simply copied out his own transcriptions for his students, but then he saw the possibility of publication. However, his first publications were for banjo: in 1927, a piece called *Eventide*, dedicated "With love to my wife [Eveline], for piano and three tenor banjos with optional fourth tenor banjo ad lib."[18] Then in 1928 came *American Fantasy, A Medley for*

Tenor Banjo Solo,[19], followed by two collections in 1930, *Twelve Graded Solos for Tenor Banjo*[20] and *Twelve Easy Duets for Tenor Banjo*.[21]

An early ad in the *Washington Daily News*[22] says that Columbia Music Co., Inc., "recently made its debut with *Favorite Collection of Hawaiian Guitar Solos with 2nd and 3rd Hawaiian Guitar Parts, ad libitum,* by Sophocles T. Papas, 'The Wizard of the Guitar'; Contains 16 Favorites, effective in any combination. Three parts complete $1.00; Canada $1.20.*"

The company published Segovia's *Diatonic Major and Minor Scales*[23] in 1953 and later his *Slur Exercises and Chromatic Octaves.*[24] Segovia was the first to organize the fingering of the scales systematically so that a student had to learn only six basic patterns (plus F major). In fact, most of the early Columbia Music publications were for teaching, not for performance.[25] For instance, *Sixty Short Pieces for Guitar* by Fernando Sor[26] included a note by Vladimir Bobri describing the publication as "a collection of graded pieces for guitar, edited by Sophocles Papas, a teacher of many years of experience...suitable for the first and second years."

Papas as Judge

On his 1963 return to Greece Papas visited his family in Ioannina and then went to Orense, Spain, to serve on the jury at the International Competition of Guitarists. From Orense he went to Santiago de Compostela where Segovia was teaching. Papas intended to leave soon, but one day at lunch Segovia asked him to be one of the judges of the guitar competition. He was also a judge in Porto Alegre, Brazil, in 1974 and 1977, and at Guitar 78 in Toronto. And he gave a Columbia Music Company prize of $200 to the competition in Porto Alegre in 1978 and 1979.

Papas was a judge in many guitar competitions; These are important for the winners, who usually receive not only prize money but a concert tour and of course publicity.[27]

Papas as Collector

Papas's love for the guitar extended to a fascination with stringed instruments of all kinds. An article in a guitar society bulletin said: "Besides being a leading light of the guitar scene in and around Washington, D.C., Sophocles

Papas, guitarist, teacher, dealer, is a dedicated collector of ancient and odd stringed instruments."[28] A 1967 feature article in a Washington newspaper shows Papas posed with part of his collection.[29]

The Papas collection ranged "from a three-stringed Japanese samisen to a Middle Eastern rabab, as well as a Spanish bandurria and a Russian balalaika."[30] Some of this collection was given to Yale University in 1984, and in October 1992 I visited the Yale University Collection of Musical Instruments. There I saw a modern lute; a modern ukulele; a short one-string lute; an Eastern European long lute; a couple of stringed instruments from China and Africa; and a Serbian gusle. The gusle is a southern Slav instrument with engraving that translates approximately "The wondrous Serbian sounds of the gusles surpass the heroic songs of the world to the eternal glory of the Serbs."[31] There are three guitars; one from Cádiz, made by Joseph Pages ("Me hizo en Cádiz, Año de 1850, Calle de la Amargura, No. 70"); another of unknown origin; and a guitarra requinto, by Telesforo Juelve, Valencia, 1940. The instruments Papas collected included a 19th-century bandurria. Inside the instrument are the words "Fábrica de guitarras de Salvador Ibáñez, Bajada Sr. Francisco, Valencia, España." Once when returning from a trip to Brazil I brought my father a berimbau, a Brazilian folk instrument consisting of one wire string, a gourd for a sound box, and feathers; but it barely survived the plane trip and is not included in the collection.

Papas as Cook

In December 1953 the *Washington Post* published an article called "That Man in the Kitchen: An Ear for Music...A Taste for Food," in which Papas cooks a Greek dish, *Makaronia Kyma*, "a traditional Greek spaghetti dish, dating back to the time of Thales, which the well-known Washington guitar soloist and teacher learned to make in his Attic youth. Half a lifetime in America hasn't dulled his culinary memory...and a score of guests will gather at his Columbia School of Music on N Street for an evening of good food."[32] I cannot remember my father ever cooking anything, but it makes a good story. He was always very generous in inviting everyone to a party, but in truth it was Mercia who did the work. Various musicians stayed for days or weeks with the Papas family, and Mercia produced many large-scale lunches and dinners—soup to nuts—such as Europeans and South Americans are used to.

Mercia loved to cook and she could prepare a meal for 4 or 50 people. She used to set up card tables in the living room and TV room, and everyone helped themselves from the huge buffet. Although she came from West Virginia, she learned to make a number of Greek recipes, such as dolmades, lamb Greek style, spanakopita, and kritharaki.

Mercia and often sent me recipes in her letters. In a letter probably written in 1962, she sent her recipe for eggplant moussaka and added, "Segovia has come and gone. We had dinner with him Sat. the 7th. The concert was Sun. the 8th. We had a reception here Sun eve. We had lunch with him Monday before he left. We had so many people—it seems everybody who was invited brought some other people. I still haven't put everything away."

Mercia was always a wonderful hostess. The receptions she put on for Segovia and other guitarists were a great deal of work. Segovia sat while everyone surrounded him adoringly, and sometimes Jesús Silva interpreted and ran errands for him while Mercia brought forth platters of food and drink.

The Lee article about my father's cooking also says: "His wife is a good cook too, Mr. Papas says with pride. He and his musician friends get together for an evening of music and good food. When Burl Ives was here last year, he came out to see the Papas' home on 29th St. in Chevy Chase for a spaghetti supper at 1 a.m. after his show at the Schubert. 'I made spaghetti,' says Mr. Papas. 'I always make double quantity when Burl is here. We both love to eat, and to play music and talk about music—and food.'"

The article includes a couple of Papas recipes (see appendix C), one for the *Makaronia Kyma* and another for *Soupa Avgolemono*, a chicken-and-rice broth with eggs and lemon. He says that this recipe serves eight Americans or four Greeks, or his wife, himself, and Burl Ives.

"Greek people have always liked good food, and we like varied menus," said Mr. Papas, recalling a quotation from the Hellenic author Athanaeus, who 1700 years ago, wrote in the "Deipnosophists":

A change of meat is often good,
And men, who tire of common food
Redoubled pleasure often feel
When sitting at a novel meal.

Papas said in the article, "I always take time out to eat, and I enjoy good cooking almost as much as playing my guitar."

Everyone who ever went to the Papas house exclaims first about the wonderful food Mercia prepared, especially the Greek dishes. Liona Boyd wrote to Papas, "Please say hello to your wife whose great pancakes I still remember." So it was fitting that, after Sophocles Papas's memorial service, everyone went back to the house on Wynford Drive where friends prepared a meal very similar to the one Mercia herself might have prepared. I kept wanting to go into the kitchen to tell Mercia how delicious the food was, and as it turned out, other people had the same feeling—that she was right out there, in the kitchen, refilling the cream pitcher or bringing on yet another delicious dish.

9: LAST THINGS

I don't know if my father knew that he was written up by Thomas Heck in 1986 for the *New Grove Dictionary*,[1] as follows:

Papas [Papadopoulos], **Sophocles** (*b* Sopiki, Greece, 18 Dec 1893; *d* Alexandria, VA, 26 Feb 1986). Guitar teacher and publisher. At the age of 14 he moved from Greece to Cairo, Egypt, where he learned to play the mandolin. In 1912 he returned to Greece, but in 1914 he immigrated to the USA. After serving in the US Army, he settled in 1920 in Washington, DC, where he began performing on radio shows in addition to teaching banjo, mandolin, and classical guitar. As a publisher he established the Columbia Music Company in Washington, and in the late 1920s he was one of very few Americans (others were Bickford, Krick, and Foden) promoting serious guitar literature, especially solo works by European masters. Papas befriended the guitarist Andrés Segovia soon after the latter's début in the USA in 1928, and later published his *Segovia Scales* (1953), a book on technique for aspiring classical guitarists, often reprinted. Papas himself is the author of the popular *Method for the Classical Guitar* (rev. and enlarged 1963). He was also the proprietor of a number of music schools in Washington, DC: Papas Studios (1938–1947), the Columbia School of Music (1947–56), the Guitar Shop (1956–68), and a private studio in the Dupont Circle Building (1968–82). Notable among his students are Aaron Shearer, John Marlow, Clare Callahan, Sharon Isbin, Charlie Byrd, Dorothy de Goede, Alvino Rey, and Joe Breznikar.

BIBLIOGRAPHY

J. Dallman: **Guitar Teaching in the United States: the Life and Work of Sophocles Papas** (Washington, DC, 1978) [interviews].

In 1973 Papas had written to his friend Jack Duarte of his semi-retirement from teaching because of some health problems. In fact, my father remained in remarkably good health until his mid-seventies when he began to lose his hearing and to show some confusion. By 1977 when he flew to Brazil to be a judge, he had already lost a fair amount of hearing. He had a cold, and the flight apparently caused much more damage. When he came back, he was noticeably more deaf and thus became disconnected from people—this man, who had always been so gregarious. During a party for guitarists at the house, I found him in his home office, sitting in his lounger, reading a magazine; I suppose the effort of trying to communicate was no longer worthwhile. He had a hearing aid but never adjusted to using it.

In August 1978 my father was hospitalized because of a prostate problem. Mercia wrote to Ron Purcell on 18 September 1978: "Sophocles is now home and recovering slowly but surely. My job is to keep him going at a slower pace."

Mercia herself, though 16 years younger than Sophocles, was aging noticeably as well. She had a stroke in late January 1980 and spent some time in the hospital and then in a convalescent home. She never fully regained speech competence or control of such matters as numbers and sequential operations. For example, she could not follow a recipe and had lost the ability to have all the elements of a meal ready at the same time. But people outside of Washington did not know much about her illness, and my father was already 86 and I think never fully comprehended what had happened to her. He kept on dictating letters for her to type, but she could no longer do the Gregg shorthand at which she had been an expert. She at last had to give up doing all the secretarial and other work she had always done for my father and Columbia Music Company.

On 23 July 1980, his friend the composer Guido Santorsola wrote from Montevideo: "I am worried by the lack of news, especially regarding the health of my dear friend Mercia. How are you, and how is Mercia? Please let me have some news. Well, dear Sophocles, I await your news and especially news of Mercia's health. A kiss for her, and an embrace for you, Guido."[2]

In the fall of 1983 Ted Papas, their older son, helped them to look for a retirement home in the area, and in late November they entered the Hermitage located in Alexandria, Virginia. Although my father was very resentful of the move at first, Mercia had realized her limitations and was quite relieved to be in an apartment there.

The Hermitage gave them a fine if not entirely accurate welcome speech on 6 December 1983:

> He [Sophocles Papas] was born in Greece and acquired U.S. citizenship through military service in World War I. He also has served in the Greek

Army. He came to Washington as a teacher of guitar at American University [sic] and established a studio. His knowledge of guitar also makes him able to play the mandolin, banjo, and related instruments. Sophocles is a linguist—he speaks French fluently, Italian, Greek, Arabic, and understands Spanish. Because of his ability to speak French, he became an interpreter for Segovia, the world-renowned guitarist, which led to a great friendship with the artist, and they still correspond. He [Papas] said, "Guitarists are all special friends." Mercia's birthplace is Roanoke, Virginia, and she was a law secretary in Washington, D.C., before her marriage and secretary for her husband after. Their romance began in the Papas studio where she was his guitar student, and they observed their 45th anniversary on July 16 [1983].

Myrna Sislen, a Papas pupil and today a recording artist, gave a program on 7 December 1984 at the Hermitage. For the recital, she played both the vihuela and the guitar. A review from the *Alexandria Gazette* of Thursday, 13 December, says: "Papas has worked with many people in the music world, including his friend, classical guitarist Andrés Segovia. Papas, who is fluent in Greek, Arabic and Spanish, worked as a translator for Segovia. Papas convinced the Washington Performing Arts Society to bring Segovia to perform for the first time in Washington during the 1930s. After the concert Sislen reminisced with Papas about The Guitar Shop, the music store Papas operated at 18th and M Sts in Washington: 'Mr. Papas was the driving force in this town for the classical guitar. His store was central in the world of guitar, everybody in the business was influenced by him in one way or another.'"

At the Hermitage Mercia spent much of her time taking care of Papas, and not enjoying the many activities the retirement home offered. So it came as quite a shock—especially given that she was so much younger than Daddy—when she died, rather suddenly, of a couple of heart attacks in November 1985. She, too, had many friends, and they all came to her memorial service held at the Hermitage.

After her death, my father really could not live in the Hermitage apartment by himself; he had become confused and tended to wander. Former student Sol Snyder writes: "In his later days in the nursing home, we talked a good bit by phone. He would phone to ask a question and then call back minutes later with the same question, which was very sad."[3] Because of his condition Sophocles was transferred to the euphemistically named Health Care Center, really the hospital wing of the Hermitage.

The last time I saw my father was on 4 January 1986. My husband and I visited him, and Daddy asked us if there was interest in the guitar in Canada and if he could come up and live with us until he found a place to live and teach. Although he would not have been capable of doing this, it seemed a harmless exercise to answer his questions positively. Thus, even near the end he was thinking of his teaching and making plans for the future.

After Mercia's death I believe my father simply stopped eating—he appeared to have no appetite the last time we saw him—and he died in his sleep on 26 February 1986. A memorial service was held for him at St. James United Methodist Church in Alexandria on 8 March 1986. The church was filled with his friends and family, including his sons Theodore Thomas Papas and David Stephen Papas,[4] and Dorothea Elisabeth Smith, one of his grandchildren. Jeff Meyerricks, Bill Harris, and Carlos Barbosa-Lima played some guitar solos. After the service Mercia's and Daddy's friends put on a big reception at the house on Wynford Drive, with food similar to that Mercia had so often prepared for parties. It was a lovely tribute to the hospitality they had all known in the Papas household.

Joseph McLellan of the *Washington Post* wrote a long obituary, part of which reads: "Papas, an immigrant from Greece, launched the guitar as a classical musical instrument in America almost single-handedly when he opened his guitar shop in Washington in 1922. Guitarists—friends, colleagues, former students and protégés—who recalled Papas yesterday talked about a multifaceted personality whose enthusiasms besides music included people, conviviality, fine cooking and good living."[5]

Later that year, in an announcement of the upcoming 1986 guitar and harpsichord festival, McLellan wrote: "The sounds [of those instruments] are not exactly unheard in Washington the rest of the year;...the guitar shop founded here by the late Sophocles Papas is internationally known. A highlight of the week will be a memorial concert in honor of Sophocles Papas, who made Washington a major guitar center."[6]

Many guitarists came to pay tribute to Sophocles Papas at that memorial concert held on 13 July 1986, and the Washington Guitar Quintet, made up of Charlie Byrd, Myrna Sislen, John Marlow, Jeff Meyerriecks, and Larry

Snitzler, performed in concert at Gaston Hall of Healy Building on the campus of Georgetown University.

At the time the quintet formed, Charlie Byrd was already a Grammy Award winner. Jeffrey Meyerriecks was a teacher at George Mason and Georgetown universities and the first American prizewinner in Brazil's prestigious international Palestrina competition. Larry Snitzler was an international concert guitarist and composer who also taught at George Mason and who hosted the National Public Radio series on Andrés Segovia. John Marlow was then head of the guitar department at American University and founder of the Licha Trio. Myrna Sislen, who taught at George Washington University, had just released an album recorded live at the Kennedy Center.[7]

In a retrospective *Washington Post* writeup in 1991, Dana Thomas reported: "They had all been students of legendary Washington guitar virtuoso Sophocles Papas. So when Papas died a few years ago, the University of Maryland asked [the five] local guitarists to participate in a memorial concert at a guitar conference. Rather than perform separately, however, the five combined talents and founded the Washington Guitar Quintet." Thomas also reported that the quintet had never planned on doing more than one concert, but that, "as Snitzler said, 'We all had such a good time, we continued to get together.'"

My brothers and I were astonished at the number of people who came to the concert, most of whom were attending the First International Classical Guitar Congress at the University of Maryland. The memorial concert was indeed the "highlight of the week."[8]

The five former students played several pieces they had arranged for quintet and also divided up and played in various subsets. In 1977 Papas and John Marlow had arranged one of the quintet works entitled *Quintet: El Noy de La Mare*. In a tribute to Papas, Larry Snitzler said: "If Washington, D.C. has become one of the centers of classical guitar activity in the United States, it is, in large part, due to the efforts of one man: Sophocles Papas."

"The possibilities are five times greater," says Sislen. "We can duplicate almost an entire orchestra."

The group performed in the Washington area and eventually started touring nationally.[9]

The Washington Guitar Quintet performed again in Washington on 11 January 1991; Carlos Barbosa-Lima filled in for Charlie Byrd, who was recovering from surgery. The *Washington Post* review was glowing: "The first half of the program reaffirmed just how well five guitars work as an ensemble when the arrangements are good and each player's personality is allowed to step out of the mix."[10] After the untimely death of John Marlow in the fall of 1992, Carlos Barbosa-Lima became a member of the quintet. But then in the late fall of 1992 Carlos was mugged—he has now fully recovered—and had to be replaced for the sold-out performance in Winston-Salem, North Carolina, in January 1993. And later, his concert schedule made it difficult for the group to rehearse, so as of 1995 Phil Mathieu has become the fifth member.

Larry Snitzler wrote a fine obituary which appeared in the *Guitar Review* of Spring 1986. "[Papas] survived through the years when it [the guitar] was viewed as a curiosity, as Segovia's unwavering efforts brought forth a tidal wave of interest and long-deserved respectability. Papas' labors on behalf of the instrument will be felt for years to come through his many students and Columbia Music's large and varied catalog."[11]

Bart Barnes wrote an unusually accurate obituary for the *Washington Post* of 27 February 1986. The headline was: "Sophocles Papas Dies; Teacher of Classical Guitar," and some excerpts follow:

> Over the years his students included jazz great Charlie Byrd, the wives of senators and diplomats, music teachers and amateurs of varying degrees of talent. It was once said of him that he could probably "get music out of a stalk of celery if he tried hard enough."
>
> He was a longtime friend of Andrés Segovia, the great Spanish classical guitarist. Segovia once gave Mr. Papas a Spanish beret after seeing him in one of Parisian style of which Segovia disapproved. "If I can't fill Segovia's shoes, at least I can wear his hat," commented Mr. Papas.
>
> During Mr. Papas' lifetime, the popular perception of guitar music as being one that was exclusively country and western changed to include classical and jazz, and Mr. Papas took some credit for that change.

Soundboard featured a picture of Sophocles Papas on the cover and a gracious but unsigned obituary in the Winter 1985–86 issue: "It is with heavy heart that we inform our readers of the deaths both of Sophocles Papas and his wife Mercia. Sophocles Papas was present in Santa Barbara, CA in September, 1973 when the Guitar Foundation of America was formed. His personality, wit, and humor will be long remembered by those of us (and we are many) who were privileged to know the gentleman."

Jack M. Smith, Jr., longtime friend and student, wrote the following eulogy for *Soundboard*:

IN MEMORIAM
Mercia Papas

Mercia Papas, wife of Sophocles Papas, leader of the guitar-lovers' community in the nation's capital since the 1920s, passed away on November 5, 1985 in the Virginia suburbs of Washington, DC. Although not a guitarist, or musically trained herself, Mercia Papas made an important contribution to promoting the cause of the classical guitar through her loyal support of the activities of her husband. Starting at a time when the classical guitar was little known in musical circles, and virtually unknown to the general public, Sophocles and Mercia undertook to promote the instrument by teaching, publishing music, and, last but not least, by cultivating the right social contacts. Mercia supported the teaching and publishing by handling all the business affairs of the Columbia School of Music and the Columbia Music Company. It was in the third area, as social hostess, however, that she was a real star. Mercia handled a program of social entertainment that was heavy, even by Washington standards. A dinner party given by Mercia Papas was an event to be remembered. Everything was perfect, from the selection of guests to the exquisite food. More important, however, was Mercia's warm and generous personality, which made even first-time visitors feel completely at home.

Mercia's decades of unselfish devotion to the cause of the guitar may be unknown to many of the younger generation of guitarists and guitar lovers. It is probable, however, they have benefited in some fashion, indirectly, from her life-long efforts. Her passing is a source of great sorrow to her many friends, and a loss to the world of the classical guitar.

Jack Smith also wrote the following article for *Soundboard*:

Sophocles T. Papas, whom the Washington Star once called the "Grand Old Man of the Guitar," died on February 26, 1986 in Alexandria, Virginia at the age of 92. Sophocles, who was also often called "S.T." by his friends, was born on December 18, 1893 to Greek parents in what is now Albania, but was then part of the Turkish Empire. After studying in Cairo, Egypt, he came to the United States in 1914 and served in the American Army during World War I. After the war, he settled in Washington, DC, and in 1922 he began teaching classical guitar, establishing the Columbia Music Company, at that time one of the few publishers of classical guitar music in the United States.

The situation of the guitar in the 1920s, 30s, and 40s was far different from what it is today. Instead of the many first-rate teachers and players we have today, there were only a handful in those days, aside from Andrés Segovia. Sophocles Papas was one of them. As Charlie Byrd has said, "There was a time not too long ago you could have made a list of the two or three most influential guitarists in the entire country, and the name Papas would have been right there."

Sophocles' qualities as a teacher have been vouched for by Andrés Segovia, who wrote in 1944, "I regard Mr. Papas as the professor of guitar most loyal to the instrument, the best informed on its history and its scope, and the most devoted to the cause of disseminating a better understanding and a wider knowledge of the guitar, of any teacher I have met in the United States. Besides, due to the many hours we have spent together since 1928, he is the teacher who is most thoroughly acquainted with my school and with my technique."

In addition to teaching, Sophocles served the cause of the guitar by undertaking to publish music for the instrument. He kept up this publishing activity almost until his death, and, in fact, accelerated the output of publications during the last few years of his life, printing new compositions for the guitar, as well as new arrangements of music originally written for other instruments.

Last, but not least, Sophocles, with the help of his charming wife Mercia—one of the most gracious hostesses in our nation's capital—promoted the cause of the guitar by a program of social entertaining aimed at bringing guitarists together with members of the musical "establishment." The energy and finesse they devoted to this activity certainly contributed to the acceptance which the guitar has achieved in the musical world today.

Sophocles followed by only a few months his loving wife, Mercia, who passed away on November 5, 1985 (see above). The passing of these two fine people marks the end of an era in the history of the guitar in America. Sophocles is survived by a daughter, Betty Smith, and two sons, David and Theodore.

Jack M. Smith, Jr.[12]

I never thought to record my father's playing, I am sorry to say. The only recording of him was done by Joe Orso at a 1961 party Papas gave for Carl Sandburg at the Virginia house.[13] Daddy played a Renaissance piece, the Villa-Lobos Prelude No. 3, and *Lágrima* by Tárrega. The sound quality is poor and his playing is accompanied by people talking and glasses clinking. Even so, his tonal quality and expressiveness come through.[14]

Although my father had never become a guitar virtuoso, he did in fact play very well in his early years and always very expressively. In 1991 Anthony Chanaka, a busy and popular piano teacher in Washington, said of my father, "He was an unusual man: very relaxed, very gentle and pleasing, humorous. He played beautifully." At this point I interposed that my father had not had time to practice once he became so busy teaching, but Chanaka said: "But when he did play he played so beautifully, so expressively. He was called Mr. Guitar....And of course his pupil Charlie Byrd brought bossa nova to the United States."[15]

Joseph McLellan of the *Post* wrote as late as 1993 of the unamplified guitar as "an instrument that has not yet found a mass audience."[16] And the guitar continues to have its ups and downs. However, Sophocles Papas dedicated his life to teaching and inspiring guitarists, and his students carry on his legacy.

Thomas Papadopoulos, father of
Sophocles Papas; 7 April 1934.

Konstantina Papadopoulos, mother of
Sophocles Papas; she wrote on the back,
"For my beloved Sophocles and Eveline,
a token of a mother's affection and
remembrance"; 7 April 1934.

Left to right: One of Sophocles' brothers; his father; Sophocles Papas; picture made in Cairo; probably about 1905.

Papas, on right, with a brother, at the Acropolis; probably about 1914.

Papas in World War I US Army uniform; he wrote on the back, "Did not get a pass that day to go out of camp."

A natty Papas by the Potomac River; Washington Monument in background; probably just after discharge from army.

A young Papas; picture by Harris & Ewing, a then-prestigious Washington photographer; probably taken in the 1920s.

Above: Papas picture in rotogravure section of a newspaper; caption reads, "ENTERTAINED POST RADIO AUDIENCE. Sophacles [*sic*] T. Papas, expert on fretted instruments, who recently appeared on The Post's radio program over WCAP. *Harris & Ewing*;" n.d.

Below: Eveline Jessie Hurcum in Cardiff; note ornate upright piano; about 1913.

Above: Eveline Monico, probably when still in Wales or England; her maiden name was Eveline Jessie Hurcum, but she took her grandfather's Italian name for her 'stage' name as a pianist; about 1920.

Below: The Sophocles T. Papas Banjo Band, one of his early orchestras, in concert at the Earle Theater; such ensembles very popular in the 30s; Papas in center; others unidentified; n.d.

Above: Andrés Segovia; dedication to Papas reads: "For Mr. Sophocles Papas, intelligent teacher of guitar, with best wishes for your work. Washington 1935." Segovia usually used Roman numerals for dates.

Below: Segovia with Papas; n.d.

Above: Segovia, Olga Coelho,
Charlie Byrd, at Papas house; n.d.

Below: Papas serenading Mercia
Lorentz; place unidentified;
probably 1937.

Papas at play; n.d.

Papas with Elisabeth Papas, age 10, after a student recital at Villa Maria Academy, in which I played a work by Mozart; I am dressed in "period" costume; spring 1938.

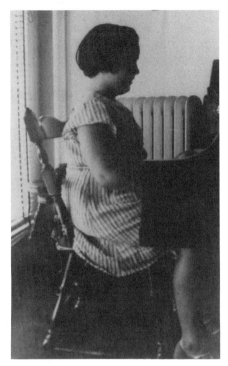

Above: Elisabeth "Betty" Papas at piano in 1508—19th St. studio; about 1938.

Below: The wedding of Sophocles and Mercia; left to right, George Lorentz, Mercia's brother; Gloria Myers, Mercia's half-sister; Papas; Mercia; Leanore Myers, Mercia's mother; Elisabeth Papas; Luise Rey, wife of Alvino Rey; 16 July 1938.

Above: Mercia in beautiful dress of lavender taffeta with sheer overskirt, tucked bodice; dedication reads, "To Sophocles with love and sincere devotion, Mercia"; probably 1940.

Below: Mercia, Betty, Papas; about 1939.

Above: Mercia in her Red Cross uniform during World War II; she rolled bandages for the Red Cross in a mansion on Massachusetts Avenue near 21st Street.

Below left: Theodore "Teddy" Papas in Dupont Circle; I used to have the summer job of taking him to the Circle for the morning; note streetcar going around Circle "wrong way;" probably 1942 or 1943.

Below right: Teddy with his beloved dog Mandy; probably 1951.

A social gathering at 2000 N Street. I can identify a number of people, many of whom took lessons for many years; Papas toward left front; Dorothy Perrenoud (de Goede) to his left; back row center, in dark suit, Papas's nephew Nicholas Papadopoulos; probably late 40s.

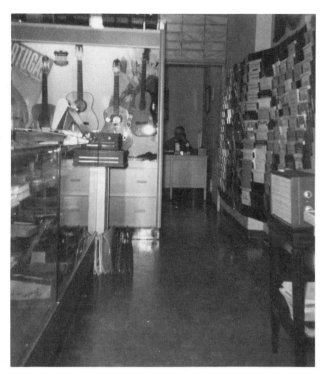

Above: The Guitar Shop at 1816 M Street, as you walked in the door at right and looked down the hall; note Papas on the phone at his desk; in front, instruments for sale, showcase, music in racks; this room also served as waiting room; September 1956.

Below: Elisabeth Papas; dedication reads, "Happy Father's Day! Love, Betty, 6/17/51."

Dorothy Perrenoud
(later de Goede),
Papas's star student;
probably 1945 or 1946.

Marcelle Jones; n.d.

Above: Gathering
at Papas's home
on Wynford Drive;
left to right,
Jesús Silva, Segovia,
Mercia, Papas, Carlos
Barbosa-Lima, other
person unidentified;
Easter Sunday,
29 March 1970.

Below: After-concert
party for Segovia
at Wynford Drive;
Silva interpreting for
Segovia; April 1969.

Above: Charlie Byrd with Papas in Wynford Drive living room; n.d.

Below: Papas showing Ida Presti a lute from his instrument collection; before 1967.

Above: Papas
with Julian Bream;
probably 1960s.

Below: Papas with
Arthur Godfrey;
dedication reads:
"For my dear old
friend Sophocles
Papas—with good
wishes, Arthur
Godfrey;" they knew
each other from
early radio days; 1963.

Papas in his studio at 1816 M Street; November 1967.

Papas playing for Carl Sandburg, Mercia in background, in house on Sleepy Hollow Road; probably 1961.

Above: Mercia with
Sandburg; 1961.

Below: Herb Block,
cartoonist, with Carl
Sandburg at Papas
house; 1961.

Below: Papas with Alvino Rey; July 1976.

Below: Papas descending from plane in Madrid, probably en route to Santiago de Compostela where he served as a judge; 1963.

Above: Papas on his
first return to Greece,
visiting family in
Ioannina; August
1969.

Below: Left to right,
Philip H. Smith, Jr.,
husband of Elisabeth
Papas Smith;
Barbosa-Lima;
Papas; in front of
Wynford Drive house;
December 1978.

Above; David Papas taping conversation with Barbosa-Lima, Papas at right; living room on Wynford Drive; note Mercia's reflection in mirror; early 1970s.

Below: Papas, Mercia, Sharon Isbin, in front of Wynford Drive; November 1974.

Papas portrait by Philip H. Smith, Jr.; Christmas 1968.

Above: Papas at his 80th birthday party held at the Virginia home of Douglas and Joan Blair; he is showing someone [unidentified] the plaque presented to him; 1973.

Below: Papas in his Dupont Circle Building studio; June 1973.

Above left: Papas at
his desk, probably
making little notes
on slips of paper
which he then tucked
in his pocket—notes
about things to do,
people to call,
business ideas, etc;
June 1973.

Above right: Papas
and Mercia on trip
to Greece and
Turkey; 1972.

Below: Papas
in his study at home
on Wynford Drive;
he liked to sit there
and read and perhaps
have a little snooze
in his recliner; 1970s.

Opposite page: Papas on 1972 trip to Greece and Turkey.

Above: Papas and Mercia in Greece; they also visited the relatives in Ioannina where Mercia met them for the one and only time; 1972.

Below: Papas; September 1972.

Above: Mercia and Papas in Wynford Drive living room; 1 January 1980.

Below: Papas teaching; student unidentified; see some of musical instrument collection on wall; 6 April 1964.

Above: Papas as judge at International Guitar Seminar, Palestrina Faculty of Music, in Porto Alegre, Brazil; possibly David Papas standing at far right; contestants unidentified; 29 July 1974.

Below: Papas; 12 December 1948.

Above: Papas; n.d.

Below: Papas; n.d.

APPENDIX A

Papas and Some Other Family Residences and Occupations

from Boyd's *District of Columbia Directory.* I have spelled out many of the
Directory abbreviations.

1893–07: Sopiki, Epirus
1907–12: Cairo, Egypt
1912–14: Vouliarates, Greece
1914–1918: Various cities in the United States
1918–1919: U.S. military installations
1919–1920: Various cities in U.S.

Washington, D.C.:
1923: 1125 Fairmont St., N.W.
1925: 1822 Vernon Pl., N.W., an apartment building called "The Colonnade"
1926: 2308 Ashmead Pl., N.W., "Le Marquis"
1927: 1861 California St., N.W.
1928–29: Sophocles T. and Eveline M., 1812 K St., N.W., #802, "The Pentilly"
1930: 1922 N St., N.W., #32, "The Lanvale" (gone as of 1991)
1931: 2100—19th St., N.W., #802 (apartment building without a name)
1932: 1722—19th St., N.W., #11, "The Sedgwick," the first place I recall living.
1933: 1221 Connecticut Avenue, N.W.; both Papas and my mother, Eveline
    Monico, are listed as music teachers and this was also their residence.
1934: 3039 Macomb St., N.W., #32, "Cleveland Apartments"
1935: Lorentz, George E., Mercia's brother, elevator operator, Tower Building,
    1401 K St., N.W., residence 1730 M St., N.W., #45; Mercia, clerk Mayflower
    Hotel Cigar Stand, residence 1730 M St., N.W., #45
1935: 922—17th St., N.W., phone National 6530
1936: 1508—19th St., N.W., same as studio; he was living there when he and
    Mercia married.
1937: Lorentz, Marcia [*sic*], stenographer, Barber & Ross, 5th & V Sts., N.E.,
    residence 315 Evarts St., N.E., "Evarts Apts.," also Myers, Jerry (Leanore A.,
    Mercia's mother) 315 Evarts St., N.E., Apt. 1A
1938: 2000 N St., N.W.; Papas married Mercia in July 1938 and moved to this
    address.

1939: Papas, Mercia L., stenographer, B&R [Barber & Ross as above] and Papas, Sophocles, music teacher, 2000 N St., N.W. 1940: Mercia same but stenographer for R. Golden Donaldson, lawyer at 815—15th St., N.W; residence 2000 N St., N.W.; Lorentz, Geo. E; elevator operator, Navy Yard, residence 1247 I St N.E.

1941: Papas, Marcia [sic] L., clerk, Navy Dept; residence 2000 N St., N.W., and Sophocles, same as in 1939

1942: Mercia clerk, Navy Dept.

There is a big gap from 1942 to 1948, possibly because the directory was not published during the war, but my brother Ted and I have recalled:

1946: 1902 Calvert St., N.W.

1947–56: 5357—29th St., N.W.

The directory resumes:

1948: Papas, Sophocles T. (Mercia L.) president, Columbia School of Music, Inc., home 5357—29th St., N.W.

1948: [separate listing] Columbia School of Music, Inc., 2000 N St., N.W.; Sophocles T. Papas, president; Thomas Simmons, secretary; Mrs. Alba Rosa Vietor, treasurer

1956: 217 Sleepy Hollow Road, Falls Church, Virginia

1965: 3222 Wynford Drive, Fairfax, Virginia

1983: The Hermitage, Alexandria, Virginia

APPENDIX B

Addresses of Papas Studios/Columbia School of Music

from Boyd's *District of Columbia Directory.*

1922–25: 1306–08 G St., N.W., in J. Edgar Robinson's Music Store[1]
1926: Room 303, 1417 G St., N.W.
1927: 1416 Pennsylvania Avenue, N.W.
1927–34: 1221 Connecticut Avenue, N.W.
1935: 922 — 17th St., N.W., National 6530
1936–38: 1508 — 19th St., N.W.
1938–56: 2000 N St., N.W., Columbia School of Music
1956–67: 1816 M St., N.W. The Guitar Shop
1967: 914 Dupont Circle Building, 1346 Connecticut Avenue, N.W.
Sophocles gave up this last studio in the early 1980s.

APPENDIX C

Papas Recipes

MACARONIA KYMA

1½ pounds lean ground beef
2 onions
2 cans tomato paste
1½ cups water
1 teaspoon ground cloves
2 pounds spaghetti

Chop onions fine; cook on top of stove with beef in butter until onions are soft. Add tomato paste and water, salt to taste and cloves. Cook slowly (simmer) about 2 hours or until water cooks away. Boil spaghetti in salted water 20 minutes. Drain well. When ready to serve, pour spoonfuls of sauce over the spaghetti to color it. Serve with sauce and cheese (grated).

Mr. Papas says he uses either whole cloves tied in a small piece of cheesecloth or the powdered cloves in his spaghetti, but no garlic. With this he serves a mixed green salad, oil and vinegar on the side, Greek cheese and Greek olives, fresh fruit and red wine. This recipe, he says, serves 8 Americans or 4 Greeks, or my wife and myself and Burl Ives."[1]

SOUPA AVGOLEMONO

1½ quarts chicken broth
1 cup rice
2 lemons (juice)
2 eggs, separated

Boil rice in chicken broth until tender. Turn off heat. Beat two egg yolks and two whites separately, then mix. Add juice of two lemons. Put a spoonful or two of the soup into the egg and lemon mixture, warming it gradually. Then add lemon and egg mixture to soup. Serve at once.

APPENDIX D

Segovia-Papas Correspondence

The forty-year correspondence between Segovia and Papas turned up among my father's papers. Sometimes Segovia typed his letters, sometimes he wrote them in longhand, and he wrote variously in French, Spanish, and English. I have translated those not in English. Some letters bear no date, but I have placed the letters where they seem to fit chronologically. When he did date a letter, he often used roman numerals, such as 21 Fevrier XLVI. A perpetual calendar has been invaluable, but there are still some problems about dates. I have been unable to identify all the people mentioned in the correspondence. The majority of the letters from Papas to Segovia are carbon copies without signatures. Segovia's addresses have been included when given.

While I have attempted to retain the flavor of his style, I have simplified the flowery good-byes. I have also left in many of Segovia's charming misspellings and the like.

SEGOVIA 1

171 W. 71st Street, N.Y., 26 January 1937
Dear Mr. Papas; thank you very much for your letter. I appreciate deeply the organisation of the Segovia Guitar Society and shall do my best to help her finality.

Will be pleased to see you next Saturday and would like if you could arrive earlier to New York, because we three, you Mres Segovia and I could have dinner to-gether some place out and then, we would be able to talk long. Of course you could wear your traveling suit.

Please, let me know when you will arrive definitively and with kind regards from Mrs. Segovia and myself to your nice family,

I am yours sincerely
[signed] Andrés

SEGOVIA 2

Essex House, 160 Central Park South, N.Y., 3 January 1938

Dear Mr. Papas: I am very happy that you will arrive the eve of my concert. Unfortunately I am busy for dinner Saturday; but if you, Miss Tugwell, and Miss Valiant would not mind coming to see me about 11:30 p.m., I will certainly be back at Essex House by then.

I am reminding you to bring a footstool with you.[1] You know that I prefer that it be rather large and about 13 centimeters high. Perhaps you have one like that? I thank you in advance.

It is too bad that you must leave for Washington right after the concert. Because a group of friends and I had thought of going to dinner all together and of going afterward to my brother-in-law's.

I am looking forward to the pleasure of seeing you again. Remember me to Miss Lorentz, hug your little girl,[2] and accept my warm wishes.

[signed] A. Segovia

SEGOVIA 3

Av. 18 de Julio, 948, Montevideo, 8 March 1939

Cable address: Segovia, Palacio Lapido, Montevideo

Dear Mr. Papas: It has been a long time since I wrote you. But please do not be angry, because many other people, to whom I am linked by longstanding friendship, wait, like you, for news of me. One way or another, my days are always full and, without meaning to delay my correspondence for such a long time, I always put off until the morrow this pleasant task.

Before leaving for Europe I had the worry of seeing my wife have a serious operation. I had to leave her in the convalescent home. Fortunately a month later she was able to rejoin me in Italy, where she has been rapidly recovering.

As for you, I can imagine that you are enjoying the happiness of linking your destiny to that of the charming Miss Lorentz. In becoming Madame Papas, she has taken on herself the noble task of being a colleague of yours in the promotion of the instrument that you and I love. I am sure that she will be responsible for many new converts.

I played in Europe with great success: England, Germany, Italy, and Hungary. We were ready to leave London for the U.S. on 18 January, when we received a cable from the reptilian Mr. Coppicus telling me that he had obtained four concerts for me to be given over a period of three months. You can imagine my reply.

For reasons concerning my Nationalist affiliation, and also because I played in Germany and Italy, and, finally, for other reasons whose source one must seek within the Columbia Concerts Corporation, I already know that it will be particularly difficult for me to play in North America this year. I must tell you that all summer Mr. Coppicus hid from me this blow which he was preparing, no doubt with the aim of making it more effective.

At about the same time I received Mr. Quesada's proposal for making a concert tour in Puerto Rico, Havana, Jamaica, Panama, Colombia, Venezuela, etc., etc. I would have had to fly and therefore I refused him. Because after traveling by air as much as my wife and I have had to do, both of us at this time have an unconquerable dislike of flying again. We will limit these exploits to the strictly unavoidable.

But to tell you the truth, I had a secret reason for attempting to put off this tour until later. It was of great artistic importance, as you will see, and justified my negative answer.

Actually, during my visit to Florence, Castelnuovo-Tedesco completed the *Concerto* for guitar and orchestra; and I had a irresistable desire to shut myself up at home to work on it. Now you understand.

The *Concerto* is a marvel. The greatest, the freshest, the most heartfelt inspiration of this musician presided over the birth of this work. I am filled with enthusiasm for it and I am preparing to perform it with zeal. The orchestra will consist of about 20 musicians: the guitar is treated poetically and with technical dexterity, and extraordinarily delicate care governs the dialogues with the orchestra. I am certain that its performance will be an event of high artistic quality next season in Europe.

You can imagine how happy I am to have brought the guitar to the highest degree of its triumphal ascent.

Now let us pass on to other matters.

I have just made six new recordings in London: Suite by Visée, Two Dances by Granados, and two works by Albéniz. They will be available very soon.

I had also intended to record a collection of 20 études chosen from among the most useful and progressive of different composers. But the president of His Master's Voice has doubts about the commercial value of such a recording because he does not know about the current surge of interest throughout the world in the study of the guitar. Instead, he sent me the request, made by I do not know what group of madmen, to record "La Paloma."

Nevertheless, something good has come of this: and that is to give me the idea of asking you to gather gradually a fair number of signatures on a petition addressed to Victor [Records], to the effect that I should record this kind of "Methode sonore." One could also present this proposal to the Victor agencies here, in South America, in Europe, and in Japan.

I am curious to know what change you have been able to make in the Segovia Society. I would like to say to you confidentially, that, if it is possible to do so diplomatically, you should remove from the presidency the name of the wife of the Mexican ambassador. Personally I have only warm feelings and respect for her. But the official representation with which her husband is invested offends my Nationalist sentiments. You know that Mexico has been one of the countries most hostile to the noble Spanish Cause, and that it provided Valencia's government with an abundance of arms and munitions. Twice during the past year I have refused the opportunity to play there.

And finally, Mr. Papas. After this letter I fear that you will not complain about my silence but quite the opposite. Write to me. Give me news about Bobri and other friends. And with best greetings from my wife to Madame Papas and to yourself to which I add my own, I beg you to believe in my sincere friendship.

The war in Spain is almost won, with the victory of our ideals! I cannot finish this letter without setting down, in Spanish, our Nationalist cry: ¡Arriba España!

Yours,

[signed] Segovia

SEGOVIA 4

Av. 18 de Julio, 948, Montevideo, Uruguay, 18 April 1939

Dear Mr. Papas: About a month ago I wrote you a rather long letter. Your silence makes me fear that it went astray. Perhaps it was not addressed properly or the airplane which was carrying it has secretly crashed.

So I send you another little note, not to tell you again what I wrote in the aforementioned letter, but to ask you to do a favor for my friend the great composer, Castelnuovo-Tedesco. You know that he is a Jew and, consequently, has been dropped by Schott, the German music-publishing house, as well as by Ricordi, the Italian one. Neither is willing to publish the beautiful Variations that he wrote last year for my guitar, on the theme "J'ai du bon Tabac." Now I would like it if you would take some steps in regard to some publishing houses in New York, etc., to see under what conditions this work could be published. I will not say anything about this to Castelnuovo until you tell me the results of your efforts. I thank you, in advance, in his name as well as mine, for your trouble.

In a few days Schott will publish 20 new pieces that I have just sent them. Among them is a magnificent Sonata by Mr. Alfred Uhl, an Austrian; the Mazurka by Ponce; a Passacaille by Couperin; 6 pieces by Frescobaldi as beautiful and important as those by Bach—allowing for the different period—and some others by Rameau, Alonso de Mudarra, Pachelbel, Vanhall, etc., etc., and finishing with a piquant Tango by Albéniz. You will have a lot of work including all of them in your new catalogue. In addition, I have also made some new recordings in London. But I now remember that I wrote all of this to you in the letter that went astray.

Goodbye. Kindly give my respects to Madame Papas and believe in my sincere friendship.

[signed] A. Segovia

SEGOVIA 5

New address: Banco Francés, Montevideo, Uruguay, 1 October 1939

My dear Mr. Papas: I thank you for your letter and even more for your affection and kindness. We are deeply saddened by the war which is going to rage all over our poor Europe. Equally sad is the suffering of poor, brave Poland and the fact that, if providence does not intervene, other countries as noble and civilized as Germany, France, and England will know the same torments. Politics has no heart. It has a terrible ferocity when it is concerned with power. If the current leaders do not moderate their ambitions and come to an agreement for making peace, this will be a catastrophe without parallel from which not a single country of the old world will escape. And even on this continent one senses hellish repercussions of disorder.

In the face of all this, individual losses are absolutely negligible. However, I cannot regard with indifference the collapse of my tour because of these events. I was to give a brilliant series of concerts in Europe this year. We are already booked to sail on 17 September, to begin in England with a public recital on 4 October with others added in the same country. After that I was to play in Switzerland, Norway, Sweden, Denmark, Germany, Czechoslovakia, Hungary, Lithuania, Romania, Yugoslavia, Italy, France, Spain, and Portugal. In spite of the fact that Europe, birthplace of artists, has neither the tradition nor the means to pay virtuosos as well as the U.S., the consumer of music, and will pay me modestly, I have received the best available terms, and that somewhat compensated me for my absence from the great North American marketplace of concerts.

But what am I to do! One must be patient and philosophical. What I regret most is the loss of favorable opportunities for making the Castelnuovo's Concerto for guitar and orchestra known in Europe. It is is a jewel. I had promised to premiere it on the BBC in London. After that, it would have been played again in Switzerland, Scandinavia, Paris. I am angry to be forced to delay this, even more because the performance of this beautiful work would have inspired a cycle of similar guitar pieces which would have enriched the repertoire in new and important ways. God knows in what state Europe will be in after the catastrophe which now threatens her, even to think of such things.

I congratulate both you and myself for the burst of interest in the guitar in the United States, thanks to the society which you founded and to the efforts of all of its members. I hope that, as before, I will soon be able to gather together more performers. There can be no doubt whatsoever that the guitar will triumph more and more, in the noble sense which I have impressed on it. In recent years I have turned my back on Europe a bit in favor of America, but as soon as I was able to make my beautiful instrument heard in the most musical centers over there, everyone was again taken by it and artists, critics, and audiences rivaled one another in enthusiasm. All the Coppicuses of the world, even if they ally themselves with the devil, can not stop the triumphal march of the guitar and its true apostles.

I will not go to play in America any more this year. I have not exchanged a single word with the Metropolitan Musical Bureau since my cable from London dated 18 January this year. But that will come. I am not old yet and I know how to wait.

If the European war does not have negative repercussions in the musical life of this part of Spanish America, it is possible that I may play in Cuba, Puerto Rico, Colombia, Venezuela, Mexico, etc., etc., next January or February. To go directly from here to the first of these countries I intend to take a North American ship as far as New York and leave from there for Cuba where I may begin my tour. If the project comes off, I will let you know so that you can come to New York for a few hours. We then will talk copiously.

Now I will briefly answer your questions. I prefer the name *Symphony* for the magazine rather than *Rasgueado*. The latter term is already popular and would imply a restricted musical sense of the guitar. On the contrary, we must broaden the thinking on this subject and not limit it.

As to the honorary presidency of your Society, it seems to me that that would be as if I myself were to preside. The Society bears my name, to my great honor, and that is enough. I leave you free to offer the presidency to another member, or to assume it yourself, which would be the most appropriate, in view of your dedication.

I will send you the article which you ask of me but not for the first issue of your magazine because I do not want to delay its appearance. I will probably write it next week.

Your idea about the Chicago exhibition seems to me very useful.

At present we are in the country, at a large, extremely beautiful property belonging to my wife. Life here is paradise. I am able to work on many of the things which enhance the prestige of the guitar.

Well, I have nothing more to say for the moment. Only I ask you once again not to ask anything from either the artists or my friends toward the development of the Society. You have enough experience of life to know that there are few true friends. An artist has even fewer, in spite of the enormous number of his admirers. The more people are dull, the less they can tolerate the explosion of talent from whatever direction. As for the other artists, the majority are composed of sensitive spirits when it comes to the success of others.

Best greetings from me and also from my wife for Mme. Papas and your little girl. And believe, my friend, in my cordial friendship.

Please extend my thanks to the members of the Board of Directors of the Society for all their efforts for the guitar, as well as in my honor.

Your,

[signed] Segovia

SEGOVIA 6

Montevideo, 16 December 1940

My dear Mr. Papas: It has truly been a long time since I wrote you. You are no doubt familiar with the anti-epistolary nature of artists, among whom I have certainly been an exception in regard to you. I believe that you have a number of letters from me, of which many of my friends would feel jealous.

I do not want to wait for the birth of your baby to wish him a gracious welcome into this frightful world. If it is a boy, do not make an artist of him, at least not until someone has first killed off all the impressarios, and until there remain, in the world of music, only the listeners, gathered together into societies, and the artists. If it is a baby girl, since she will be like her mother, she will inspire artists, which is much better than becoming one.

I congratulate you also on the prosperity of your School of Music. Try to have good teachers of the other instruments because that will reflect on the prestige of the guitar. If one combines teaching the guitar and the mandolin, for example, the guitar loses. But when taught with the piano, cello, or the violin, the guitar gains in the respect of those who are ignorant of its possibilities.

My tour last year, throughout the Spanish-speaking countries, was actually a great success. Everywhere there was a full house and enormous enthusiasm. I often played the Concerto by Castelnuovo which the public loves to the point of delirium. I always had to repeat the last movement which is quite rare in an orchestral concert or when there is a soloist.

It is for that reason, dear friend, that I am more and more afflicted by the ostracism to which the impressarios of New York have condemned me. I am persuaded that this Concerto by Castelnuovo, and still another which Manuel Ponce has just sent me and which is a festival of glittering harmonies, would be a mad success in New York and throughout the United States. But I can do nothing against the monopolists which have declared me persona non grata. If Europe were not at war I would happily dismiss them because, in view of the enormous success of this new work in the most respectable musical circles, they would have ended up by asking for me in order to satisfy their appetite for profit. But Europe is at war, and unfortunately for a long time, and while waiting it out, I am immobilized.

It is too bad that you did not choose to be a concert organizer, without actually becoming an impressario. We would have made an agreement together, and believe me, we would have earned a lot of money. Joking aside, right now what I have need of is a secretary who knows all the resources for organizing concerts in your country—the halls, the local managers, etc., etc., and who would throw himself, after setting the dates in advance, into following them through. Just think, in the ten years during which I have played in a large part of the United States, I have had only one single concert with poor attendance: the last one in New York, and you know very well the political reasons. The newspapers and the critics everywhere, which anyone can see, testify that what I say is not empty pride.

Well, enough of that. It is quite possible that this year I will repeat last year's tour. If I pass through your neighborhood, I will pay you a visit.

Thank you for the care which you lavish on the "Segovia Society." I promise you the article for which you asked, but I cannot say just when. You will receive it when you least expect it. At present I am absorbed in studying the Ponce Concerto, which is difficult, and by other concerns such as the failure of the Banco Francés, which was managing the affairs of my wife and daughters and in which a rather large part of my bank account has been shipwrecked. I take advantage of speaking of this in order to ask you no longer to address your correspondence there, but to our private house, Massini, 3410. We are finally settled there; it is a villa belonging to my wife, with a beautiful garden facing the sea, where I can work in peace.

I regret enormously that the firestorm in Europe has also affected your beautiful country. It presents to the world an admirable spectacle which recalls past glories. I hope, in the end, that all will soon come right.

Keep me informed of the coming family event,[3] which I hope will be happy and without suffering for the beautiful Madame Papas.

My wife wishes to be remembered to you two, and believe me, dear friend, in my sincere sympathy,

[signed] A. Segovia

SEGOVIA 7

Biltmore Hotel, Los Angeles 13, California, [probably 1943]

[Dear Papas] I begin this letter by asking you for a favor. Mr. Barnett, of the National Concert and Artists Corporation, wants me to send him a work for guitar whose duration should not exceed 2 minutes, to have it arranged for guitar and orchestra, and he wants me to play it on 26 March, I think, on the radio (Carnation Hour).[4] The only piece which is both of the required length and is also by a Spanish composer is the *Fandanguillo* by Torroba from the Suite Castellana. Would you do me the favor of making a photocopy of it and sending it to Mr. Barnett, N.C.A.C., 711 Fifth Ave., New York City, as quickly as possible? Thanks, and à bientôt.

I did not see the Albinos [Alvino Rey and his wife Luise]. They left me a message at the hotel. I telephoned several times, without success. Finally, on the day of my concert, Mme. Albino phoned me to say that her husband was away, but that he would like to see me at the concert. That is all. I am telling you this so that you will not ever ask anyone to put me up overnight. That is one thing I have always detested. I wanted to be in touch with them by phone only to be polite and to thank him for his kind remarks, but also I was ready to refuse any invitation he might make.

[Andrés]

SEGOVIA 8

[about 1943]

My dear Papas: Finally I am able to write you. I am at home again, after having traveled around almost all of America. I collected my wife in Mexico, after leaving New York. We have given concerts almost everywhere: in Mexico, Guatemala, El Salvador, Costa Rica, Panama, Ecuador, Peru, Argentina, etc.; and the preparation of programmes, the social obligations, the trips, and many other things have kept me from writing, not only to you, but to other close friends as well.

And I haven't finished yet. I still have to give three radio programs of a half hour each, and I am in the process of preparing new works for them. Add to this my own personal work, that is, the pieces, exercises, studies, and compositions which I never stop working on, and you will have an idea of how full my days are.

In spite of this, here I am chatting with you. And I will tell you frankly that I have great hopes for this talk. Indeed I never forget how you have always been ready to help me, and that is why I have not hesitated to ask favors of you. And here is what it's about this time.

You certainly know about the death of my New York impressario, Mr. Paul Schiff, who was the president of Inter-American Artists. There were many of us artists in his circle, such as Artur Rubinstein, Wanda Landowska, Argentinita, myself, and others. I have sent my condolences to one of the members of the Inter-American, a man named Mr. Libidnis, and also I wrote to Mr. de Quesada, another of its members. I have not received any answer. The worst thing about all this is that, since I signed my contract for the next U.S. concert tour, not directly with Mr. Hurok, but with Mr. Schiff and his group, which was the intermediary between Mr. Hurok and me, I don't know at this moment if Mr. Hurok is going to continue to represent me and thus to arrange my concerts, or if in fact he has stopped doing so. For the other performers, who live in New York, this is a matter of finding another impressario who can replace Mr. Schiff. But for me, since I am so far from there, it becomes extremely difficult because, before doing anything, I must be sure that my contract with Mr. Schiff has been cancelled, and that this organization of which he was the president no longer exists, that Mr. Hurok has given up planning my tour, etc., etc. That is why I am bothering you. It would be helpful to me if, during one of your trips to New York, you would be so kind as to go to the Steinway Building (113 West 57th Street, Suite 1015, phone Circle 6898) and to try to find Mr. Libidnis—I am not quite sure how to spell his name—or the secretary, Mlle. Carmencita, and if you would ask them about the arrangements concerning me. I hope that they will not refuse to give you this information because they must understand how deeply concerned I am not to drop my U.S. tour for next year, especially after the success which I have been fortunate enough to encounter in that country.

If my contract is still valid, I ask you to find out from them or else from Mr. Hurok's office... [rest of letter missing]

SEGOVIA 9

Biltmore Hotel, Los Angeles 13, California, 21 February 1946

My dear Sophocles: In great haste, I write you these lines to give you my impression of Mlle. Perrenoud. She is young and gracious, pleasant to look at, and of an agreeable temperament. She has some ability for the guitar and for music, but she is *totally* ignorant of some matters. Her technique is bad, and her knowledge of the most elementary matters of the art is *nil*. In spite of these negatives, one glimpses a temperament open to the beauties of music, and some facility for the instrument. It would be necessary to make her forget all she has done up until now, to make her begin from the beginning, with strict discipline, and to teach her solfège and theory from their basics. Perhaps after a year and on the condition that she give to this test the cooperation of her will and her modesty, one could see serious progress in her, rising from her current state, which is that of a poor amateur, toward the concentrated study and stature appropriate to a professional who has aspirations.

No more. I told her all that I have just written, and with almost the same frankness, and I added that I intended to give you my impression of her, so that you could decide whether it would be convenient for you to help her or not. In any case, I believe that she deserves to be helped, if she takes her work seriously.

Someone told me, but vaguely, that you had the idea of organizing a competition for guitar, and that the first prize would be 500 dollars; would you write to me about this? Because it would be necessary to inform Ponce, immediately and later Castelnuovo and Tansman. Write to me, please, about the details of your project.

This evening I leave for Seattle, and I will be back in San Francisco the 26th where I will stay at the San Francis [St. Francis] Hotel—until 3 March, after my concert.

Thank you, dear friend. My best wishes to Mercia and a kiss for your children, and believe me your friend

[signed] A. Segovia

S E G O V I A 10

Hotel del Caribe, Cartagena, Colombia, 5 April 1946

My dear Papas: In the enclosed I'm sending you the song which I mentioned to you, and of which I want to be sure about the copyright. The name which it must bear is as it is on the manuscript "Canción Andaluza." I'm asking you to find out about it right away, because I fear that the evil people in whose hands it was could cause me trouble.

I am thinking about the method; and I think that that would be a good idea; all the better because I don't have to respect the conventional principles but rather the actual experience I have had with the instrument. I hurry to return home and there to lead a peaceful life, to devote myself to writing. The only thing that might hinder my plan would be a cable from Hurok calling me back to the United States.

I have left you the care of many things in my suitcase. I would like it if your charming wife could from time to time take a bit of care of the clothes which I put there, so that they are not eaten by moths. There are also some music and books there. Make use of them to satisfy your curiosity, but don't let them go astray because they are quite important to me, especially the music.

As soon as I have a moment I will write the second article for the Bulletin [of the Segovia Society, presumably]; also the letter for the Brigadier General. I want to tell you on this subject that I had to put on a nylon first string because of the heat and humidity in this tropical city, so as not to exhaust the small reserve I keep of Pirastro strings, and which, for the time being, work very well.[5]

No more news at the moment. My most cordial greetings to your household, and also greetings to the La Farges and Mr. Creel.[6]

And believe in my faithful friendship.

[signed] A. Segovia

SEGOVIA 11

Massini 3410, Tel. 41.19.84., Montevideo (Uruguay), 18 May 1946

My dear Sophocles: It hasn't been very long since, at last, I am settled in my new home, not without some problems, happily overcome. I will soon be able to devote myself completely to my work.

I have delayed writing you just because I didn't know what I was going to do before returning home. At the moment, the wedding of Paquita's youngest daughter is set for 25 May, after which I will undertake study of the following works: 1. A Rondeau by Castelnuovo, rather long and important. 2. A Suite, by Guillermo Uribe Holguín, a Colombian musician who has worked very well in Paris and who has composed very well and abundantly. His fortune has been the greatest obstacle to the spread of his talent and reputation. 3. The Concertino, by Alexandre Tansman, for small orchestra and guitar. 4. The Serenade, in four movements, also for guitar and ensemble orchestra, by Castelnuovo. 5. The Concerto that Torroba is presently writing and of which I will soon have the first two movements. Add to this work putting together the Method and the arrangement of the Ponce piece— about which I still know nothing—and you can tell me if my time is not well taken up.

I have received three letters from our friend Bobri, three letters in the course of a short time, to tell me that he has reorganized the old Society of the Classic Guitar in New York and that he has named me honorary president. He asked me also to send him a message which would be read at the first meeting of all the members, set for the 20th of this month; and, since I forgot to do as he asked, he cabled me yesterday evening, with prepaid answer, asking me urgently to send this message, which I did rather briefly.

I am bringing you up to date on this because, while considering that the creation of new societies of the guitar is good for its development and expansion, I wouldn't want you to imagine that I am spending my energy on groups other than yours. It is particularly satisfying for me that Bobri and his friends are creating an association whose goal is to intensify love of the guitar, but I feel strongly that, for them, the meaning of this beautiful instrument is not so clearly established as it is for the members of the Segovia Society, which is to say, that it is not the strictly *musical* sense of the guitar that they intend to develop and improve but more the popular side, and, what's worse, the pseudo-popular aspect which Bobri himself and some of his friends love so madly. Because I am Andalusian, and I love the songs of my part of the world, I recognize better than they do the value of this second aspect of the guitar; but it must be kept completely out of our project and it is incompatible with it because the guitar is destined to attain the status of a noble instrument, like the cello, the violin, and the piano, and, in order to attain this rank, the guitar must never depend on the support of the ignorant and lazy.

I don't want you to make the above words public. But at the very most do communicate them verbally to Mr. La Farge and Mr. Creel. I would like to be proved mistaken and shown that the designs of Bobri and Co. are as right for the instrument as ours is. Also I would like very much if this New York society would combine its forces with the Segovia Society for the good of the guitar.

I ask you also to tell Bobri, if you see him or write to him, not to send my letters to the Nirvana Hotel, not to speak to me about arrangements for guitar and voice, and to remember that I am at home.

While I am waiting for your news, dear Papas, I ask you to give my best wishes to Madame Papas, to your daughter, and to hug your young child.

Cordially,

[signed] A. Segovia

SEGOVIA 12

Hotel Nirvana, Nueva Helvecia, Uruguay, 28 September 1946

My dear Sophocles: Thanks so much for your cable. The day after I mailed you a letter, I received word from Miss Ward telling me extremely warmly that she expects me to visit her in November. I will certainly not give up the pleasure of spending several days in your new house. It is very likely that I will arrive before November.

Your letter still has not reached me, not even the one you told me about in a cable about two months ago. You should always use registered mail because in this country the postal system doesn't work very well.

I am working a great deal, I read, and I write. The time passes pleasantly enough. This hotel, which is one of the best in South America, is full at present, but I flee from everyone to the point that I begin to seem mysterious and anti-social. For relaxation I take long walks or go on long horseback rides through the countryside.

Until next time. My best wishes for your wife and children, and believe in my sympathy and friendship.

All the best to you,

[signed] A. Segovia

SEGOVIA 13

Montevideo, 14 October 1946

My dear Sophocles: I am enclosing a letter which I wrote several days after receiving your cable and which I would have sworn that I had sent. When I returned home I put my music and books in order, and my epistle arose like a phantom.

I am very happy that your school is prospering. It is the natural result of the effort and enthusiasm and intelligence that you put into your work.

Thank you for your offer of hospitality. Be sure that I will accept it soon. At the moment I must be on the scene here to take part in our house moving, which will begin next week. Pity me, because it is a crazy business.

I had thought of going to Europe, because I have received letters proposing concerts in Italy, Spain, England, Switzerland, and Sweden. But Portugal, which I forgot to mention, is rather restless; Spain will be, I fear, from one moment to the next, and the other countries will be in a better situation in the spring in both food supplies and politics. Thus I have decided to stay here and wait until time for my departure for the U.S.

I am quite unhappy with Hurok this time. He cabled to announce that it would be quite difficult to get me the 15 concerts he guaranteed me. Is it not heartbreaking to see how little sympathy an organization as powerful as the N.C.A.C. which has 600 concert societies, I believe, affords me when no other artist has had such success among critics, the public, and musicians as I have had in the past year. Hurok and his colleagues will have put on more than 40 concerts this year. You were present at my concerts in Carnegie Hall and Constitution Hall, you have read the critics; and this was true in California and everywhere else. Am I not right to conclude that there is a powerful animadversion against me on the part of these managers who refuse to have me play?

I am thinking that it may be much better for me to spend some time in New York this year, after the concerts that I will give, in order to find someone active, congenial, and intelligent who could organize my tour for 1948, certain of sharing in a fairly large profit; because the secret of the matter is simply to find halls and to have me play. This way I could free myself from this group of impressarios and work better. What do you think of that?

Au revoir, dear Sophocles. Best wishes from Paquita and me to you and yours, and believe in my friendship.

[signed] Andrés

Because we are moving I ask you to send your news to the address of our lawyer: c/o Aparicio Mendez; Calle 18 de Julio 1417, Montevideo, or even to wait until I give you our new address.

SEGOVIA 14

[This is a handwritten copy of a telegram from Sophocles Papas to Andrés Segovia.]

26 October 1946
To: Andrés Segovia
Avenida Brasil 2645
Montevideo, Uruguay
Cognizant Hurok's contract new developments are new artistic recording company. Possibility of Professorship on criticism and analysis of music, Creel's University. Also your presence here helpful planning for next year. If you need thousand or two advance Royalty now wire. If no business keeping you in Montevideo come to Washington, we can accomplish many things here in two months.

Papas

SEGOVIA 15

[Montevideo], 12 November 1946

My dear Sophocles: I am sending you this letter which will probably arrive two or three days before me, to say that I will stay for a few at Miss Ward's. She has been so kind that I don't want to hurt her feelings. After the time spent at her house I will join you.

I have not had any answer from Hurok to the last letter I wrote him asking about the date and hall of my first public recital in [missing]. I cannot explain his silence, especially since I asked him for this information in order to plan the program according to the dimensions of the hall because, if I play in Carnegie Hall, I must play works more powerful than one plays in Town Hall.

I don't understand his attitude if it was not because of some antipathy on the part of the president of the N.C.A.C. toward me, which would have the negative result of giving to Hurok some concerts on my account. You know well, dear Sophocles, that most of the artists who give concerts in this country have neither the favorable criticism nor the public following that I have. Living in New York, they gather their cronies together once a year in Carnegie Hall, thanks to the assiduousness of all the members of their families who work for them. And after this single concert and the lukewarm, negative, or somewhat enthusiastic write-ups that appear the next day, they manage to turn that into a tour of 40 concerts.

If Hurok has not gone along with those who refuse me work, he stands to profit from my renown and from the varied character of my instrument in order to organize a series of public concerts throughout the country, which, if heralded by good advertising, will give magnificent results.

Well, we will talk at length about all this and perhaps lay the foundation of a collaboration, in that way which could be useful to both of us.

My best greetings to your wife and believe, dear friend, in my affection. Hug your children.

[signed] A. Segovia

I will notify you of my arrival.

SEGOVIA 16

St. Francis Hotel. Union Square, San Francisco 19, [California], 29 January 1947

My dear Sophocles: I received your letter accompanied by that of our charming friend Mr. Creel. I can answer you now because I am alone in the bedroom of a train carrying me to Aberdeen.

Mr. Creel writes that the "faculty of Music" wants me to give a concert on the campus. I think this will work out, and I will speak with Mr. Hurok about the price, in such a way that he won't make it too expensive. But I prefer for many reasons to do this not by letter but verbally as soon as I get to New York. Please be kind enough to tell this to our friend, to whom I don't want to write until I can do so in English without too many mistakes. I will not delay too long, I promise.

My concert in Chicago, for 23 February, has been announced. If Mr. Creel is there and also Mr. La Farge, it would give me great pleasure to invite them and their wives to have lunch or dinner with me. Please let them know about this. I will probably arrive the night before my concert and I will not leave again until two hours afterward.

I have been told of the awful conditions in which Madame Guiomar Novaes played in Washington, of the noise people made in the hall, and of the thoughtless and unmusical conduct of the audience. I fear greatly that the charming lady who is in charge of this organization and whose name escapes me at the moment, does not keep close watch on these things, and it's really a shame, because this poor reputation could easily fall on the Society, and neither the good public, nor the impressarios, nor the artists would attend from then on. You who know the guitar and who are a good friend of this lady—please make known to her the atmosphere of silence, respect, and behavior that such an instrument requires, and add that my character is not able to surmount such troubles. Because of similar circumstances, about 20 years ago, in the Spanish Embassy in Paris, in the presence of the King of my country and Doumergue,[7] then President of the French Republic, I got up and I left without playing, leaving everyone stupefied. I was then at the beginning of my career; this is not to say that I would have been any more tolerant about this.

My concerts in California were magnificent, above all in Los Angeles and San Francisco which are the most important places. I played the Chaconne there. One of the good critics there, the one who writes for the San Francisco Chronicle, making reference to Pincherle's note, wrote that "as far as he was concerned, I am authorized to play the Mass in Si Minor, the whole work, on the guitar, if I wish, because this would be excellent."

In Los Angeles, Mrs. Jones came to greet me and told me that you have written asking her to join the Society as a member. Perhaps she made this up, but if it is so, dear Sophocles, I am sorry to tell you that that does not please me at all. The critics always have justifiable suspicions about the secret desires of artists to win for themselves their goodwill, and to do so in any way possible. They defend themselves in the most energetic way, and they are right. But in the present case, they cannot imagine that I was not told of your overture and that I do not approve of it. And the meaning that she would attribute to them is that of them thus to favor me. I do not understand how these things can fail to dampen your spirit and get in the way of some of your projects. I am sure that if you had consulted Mr. Creel, who last year recommended that I not thank Mr. Virgil Thomson, he would not have agreed with your way of thinking, for that which concerns the affair of which we are speaking. The same for Mr. La Farge. Your desire to promote the Segovia Society, for which I am grateful to you, could do me a lot of harm in certain milieus which you do not know as well as I, for the simple reason that you are located in Washington, peacefully in your school, while I circulate in the whole world and understand the different characters, habits, and fads of people who make up the musical world. I have already told you of my profound wish not to disturb my friends or my colleagues or the critics, asking them for things that would help out the Segovia Society. It is completely natural that they identify with me and, if on the one hand they know all too well that I have never bothered them in order to obtain the least advantage in my favor, they must see also, not without an ironic smile, that this society which bears my name is extremely active and contradicts, consequently, my direct passivity. This makes me appear to be a subtle hypocrite.

I would like it very much if you let the president of the Society know these things, by translating the foregoing paragraph into English, because I would not wish to seem to be an ingrate nor to paralyze the methods which the Society can use to prosper. If you can find a way of serving it [the Society] without bruising my sensibilities, I will be delighted and prompt to cooperate in its development.

You have forgotten, dear Sophocles, to send me the translation done by Mrs. Ward, of the note on the Chaconne. Give a copy to the secretary of the Society where I am going to play in Washington and keep the original safe to give me on my arrival.

No more for now. My best wishes for Mercia, a hug for the children, and believe in my sincere friendship.

Your

[signed] Andrés

SEGOVIA 17

Washington D.C., 4 March 1949

Dear Andrés, We are coming to hear you on Sunday en famille. You no doubt know by now why we missed the concerti; we are all very disappointed.[8]

Anna Cajigas is giving a surprise party for Tomas' birthday on Monday and she asked me to invite you to come. Knowing how they feel toward you, you can imagine how much pleasure you will give them, and I hope that your schedule permits you to do it, if you feel so inclined.

We are driving to New York tomorrow and you can drive back with us on Monday. If you have never driven to Washington from New York you will find the trip interesting.

We are looking forward to seeing you on Sunday.

Cordially,

[signed] Sophocles

SEGOVIA 18

248 Central Park West, New York City, 30 December 1949

My dear Sophocles: I have been home for 5 days from Europe, and I have learned that you have lost the newborn. I send you my sincere condolences, although, in these uncertain times that we suffer, it seems to me that your young one has had the intelligence not to want to remain among us and to return to Infinity, in great joy. There is thus no reason to commiserate, even if his departure makes you sad.

Never call other children to come into this world, dear friend. Be aware, you and Mercia, of the moral responsibility that you take on in launching a new being into this whirlpool of selfishness and cruel wickedness. Content yourselves with matters less transcendent.

I have scarcely arrived home from a tour, in Europe, of 42 concerts— Scandinavia, England, Belgium, North Africa, France, and Italy—and now I have to leave home the first of the year to begin to play. With small breaks, I will be traveling until the month of April.

It is possible that I will stop in Washington on one of these trips and that I will come to see you. Thus you will receive in your school a surprise visit from me.

Until the next time, my best wishes to Mercia and believe, dear friend, in my affection.

[signed] Andrés

SEGOVIA 19

New York, 1950

My dear Sophocles: It has been three or four months since the young lady who brings you this letter came to Mr. Augustine's, where I saw her, and I have promised to introduce her to you. Afterward I totally forgot, even to speak of it to you, when I was in Washington. Now I am correcting my guilty oversight in introducing her to you. Be so kind as to give her your attention. She wants to study seriously.

I am still here, but not for long. Give Mercia my greetings, as well as your daughter and give a kiss to Teddy.

Cordially always your,

[signed] A. Segovia

SEGOVIA 20

Hotel Hassler-Roma, Trinità Dei Monti, 16 December 1950
My dear Papas: A few words of greetings for Mercia, you, and your children on the occasion of Christmas and the New Year.

You have written to me several times, but I have traveled around nearly half of the world without having time to answer any letters received.

Hauser made me a magnificent guitar, which he sent to Zurich for me to try out. But the war has very much changed his character. Don't be astonished if he does not answer you. Knowing that I have never disputed his prices, neither for the guitars he made for me previously, nor for the strings; now he dares to ask me to pay him before sending me the guitar, which I have of course done without delay. You see what bad spirit there is in all of this.

The European public continues to approve of me. Everywhere I have overflowing and enthusiastic halls. And the critics add their praise to these demonstrations of support. That obliges me to work a great deal, in order not to disappoint either the one or the other.

Many greetings for Mercia. I hope that she continues to bloom[9] like the time when I had the pleasure of seeing her in New York. Also hugs for your two children, and believe in my friendship of [illegible].

Your
[signed] Andrés

SEGOVIA 21

[n.d.]
My dear Papas: It has been a long time since I sent you my news or heard from you. Your cable told me of a letter which has never come. And I am anxious to hear from you about Ponce. He must be very ill not to have answered the letter I sent him about two months ago. Or perhaps his physical energy was spent in writing to you or Bobri. Do let me know what's going on with him.

I had intended to go to Europe in October but I was very alarmed by the situation there. I would not want again to fall into the inferno.

It is because of this, and because of the work of making new recordings, perhaps for Victor, Columbia, or some other company, that I foster the plan in advance of my departure for the U.S. Perhaps I will be there about the middle or the end of November. I could then work peacefully on the pieces to be recorded—the Chaconne and other Bach works, the two concertos, and some guitar solos—and those which I will play on my next tour. The problem is that my presence in New York will coincide with the members of the UN which will make it more difficult to find a hotel room. I have already written to several friends asking them to find me a place to stay. Among other people I have let Miss Justine Ward know of my wishes, because I am in debt to her, having promised to return to her from Colombia, in accord with certain plans that I then had, but at the last minute it was not possible for me to carry them out. I don't know if she is still in Washington and, consequently, if she will receive my letter; and if she does receive it, if she will be able to offer me hospitality. In any case I always have the Spanish Embassy—because I rely upon the friendship of M. and Mme. de Cárdenas—but I fear greatly that it is really the place least conducive to work, because it is nearly impossible to avoid the invitations and friendly gestures of the hosts.

In any case I ask you urgently not to say anything either to Miss Justine Ward or to the Embassy about the above. First I will wait for a reply, and I will write to the Ambassadors later.

The Method continues on its way. And my book also.

I will go to Buenos Aires in two weeks. I am asking you to send your answer there, in care of Mr. Miguel del Pino, Corrientes, 1309.

My affectionate greetings for your wife and daughter, embrace your infant, and believe in my truly sincere friendship.

[unsigned]

SEGOVIA 22

New York, 9 March 1952

My dear Papas: Here are the conditions of the Concours de l'Academia Chigiana, as I promised you.

I have just returned from Florida. I am getting ready to make some recordings for Decca and when I am too tired, I will phone to ask you to reserve a room for me in the small hotel we spoke about. I will go there to rest for several days.

Greetings to Mercia, and embrace your children.

Cordially your

[signed] Andrés

Don't say anything in the letter about the possibility of my going to Washington, I beg you.

S E G O V I A 23

Palazzo Ravizza, Siena, Italia, 31 August 1954

My dear Sofocles: Thank you for your two letters. I would like to know if the sound of the Decca disk, which has just come out, is appreciably better than that of the preceding disks. In the Studio, it was. I don't know if the recording lost quality during manufacture.

It's not worth the trouble for you to send it here because I am planning to return to New York toward the end of October.

Grace Schwab is here. She continues to battle, I think without positive results, against herself. On the other hand your friend[10] is making progress. He pays close attention and works hard.

The day is not long enough for all that I have to do. I teach twice a day; in my hotel room I received a young English guitarist of astonishing abilities; and other students always come to confide in me both their problems both musical and non-musical; and, in addition, students of instruments other than the guitar; I have to go frequently to the home of the Count, who always wants me to be present at lunches or dinners where there are guests of note from the intellectual, artistic, or aristocratic world. Add to this my own visitors, who come to Siena from the four corners of the earth, and my hard labor on new works—concertos, chamber music, solos, etc.—and you will understand well that my life here is very full. And still I find a few minutes to pay confidential compliments to the beautiful women of which Siena is full.

And now, dear Sophocles, until the next time. Don't forget to let me know, after comparing them, if in fact the disk that Decca has just put out differs in sound quality and in fidelity of timbre, from the others.

Thank you, and with many greetings for Mercia and the young mother,[11] and believe in my friendly feelings.

[signed] Andrés

Have you read any reviews of the disk?

SEGOVIA 24

Madrid, 15 October 1959

Dear friend: I presume you have already heard from Mr. Vidoudez about the case that you ordered. Inasmuch as mine (which I also obtained from him) has travelled too much, I will give you the one that I have recently bought. They are both identical.

With regard to Hauser, Jr.'s guitar which I have here in Madrid, I want you to know that it has a couple of cracks or more. I think the best thing for me to do is to send it first to Hauser for complete repair and get it back from him on my trip to Germany, or, if I should find a better one, to exchange it for the latter and bring it over to you as agreed.

I have been notifed by Decca that Olga's album will appear within a few weeks. I am very happy for all the good this can do for our special friend.

Kindest regards to both you and Mercia.

Sincerely yours,

Affectionately,

[signed] Andrés

AS/ec

[letter typewritten in English]

SEGOVIA 25

This letter was apparently sent to Ramírez, the guitarmaker, as an introduction to Sophocles Papas.

Washington, 18 January 1960

My dear Ramírez: Your guitar withstands the temperature and dryness of this country and sounds better every day. I broke a finger-nail recently, and when it has grown out I will try the guitar in one of my concerts.

I am writing to you to introduce a friend of mine, Mr. Papas, who has a music school where he himself teaches guitar. He likes your instrument very much. He would appreciate knowing the conditions under which you might enter into a commercial relationship with him. You may be assured that he is serious and financially responsible.

Greetings to your wife and the Rubios, and a fond embrace from

[signed] Andrés Segovia

SEGOVIA 26

Falls Church, Virginia, 17 February 1961

Dear Andrés, Mercia and I will not be able to come to your concert again this time, but we are definitely planning to come to the April 29th concert. Of course we are looking forward to hearing you in Washington and to having you and Olga as our houseguests as usual. We hope you will allow us to plan a reception in your honor after the concert.

I received a new guitar from Ramírez and it is magnificent. I am grateful to you for recommending me to him.

Next December I will be 67 [*sic*] years old and would like not to have to teach forty hours a week, which I am now doing. At present my main income comes from teaching, and I must develop the publishing business I started in order to have an income which will enable me to partially retire. For this reason you can readily understand why I am anxious to publish the Milan Pavanes. Since I did not have the Pavanes last year I went ahead and reprinted six of your arrangements which are in the public domain since Casa Núñez never copyrighted them. I also published your Estudio-Vals, which you were kind enough to dedicate to me. You will receive royalties on this. I feel sure that you will like the quality of the new edition, which I hope has no misprints.

You will notice from the enclosed Ricordi editions that all they did was to photograph the old Romero y Fernandes edition with misprints and all, especially the Leyenda. I had new plates made for my edition.

I understand that Bérben of Modena has published the Weiss (Ponce) Suite without giving Ponce credit for it. Furthermore, Mrs. Ponce does not

benefit. I will be glad to publish the Weiss as well as the Scarlatti suite if edited by Ansetonius, and to pay Mrs. Ponce royalties.

I wrote to Castelnuovo-Tedesco to ask him to write some easy preludes.
He sent me a very nice letter but did not promise to write the preludes because he "does not want to be restricted." I sent him the Ponce preludes, and
perhaps after seeing them he will reconsider—under your influence.

Tell Olga that I received the material from Gaspar and hope to present it
next week to Edward R. Murrow, who is the new chief of U.S. Information
Agency.

Mercia joins me in wishing you a successful (if not restful) tour. Again in
anticipation of April 8th, I am

Affectionately,

[signed] [Sophocles]

SEGOVIA 27

15 April 1963

Dear Andrés, I delayed sending you the clippings because I was waiting for
the photographs, which I am enclosing.

Washingtonians, and especially Mercia and I, were very fortunate this year
to hear you so many times. The inner peace which pervades you is reflected
in your playing, and it was evident to all those who admire and love you.

Everyone, too, was so impressed with Emilita's charm and devotion to
you. Mercia and I already feel very close to her, and as though we have
known her for a long time.

Larry Snitzler (the red head who played your compositions) visited Clare
Callahan since her latest letter, and in it he gave her the information that she
had requested. She plans to be in Siena as well as Santiago. There will be at
least three of my pupils going to study with you this summer.

I wish I were able to attend too this year, but I will at least attend your
classes in California in June of 1964 and probably Europe as well.

Affectionately,

[signed] Sophocles

SP/kjm

[typed by someone other than Mercia]

SEGOVIA 28

Hostal de los Reyes Católicos, Santiago de Compostela, 3 September 1963
My dear Sophocles: Thank you for the strings, the books, and the piano
bench. Everything came, a bit late, but without loss or damage.

Recently I spoke with Alirio Díaz, with Ghiglia, and with Thomas abut the
university offer and your own contribution. Alirio fears that it will paralyse
his career if he takes on the daily obligation of teaching in a university.
Ghiglia is horrified at the price of the round tip if the classes don't suit him.
And Thomas has not openly answered me. I think that his wife and two
children keep him in the provincial conservatory of Alicante. In any case do
correspond directly with him. The others have also told me that they will
write to you.

I left Helga Sandburg's address in Madrid. Please thank her for me for the
kind dedication she put in her book. As soon as I return home I will write to
her directly.

Siena has taken up a month, from 15 July to 15 August. Santiago, another
month. On the 13th, the University of Santiago is going to honor me with the
degree Doctor Honoris Causa. I am very proud! From here, Emilita and I will
go to Mallorca. We are invited to stay at the Cárdenas' home. I will close the
Festival of Music, which is given in Pollensa, with a gala recital. I have offered
my fee to charity. We hope also to see Consuelo Landa[12] there.

Greetings to Mercia from both Emilita and myself, and from both of us to
you.

[signed] Andrés

SEGOVIA 29

Washington, 11 September 1963
Dear Andrés: I was happy to receive your letter and to learn that you have by
now received all the things I sent. A friend of mine in the State Department
had promised to deliver the bench and at the last moment could not do so.
Hence the delay in shipping it to you.

Helga Sandburg's address—1673 Columbia Road, N.W., Washington,
D.C.

I know Consuelo will be glad to see you and Emilita when you arrive in Pollensa. Please give my regards to her and to Mr. Cárdenas. I wrote Consuelo about two weeks ago. Incidentally, she divorced Landa about five years ago and has returned to her first husband's name, Consuelo Thaw.

My pupils write enthusiastically about your classes and of your kindness to them in particular. I appreciate that too. We are happy here about your receiving the doctorate in November. We think there are several universities that should recognize your life's work in the world of music, especially American University here in Washington.

With love to both of you from both of us.

Affectionately,

[Sophocles]

SEGOVIA 30

Washington, 18 March 1964

Dear Andrés: I am sorry you missed me when you phoned. Mercia gave me your messages and everything is taken care of. I had the new program typed and sent to Mr. Hayes.

The enclosed clipping should bring interesting news to you, and I hope the new Ambassador is more musical than his predecessor.

The Lagoyas spent three days here with us, and they gave a very successful concert. Business took me to New York and gave me the opportunity to hear them again in Town Hall. Both Hurok and Shaw were enthusiastic about them and are planning a longer tour next season.

Mercia and I are glad that you and Emilita are going to have some extra time in Washington in April. The weather is usually pleasant and the cherry blossoms should be in bloom. If you wish, we can plan a trip to the Blue Ridge mountains.

If time permits, and you feel inclined, I would like to arrange for you to hear some of my advanced pupils, and invite a few of the less advanced, but promising students, to sit in as auditors.

I will telephone you at the Ambassador Friday evening to discuss the details of your visit, and also about Aldo Minella.

With affectionate regards to both of you from both of us,

Cordially,

[signed] Sophocles

[enclosure missing]

SEGOVIA 31

Washington, 9 September 1965

Dear Andrés: I am happy to enclose a check for $243.10 which represents royalties from your works for the first six months period of 1965.

I have just completed an agreement with the Theodore Presser Company of Bryn Mawr, Pa. who will distribute my publications. This should increase the sales considerably and will also give me time to edit and publish more works.

My copyright lawyer told me it was possible to register a composition with "as played by Andres Segovia" and suggested that we try it with one piece first. I hope you will send me such work.

Patrick Hayes has your schedule for two concerts in Washington January 15 and March 13. We are looking forward to hearing you and to seeing you and Emilita again.

We are now in the process of purchasing a new (and larger) house with an extra bedroom for guests, and we would very much like to have you two stay with us your next trip here. I know you will be comfortable and Emilita will enjoy our new kitchen. The new house is in a much quieter neighborhood.

Affectionately,

[signed] Sophocles

SEGOVIA 32

Washington, 15 November 1965

Dear Andrés: About two months ago I sent you a letter together with a check for royalties which I hope you have received. It was sent to Santiago. Under separate cover, I am sending you copies of my recent publications. You will recall that you gave me permission to use your version of the Dominant 7th chord in the "Leyenda."

I still hope you will send me one piece to publish under the caption "as recorded by Andrés Segovia" and if such a title can be copyrighted then I am willing to destroy all the copies I have of the following publications and publish your version of the same pieces again with your name and pay you royalty. Destroying the copies on hand will not be a loss because I will sell many, many more with your name on them.

A friend of mine went to Mexico and was able to see Mr. Carlos Vázquez who seems to be taking care of Clema Ponce's affairs. Mr. Vázquez gave my friend a photostatic copy of Ponce's unfinished quartette and I am glad to have it even though Ponce failed to write the dedication to me as he had written me he would. God rest his soul.

In my last letter I wrote about our having bought a new house. We are now living in it and are very happy and more comfortable. In addition to the extra space we have in the house itself, we have an acre of tall trees which are magnificent. Photo and plan enclosed.

Mercia and I want you and Emilita to stay with us during your visits to Washington. We have a separate guest room now and you will be comfortable. Tell Emilita we have a beautiful new kitchen with two ovens and many other innovations. She can experiment with it if she likes.

Tom Hartman (the bearded one) gave me a glowing report of your large class in Santiago and that Larry Snitzler played well.

The Peabody Conservatory did not take our recommendation to engage Guillermo Fierens as guitar instructor and chose Aaron Shearer instead. Qué lástima! I will offer Guillermo a teaching position here and will help him to give concerts.

The American Music Conference has engaged a public relations firm to gather information about the classic guitar.

The University of Florida is investigating the guitar with the purpose of developing and increasing its volume. This is a big project on which they have two men and are spending several thousand dollars.

Hoping to hear from you soon, and with affectionate regards,

Sincerely yours,

[signed] Sophocles

SP/ml

[Mercia always signed her letters with ml for Mercia Lorentz]

SEGOVIA 33

Washington, 14 January 1966

I rejoice, my friend Papas, that you have succeeded in reviving the moribund Washington Guitar Society, converting it into a thriving and active entity. Its members should not limit themselves, as so often happens in other places, to the selfish pleasure of organizing evening gatherings for the purpose of listening to each other. This has limited value for the development of the instrument. They should, among other things, make an appeal to their sister societies throughout the country, with the altruistic purpose of jointly accumulating funds which could be used for the complete training of some youthful guitarist of real talent, in musical conservatories or academies, national or foreign. Also they should collectively undertake the organization of concerts for those who are ready to present themselves before the public, requiring them to pass through each of the groups that have embraced these ideas. In this way it would be possible to overcome the awkward difficulties encountered by the young artist of merit at the beginning of his career.

Finally, it is not necessary to specify in detail all the good that would be achieved for the guitar and its performers if the societies then put these and other ideas into effect. Try to inspire what has just been reborn in that direction.

[signed] Andrés Segovia

SEGOVIA 34

Washington, 27 April 1966

Dear Andrés: I was very happy to be with you and Emilita in Winston-Salem. Even in only three classes, one is able to learn a great deal from your instruction. I am sorry that the quality of the students was not what you expected and deserve, but their appreciation and gratitude for your help is genuine.

The album I want to publish will contain only the following pieces which I have already printed separately. You have seen them and I am sure you would have pointed out the errors if any. I have been using these pieces in my teaching.

If agreeable with you, please sign the enclosed agreement and return it to me in the enclosed envelope or together with the Chilesotti pieces.

I hope that Emilita has fully recuperated by now and that you are both enjoying the freedom from the pressure of traveling.

Affectionately,

[signed] Sophocles

SEGOVIA 35

Washington, 29 November 1967

Dear Andrés: Mercia and I were saddened by the news of Beatriz.[13] Although we met her only once, we felt close to her because of you. We are sorry we did not learn of this tragedy sooner.

Alicia de la Rocha played here last week with great success, and it was she who gave us the news that Beatriz had passed away. We know how much she meant to you and hope that time will heal the wound her death has brought upon you.

Please give our love to Emilita.

Affectionately,

[signed] Sophocles

SEGOVIA 36

Washington, 19 June 1968

Dear Andrés: Mercia and I went to New York in April to see you and Emilita and found that you had left for Madrid the day before. We are sorry to have missed you. Dr. Castroviejo told us he was to perform the second operation in Madrid. We are glad to learn from the newspapers that the operation was successful.[14]

Your royalty check for 1967 reflects the general business situation all over the United States. The Theodore Presser Company who distributes my publications, told me 1967 was a bad year for all music sales, not guitar publications alone. They also advised me to publish the single pieces of your arrangements in one volume. I hope you like the production.

The civil disturbances we had here in the city in April[15] had an adverse effect on business in general, and we do not hope for much improvement until after the summer is over.

The $400 scholarship check is enclosed, so that you may present it to the proper person.

Our love to Emilita.

Affectionately,

[signed] Sophocles

SEGOVIA 37

Washington, 5 May 1969

Dear Andrés: I hope this letter finds you recovering and resting and enjoying the nice weather.

You remember the Alvino Reys. They are members of the King Family who appear on television. They have been close friends of ours for many years. Their daughter, Liza, is in Madrid studying the harp. We sent her your address because we know she would like very much to meet you. I am sure you will find her charming and artistically gifted. If there is an opportunity for her to play for you, it would be to her advantage and her great joy if you would give her some advice.

We are looking forward to your next visit to Washington. Give our love to Emilita.

Affectionately,

[signed] Sophocles

SEGOVIA 38

4 April 1970

My dear Sophocles, Please send me by return mail the home address of Mr. Arthur M. Bernstein. I promised to send him my opinion of his sound system while I was on the plane going to Madrid, and I unfortunately mislaid the piece of paper where his address was written. I don't want him to think that I reneged on my promise.

Have you received the "English Suite" by Duarte? After I was in New York I spoke with the reception desk of the Mayflower,[16] telling them that you would stop by to pick it up.

Greetings from Emilita to Mercia and for you and my affection for both of you. Your,

[signed] Andrés

SEGOVIA 39

Washington, 24 June 1970

Dear Andrés: Mercia and I, along with the whole world, are delighted to hear of the arrival of Carlos Andrés. In the enclosed photo he looks very healthy and we wish him a long and happy life.

The enclosed letter is from a scientific magazine and self-explanatory. Mr. [blank] called me over long distance telephone to ask me about the Kasha guitar. I was not very enthusiastic about it because Carlos Barbosa-Lima used it when making a record for Westminster and it was "dead" He had to tape the piece over again.

I am enclosing Duarte's "For My Friends," and the Ponce Scherzino which I hope you will find time to transpose for guitar solo as you promised.

Affectionately,

[Sophocles]

SEGOVIA 40

"Los Olivos," 15 July 1970
Dear Mercia and Sophocles: We have been visited today by the legendary kings from Far East loaded with your presents to Carlos Andrés. Emilita and I we are sending you our thanks for so many and useful things.

The boy is gaining every day in strength and good appearance. In few days he will have two months and he begins to follow with his eyes, his mother's movements and my voice. His interest in the spectacle of life is awakening in his foggy mind. As soon as we will have a good picture of him, we will send it to you. The echo that the birth of this boy had throughout the world makes me think that I am now more famous for being a Father than an artist.

Emilita and I we send you our thanks again and our affection.
Andrés

SEGOVIA 41

P.O. Box 19126, Washington, D.C., 22 July 1970
Dear Andrés and Emilita: Mercia and I were delighted to receive your letter and to learn of Carlos Andrés good health and progress.

Duarte told me he has written "Three Songs Without Words" for Carlos Andrés and I told him I would like to publish them. Bobri, who is now Art Director of the Columbia Music Company, will design the cover in color. I hope you will agree to that. It will be a work of love for Bobri and me as it is for Duarte.[17]

I think the enclosed clipping will amuse you. Incidentally, El Dopa is not an aphrodisiac but a new drug for sufferers of Parkinson's disease.

Our best to your lovely family,
Affectionately,
[signed] Sophocles

SEGOVIA 42

Washington, 14 December 1970

Dear Andrés: "The Guitar and I"[18] was a great idea and should inspire students to practice seriously. Mercia and I enjoyed the photographs on the jacket, especially that of Carlos Andrés with Emilita. You look happy and serene standing there on the balcony.

I don't know whether to call it mental telepathy or prescience but three weeks ago I began taping "Forty-two years of friendship with Andrés Segovia" and am reliving those years with joy and gratitude.

Bobri showed me the book he is preparing with drawings and photographs depicting the various positions of your hands, etc. If you recall, last year I showed you rough drawings of the right hand playing the scales. I showed them to Bobri too, and I hope it was I who inspired him to undertake the preparation of this valuable book.

When I showed you my method you told me you liked the material, text and organization but suggested that I eliminate the flamenco and that I should have more written instructions. Your advice was heeded and I am now in process of revising and enlarging it. I hope to have the new edition out by next fall and it will appear in two or three volumes. I will be able to show you many of the changes next month and anticipate your approval.

As always, Mercia and I would like to have you stay with us while in Washington and also to give a small reception in your honour after the concert.

Duarte agreed to have me publish "Three Songs Without Words" dedicated to Carlos Andrés if you approve. Bobri will design the cover. Three of your best friends will treat this work with loving care.

Our love to Emilita and best wishes for the holiday season.

Affectionately,

[signed] Sophocles

SEGOVIA 43

Post Office Box 19126, Washington, D.C., 30 July 1971

Dear Andrés: Mercia and I were happy to receive your letter and the good news of the successful operation. I hope by the time you receive this your sight will be fully restored. Don't forget your promise to send us a photo of Carlos Andrés. Perhaps we could have one of the baby with Mama and Papa together?

Last week I mailed you two books of Scarlatti and other music which I hope will arrive safely. In the same package I included two volumes of Giuliani by Dr. Thomas Heck which I am sure you will find interesting. The two books are a gift to you from the author. The sets are numbered and yours is number one. If you wish to write to Mr. Heck, his address is Box 182, Bozman, Maryland 21612 U.S.A.

Dr. Heck is currently helping me to organize the American Guitar Foundation as a national organization, which we eventually hope to change to international, and renamed "Segovia Guitar Foundation." In the next few weeks you will receive material about the AGF which I feel sure will please you.

Concerning the Scarlatti Sonatas, Carlos transcribed twelve but only seven could go on the record. When you see the music you will see that some of the notes and finger indications are not like yours. When working on the sonatas Carlos remarked about the similarity of the transcriptions and I reassured him that with most of the sonatas he undertook to transcribe, there was not much else one could do because some of them can be played from the harpsichord score. For example L 483 same key A major. L 454 by changing the key from C to D. L 352 from F minor to E minor. I had four volumes of Scarlatti which I gave to Carlos so I don't have the harpsichord part of all nine to make more comparisons.

About ten years ago I had telephoned you and asked if I could come to see you "next Sunday afternoon" and you said yes. When I arrived I found you in bed suffering intermittent but excruciating pain from kidney stones. I had brought with me a transcript I was working on of Moussorgsky's "Old Castle" but noting that you were ill and there was nothing I could do, I offered to return to Washington. You insisted that I stay which I did, and after looking over my transcription you said "Well Sophocles there isn't much to do in transcribing this work for the guitar. All that is necessary is to change the music to the key of D minor and finger it." Now don't you think that is an analogous situation between Moussorgsky's "Old Castle" and most of the sonatas of Scarlatti which Carlos transcribed?

Of all your pupils I don't believe there is one who is more faithful to you musically or more grateful for your help and generosity than Carlos. It would break his heart to think you suspected him of wrong doing. When I told him you were too busy to write pieces for me to publish, he made copies of your transcriptions (enclosed) for you to check their accuracy and then send them to me for inclusion in an album. I believe Carlos is totally dedicated to his art, and he will be one of the most successful artists from among your pupils. In my humble opinion, Hurok will be the loser for having rejected him from his management.

Parkening played here last April and will play here with orchestra in the Post Pavillion on August 22nd. Lorimer paid us a visit last month and he will play here next season. Sharon Isbin, the 13-year-old girl who played for you in January, came to Washington for lessons again. She has made tremendous progress and will attend Ghiglia's class in Aspen, Colorado next month.

Jorge Crespo died from pulmonary emphysema. We saw Dr. Cajigas a few weeks ago. He [Cajigas] still goes to his office three days a week, but Anna Cajigas is an invalid and is confined to a nursing home. They sold their lovely big house and distributed some of the rugs and other furnishings among the grandchildren.

Again we hope your eyes are now in good shape and with kind regards to Emilita,

Affectionately,

[Sophocles]

SEGOVIA 44

Los Olivos, Almuñécar, Prov. de Granada, 4 August 1971

My dear Sophocles: I have not yet received the letter which you mentioned on a scrap of paper found inside the package which you sent me. The best things that package contained were the two books by Mr. Heck on Giuliani. I have brought one of them to read carefully during my next trips in Europe and the other I have kept for my American tour. And then, either directly or by letter which I shall send you via your intermediary, I shall give you my opinions—which, I feel sure, will be generally favorable.

I was disagreeably surprised at the lack of integrity and intelligence on the part of your adopted son, Barbosa Lima. He showed not the least scruple in expropriating the artistic property of John Williams, Alirio Díaz, and myself in publishing the Nine Sonatas of Scarlatti under his own name. And I am even more astonished that you, who know the entire guitar repertoire, and Scarlatti's music in particular, did not point out to him the dishonesty of what he was doing. I believe that your paternal affections have blinded you.

In addition to the fog in which he clothes his conscience he has also clouded his own intelligence, of which he does not have much. He has not taken into account the fact that two of the sonatas which he published under his name were published by Schott, under my name, before he was born. And another in G Major has not yet been published by me but was included on one of the disks I recorded, with Decca, around 1948. The Sonata in A Major was transcribed by John Williams and I have also recorded it on a Decca disk, around 1960–1962; at that time I stated, in the explanatory material which accompanied the disk, that the transcription was by Williams and not me. Alirio Díaz must also have recorded his transcription of the Sonata in G Minor for the recording company with which he works. He gave me a copy a very long time ago in Siena. The most cursory glance at this matter shows Barbosa as a petty thief, which will not add a bit to his reputation.

In some of his transcription he has changed either the key or the fingering. For example the short Sonata arranged by Alirio he has transposed to E Minor from G Minor, while in the three I transcribed and the one by John he has changed the fingering—for the worse of course. That is the only bit of originality which he has contributed to the work. One of the great French writers said that, in matters of art, theft is permitted only when followed by murder. In other words, when a painter, a poet, a musician takes from another a work which is definitely inferior and transforms it into something brilliant which totally kills the original version. This is not the case with your child prodigy.

Llobet did a transcription of Chopin's "Nocturne" in E-flat Major and the one by Tárrega at almost the same time. He always gave credit to the Maestro whenever he played them. For my part, I have never wanted to publish either "Sevilla" or "Cádiz" by Albéniz, despite the essential changes which I introduced, because the former was done by Tárrega and the latter by Llobet. I did publish "Granada" because, so far as I knew, that piece had been badly done by Tárrega's brother who was a bad violinist and published by the Maestro's son who was good for nothing. As regards the Granados "Dances," I refer you back to my comment about theft and murder, and you will understand me.

But your publishing enterprise, at least in some of the works which I have seen, is a little nest of plagiarism. Take care, my dear Sophocles, because you, too, are subject to the law that a disgraceful act is a disgraceful act, anywhere in the world.

To sum up: I believe you know me well enough not to imagine that I have some material interest in these remonstrations. It is very painful for me to note that a young guitarist at the beginning of his career can calmly commit such disgraceful things. Parkening, who after John Williams is the best artist of the guitar of this generation, upset me profoundly when I learned that he is so vulgar as to play flamenco at the ends of his programs. Nor did I flinch when I saw that Lorimer, the day after my concert in New York, himself gave a concert in which he played a number of pieces which I had played the evening before. I attended his concert and I had to smile. In Europe we have more delicacy, and we respect our masters.

Well, enough. I had to be at my country house, free from haste, to write such a long letter.

Emilita joins me in sending our affections to Mercia and to you as well.

Cordially,

[signed] Andrés Segovia

Author's Note: In 1969 in Washington Segovia had written (in English):
"The young Brasilian artist Carlos Barbosa is gifted by the Godess of Music with warm sentiment for playing serious and beautiful compositions in his guitar. He learned quickly my technical advises and extends his right interpretations to classical and contemporary authors. I wish him the success he deserves.

[signed] Andrés Segovia
Washington 1969"

SEGOVIA 45

Washington, [n.d.]

Dear Andrés, Your letter of August 4th crossed my letter of July 30th. I feel sure you would not have written as you did if you had received mine.

Your letter made me sad not because of what you said about me and about Carlos but because you must have been in a state of rage to have written such words to a friend of 40 years.

It was January 9, 1928 when we first met back stage at Town Hall and I still have the photo you autographed for me in your hotel room the following morning.

To transcribe Scarlatti is a comparatively easy job for a skilled guitarist, but to transcribe Bach's Chaconne from a simple violin solo to the monumental transcription you made of the work requires Segovian musicianship and imagination. And yet, out of the six guitarists who recorded the Chaconne (two of them twice) only one gives you credit for the transcription and he also states "Segovia added a few guitaristic chords to his edition." The Chaconne was 8 times recorded. I have the above information properly documented and will give it to you if you don't already have it.

I am wondering if your reaction to not having gotten credit for the Chaconne was the same as for the Scarlatti. I hope not for your sake.

Andrés, you are a great man, an intellectual and musical giant. No one can dispute that fact. But you are also a human being. And a very kind one too.

You could have shown your displeasure with Carlos in a less vehement way by accusing him of using bad judgment and not of deliberate dishonesty. Shakespeare said, "Oh, it is excellent to have a giant's strength, but it is tyrannous to use it like a giant."

[signed] Sophocles

SEGOVIA 46

Author's note: I have included this letter from Papas to Barbosa-Lima because it is pertinent to Nos. 44 and 45.

Washington, 20 August 1971
Mr. Carlos Barbosa-Lima
Rua Pedro Taques 467 (Brooklyn)
São Paulo 17 S.P. BRAZIL

Dear Carlos: I received your letter and am glad things are going well for you. The Scarlatti books are selling well and I hope will continue to do so. The Weiss Suite is at the typographers and so is the Unamuno piece. I am holding Mignone's work for your arrival.

Maestro Segovia became upset about the Scarlatti Sonatas which he had recorded. I wrote to him and explained to him that, while working on them you had remarked to me about the similarity of the arrangements to those of the Maestro's and that I told you at that time it was okay, because with most of them all anyone had to do was to change the key and the piece can be played on the guitar from the harpsichord score. My answer to his letter is enclosed.

There was a time several years ago when Segovia was mad at Bobri and he would neither see or speak to him for several months. Later he found out that somebody had told him lies about Bobri. It may be possible that somebody has told him lies about you that would upset him enough to strike out at you. In any event, don't worry, and if he should write to you guide yourself by what I told him.

Next week I plan to visit my daughter in Canada and then back to Washington for another busy season.

I have moved away from the Guitar Shop and have a new studio nearby. The mailing address is Post Office Box 19126, Washington, D.C. 20036, U.S.A. My residence is still the same at 3222 Wynford Drive, Fairfax, Va. 22030.

Sincerely yours,
[signed] Sophocles Papas

SEGOVIA 47

Washington, 9 January 1972
Dear Andrés: Today, January 9th, is the 44th anniversary of your debut in New York and the beginning of our friendship of almost two generations.

Mercia and I were delighted to learn that Emilita is expecting again. It is wonderful news.

I am happy to know you will play in Cleveland this month. Besides my colleague, Dick Lurie, do you know that Helga Sandburg (Mrs. George Crile) lives there? Thomas Heck also will be there to greet you and to bring you up to date on the progress we have made with the American Guitar Foundation.

My daughter Betty and her family live in Canada. She is Mrs. Philip H. Smith, Jr. of Waterloo, Ontario, about sixty miles from Toronto. Betty and her husband Philip and two friends have tickets to your concert in Toronto.[19]

You met Philip in my house two years ago when we had lunch together and drove to New York immediately afterward. It had been snowing and it took us several hours to get there.

Mr. Weinberger phoned me last night to get news of you. He said he has not been well and may not be able to get to your concert.

Mercia and I are looking forward with great pleasure to your visit here on February 19th.

Affectionately,

[signed] Sophocles

SEGOVIA 48

Washington, 8 October 1972

Dear Andrés: Mercia and I were saddened to hear that Emilita lost the baby. When Mercia suffered a similar misfortune in 1949 you wrote to me as follows: "I send you my sincere condolences, although, in these uncertain times that we suffer, it seems to me that your young one has had the intelligence not to want to remain among us and to return to Infinity, in great joy. There is thus no reason to commiserate, even if his departure makes you sad.

"Never call other children to come into this world, dear friend. Be aware, you and Mercia, of the moral responsibility that you take on in launching a new being into this whirlpool of selfishness and cruel wickedness. Content yourselves with matters less transcendent."

The world situation is not any better now than it was then, and I hope both of you are philosophical about the event. Mercia and I wish you both health and happiness and endless joy in bringing up Carlos Andrés to be cognizant of the good things of our society, the philosophy of his parents and heritage that will be left him by his father.

Mercia and I are leaving tomorrow for a two week guided tour to Athens, the Greek Islands and Istanbul. Mercia has never been abroad and we are both excited about the trip.

Our love to Emilita and Carlos Andrés,

Affectionately,

[signed] Sophocles

SEGOVIA 49

Washington, 13 February 1973

Dear Andrés: Three years ago at the reception at the Indonesian Embassy you told me you liked Mayor Washington and would like to have a photograph of him. As you see, I did not forget. I was waiting for an opportunity to meet him again and ask him in person. This I did three months ago at the Greek Embassy. Mr. Washington loves the guitar. Let me know if you want Mr. Hayes to send him some tickets.

We are looking forward to hearing you here on the 25th. I will be prepared for any kind of weather this year. I have also donated a footstool to the Kennedy Center. And as always, I will be prepared to meet you at the airport. Please have dinner with us and let us arrange a small reception at our house after the concert.

"The Highwayman" is a famous poem which my daughter Elisabeth Smith set to music. It was published in 1963. When Bobri saw the book he was inspired by the contents to design this new edition enclosed.

Please call me at any time if you need my services for anything. My studio number is 202 293 4776 and my residence 703 560 8042.

Affectionately,

[signed] Sophocles

SEGOVIA 50

Av. Concha Espina, 61, Madrid 16, 9 May 1973

Dear friend, On my return from Italy I received your letter which contained the check corresponding to my royalty on the sale of my music and, truthfully, this figure is very encouraging.

As to the exercises of which you have sent me three sample manuscripts, you are in error: the first is not mine at all. The second and third are an incomplete fragment of those which I gave to my students at Siena and Santiago.

As soon as I am at my country house—in the first days of June—I will send you, for publication, some exercises for both hands. Before then it is impossible for me to work on anything not having to do with the preparation of works for my next recording. M. Israel Horowitz, the technician with whom I have for fifteen years made all my Decca recordings, will arrive in Madrid on the 14th of this month and we will begin our work on the 16th. I think I will be through about the end of May and right away we will leave for "Los Olivos" in order to remain there until the end of September.

Best wishes from Emilita and from me to Mercia and we send you our affectionate friendship.

[signed] Andrés

SEGOVIA 51

Washington, 23 April 1973

Dear Andrés: Mercia and I were happy to see you and Emilita in February. Both of you looked well.

Enclosed check with attached accounting is self-explanatory and most encouraging. I believe the amount could be doubled if and when you can find the time to prepare another album of pieces or exercises.

Last year I showed you the ligados which you gave me in 1929 and which I have been using with my pupils ever since. After the release of "The Guitar and I" we received many requests for the slurs. I have them ready to go to the typographers[20] but before sending them to be printed I would like your approval to include the enclosed exercises.

I also have ready for the printer your "Estudio" in E Major, together with Paquita's "Humorada." I can publish them together or separately or leave the Humorada out.[21] I will send you royalty contracts when I hear from you.

Duarte will be visiting us in May while in the United States giving classes.

Our love to Emilita and Carlos Andrés.

Affectionately,

[signed] Sophocles

SEGOVIA 52

Washington, 2 October 1973

Dear Andrés: I hope you had a restful and productive summer. Mercia and I did not go to Europe this year but we attended the guitar convention in Santa Barbara. Tribute was paid you by all who attended and your name was mentioned with reverence and affection. Guitarists from everywhere recognize your life's work for the noble instrument.

Santa Barbara is not far from Los Angeles so that we had an opportunity to visit with the Alvino Reys, and we stayed four days with Dorothy and Martin de Goede.

Columbia Music Company is progressing very well and of course CO 127 (the scales) is one of the biggest items in sales. In your last letter you promised to send me some new exercises for publication, and I hope you will bring them with you when you arrive in New York.

Some time ago you made many changes in Turina's "Sevillana." As a matter of fact, you practically rewrote the piece. I would like to issue this new edition with the sub-title "New Edition Revised by Segovia" and of course pay you the royalty, as well as any heir of Turina who is entitled to it. When I printed and copyrighted this piece it was in the public domain.

I can also publish a second album under your name, consisting of the following: "Estudio in E Major" by A. Segovia, "Humorada" by P. Madriguera, "Rondino on a Theme by Beethoven"—Kreisler, "Minueto Op 31 #3" Beethoven. "Humorada" can be omitted if you don't think it merits inclusion. Of course, you will get the usual 10% royalty which will increase the annual amount considerably. I have checked the music very carefully for any misprints and it is ready for the typographer. If I do not hear from you to the contrary, I will proceed with the above and we can sign the royalty agreement when you arrive in the United States.

My publishing business is doing so well that the income I derive from it makes it unnecessary for me to have to teach for my living. I accept only a small number of gifted pupils.

Mercia and I are looking forward to your concert here in February, and we hope to see Emilita too.

Affectionately,

[signed] Sophocles

SEGOVIA 53

Washington, 9 March 1974

Dear Andrés, I read in the newspaper that Sol Hurok died a short while after visiting with you and I know it must have been a double shock to you to see such a long time friend go so suddenly.[22] I followed his career for many years and know he was a great impresario and an astute businessman. He was interviewed on the radio about two months ago and he gave a good performance in logic and diplomacy. Reporters tried very hard to get him to make uncomplimentary remarks but they were frustrated. He would not criticize his temperamental artists but said it was a characteristic he admired in them.

I did write to Mr. Molleda[23] offering him an advance plus royalty and I will let you know the result.

Mercia joins me in sending affectionate regards.

Sincerely,

[signed] Sophocles

SEGOVIA 54

Washington, 1 May 1974

Dear Andrés: Enclosed please find check in amount of $2,145.13 for royalty for 1973.

I have ready for the typographer the following transcriptions by you: "Minuetto Op. 31 #3" by Beethoven, "Canzonetta" by Mendelssohn,

"Canción Sylvestre" by Schumann, "La Maja de Goya" and "Danza" No. 10 by Granados, "Romanza" by Jose Franco, and "Estudio" (arpeggio) by Mendelssohn. These pieces can make another volume.

Duarte told me he is hoping you will be able to have ready this summer the suite which he dedicated to Carlos Andrés, and which he has agreed to have me publish.

I am writing to Mr. Molleda about his Variations, offering to pay a royalty with a cash advance.

Mercia joins me in wishing you and Emilita and Carlos Andrés a pleasant and relaxed summer.

Affectionately,

[signed] Sophocles

SEGOVIA 55

Washington, 16 July 1974

Dear Andrés: I enclose the Sor piece you requested. I am glad you will perform it as it is one of my favorites. The theme is very well known here as a popular tune "for he's a jolly good fellow."

As to Mr. Molleda, you know me better than that—it was a typographical error. I have corrected myself in a letter to him. It should have been 30,000 pesetas.

Mercia and I are happy you are writing your memoirs. The whole world will be happy too. This brings to my mind the next January 9th; it will be 46 years since we first met in Town Hall. From the beginning you have always been kind to me and have played a great part in my life. I am grateful for the association and hope you are not disappointed with me as a friend.

Mercia and I are going to visit Argentina and Brazil the end of this month. I was asked to be a judge at the Faculdade Musical Palestrina in Porto Alegre but I declined because my schedule did not permit and also because two of my students are among those competing. However, I will have the pleasure of meeting one of your former students, Abel Carlevaro. We hope you will have a restful summer and look forward to seeing you again in February.

Affectionately,

[signed] Sophocles

SP/ml

SEGOVIA 56

Madrid, 23 April 1978

Dear Sophocles, From New York I came home for two days, going immediately to London, and from London to Switzerland. I arrived only a few days ago and already in my Studio, I begin to attend all my obligations: the preparation of the second volume of my life, a voluminous interview for the Spanish National Broadcasting lasting 20 days of half an hour each, the selection of old and new pieces for my next concert-tour in Europe and the United States and for you, the new transcription of the pieces that I have played recently, by Schumann (I have, a longtime ago, published in Schott a few of the same author, but different).

I thank Mercia and you for sending me the reviews of my last concert.

A Contest, organized for Guitar Execution and Interpretation by the Ministry of Culture will take place in Granada. The first prize will be a substancial one of 500,000 Pesetas and ten concerts throughout Spain. The second prize, 250,000 Pesetas and 100,000, the third.

According to my knowledge, there are three students who may aspire to win the first: the North-american, Eliot Fisk, the Uruguayan, Eduardo Fernández and a miraculous 16 years old Japanese whose name embroils in my tongue. Of course, he lacks the experience of the west music style, but he has a rich intuition. If you know any other worthy of trying the second prize, send him.

"Abrazos" from Emilita and I to Mercia and to you.

[signed] Andrés

APPENDIX E

"The Romance of the Guitar"

This article appeared in *The Etude Music Magazine* in four sections in April, May, June, and July 1930. Arnold Broido, President of Theodore Presser, which formerly published the magazine, has given his permission to include the entire article. The magazine's editor wrote: "This is one of the most interesting and comprehensive articles ever written on the guitar and is of immense usefulness, whether the reader plays this instrument or not. Sophocles Papas's introduction follows."

Based upon an Interview with the Great Spanish Guitarist Andrés Segovia

Secured for *The Etude* by Sophocles Papas

"The Guitar is a Miniature Orchestra in Itself." — Beethoven

What greater compliment could be paid a solo instrument with only six strings than for this great genius to compare it to an orchestra? And it is this instrument which filled with celestial sounds the temples of Solomon, which accompanied Homer as he sang the deeds of the heroes of Troy and which was used by the emperors and kings in their sumptuous entertainments and by the humble lover in serenading his mistress.

In eight words Beethoven has summed up all the merits of the guitar, for by these he means not only that it is capable of producing all the harmonic combinations of an orchestra but the effects and tone colors as well. Yet, as Berlioz said, the guitar has been treated as an orphan and has been misunderstood so often that the average person about to hear it for the first time is under the impression that the performance is to be such as we usually hear in vaudeville. This situation exists to some extent in Europe but much more so in this country—at least it did until Andrés Segovia, the great Spanish guitarist, made his debut in New York two years ago and was acclaimed by the critics not simply as a great guitarist but, indeed, as one of the greatest artists on the concert stage today.

Those who knew the guitar and its possibilities and had heard of the ovations which Segovia received in Europe were sure of witnessing another triumph. Many traveled miles to hear him. But Segovia's audience did not consist entirely of lovers of the guitar and his art. There were many prompted by curiosity among whom may be included some of the music critics, for such was the confession of the critic on the "London Times" after Segovia had played there. "And so," he says, "in the fullness of our ignorance we went, expecting we did not quite know what but hoping, since Señor Segovia's reputation had preceded him and the name of J. S. Bach appeared on his program, that we would satisfy our curiosity about an instrument that has romantic associations without being outraged musically. We did not go to scoff but we certainly remained to hear the last possible note; for it was the most delightful surprise of the season."

Segovia's Early Training

Andrés Segovia was born in 1896 near Granada in Andalusia, Spain, and, in his own words, "opened the musical dynasty of his family." From his childhood he was greatly interested in music and the guitar was his favorite instrument. The most amazing thing is that he was his own teacher, and, at the age of fifteen, was able to interpret the most difficult compositions with uncanny skill. From that time on he has appeared continuously on the concert stage, and his repertoire now embraces compositions of the sixteenth century to the moderns.

It is impossible to describe Señor Segovia's playing; one must hear him to believe. With a transcendent technic and unimpeachable musical taste, with his deep insight into the works of the great masters combined with the most delicate nuances, perfection of phrasing and vital rhythm, Segovia is a miracle. The hundreds of music critics who heard his performances all vied with each other in praising him. Never before has there been an artist who has received wider acclaim than Segovia.

When asked how he began the study of his guitar, he replied: "I cannot remember just when I did so, as I was too young, but I knew that I had an insatiable desire to play and I heard as many guitarists as possible. Then I went home to find out new ways for myself. Of course there are teachers of the guitar in Spain, but a great many Spanish boys need no further encouragement to begin than the instrument itself."

Segovia being the greatest exponent of the guitar in the world at the present time and his being so thoroughly familiar with its history and literature naturally makes this interview of unusual interest.

[Andrés Segovia's interview follows.]

Remote Ancestors of the Guitar

Before proceeding with the history of the guitar, two points must be made clear: first, that the traditional lute differs from the guitar only in shape; second, that the cithara (Greek, *kithara*) which is frequently mentioned in the works of the ancient Greeks was not an instrument similar to the lyre as some historians claim but was in reality the predecessor of the guitar which today is called the *kithara* by the Greeks and *chitarra* by the Italians.

Dr. Burney who made a most thorough research in determining this fact quotes Father Monfaucon: "It is difficult to determine in what respects the lyre, cithara and other such instruments differed from each other." And in his reflections on the construction of ancient instruments we read: "The belly of the theorbo or archlute (a lute with additional bass strings) is usually made in the shell form and the etymology of the word *guitar* seems naturally deducible from *cithara*." It is supposed that the Roman "C" was hard like the modern "K," and the Italian word *chitarra* (guitar) is manifestly derived from the Greek word *kithara*. In the *Hymn to Mercury*, ascribed to Homer, Mercury and Apollo are said "to play with the cithara under their arms." This seems to infer a guitar rather than a harp.

Like all the ancient musical instruments, the guitar and lute, as might be expected, had undergone considerable changes during the ages and were of various forms in different countries and in the same country at different periods. They also had various tunings some of which are still in use for special purposes. The Spanish tuning being the most practical was universally adopted—hence the name "Spanish guitar."

Cargo for the Ark

The guitar is so closely associated with the history of man's career throughout the ages, that we could almost believe it to have been part of the household of Adam and Eve. Padre J. B. Martini in his "Storia della Musica" reasons very convincingly that Adam was instructed by his Creator in every art and science, the knowledge of music being, of course, included. A vivid imagination could picture Adam absorbed in his guitar beneath the apple tree while the wily serpent beguiled Eve with the prohibited fruit. One thing is certain, however, and that is that the guitar was invented before the deluge, perhaps by Jubal; and naturally some member of Noah's family, if not Noah himself, was a performer on this instrument. Noah, it is believed, settled in Egypt after the deluge, and it is there that we find concrete evidence of the guitar's antiquity in the form of an obelisk supposed to have been erected by Sesostris whom some historians identify with Noah. According to Dr. Burney, on this obelisk which is now in Rome there is a reproduction of an instrument similar to the lute.

Both the lute and guitar were venerated, and the performers were held in high esteem by the Egyptians and Hebrews. David played the lute and it is reasonable to suppose that he instructed Solomon "And David and all the house of Israel played before the Lord on all manner of instruments made of firwood, even on harps, and on psalteries and on timbrels and on cornets and on cymbals." *2 Sam. vi: 5.* The same quotation in Syriac is given in part as follows: "with cithara, psaltery, cymbal and sistrum."

It is probable that the guitar was introduced into Greece shortly after the Trojan war, about 1000 B.C., and was used by the rhapsodists. Homer sang the Odyssey and Iliad to the accompaniment of the lute, and references to the guitar abound in the Greek writings. Thamyris, a guitarist, was so skilled in his art that he challenged the muses, especially Clio, the patroness of stringed instruments, and the result is described thus by Homer:

Too daring bard, whose unsuccessful pride
The immortal muses in their art defied;
The avenging muses of the light of day
Deprived his eyes and snatched his voice away.
No more his tuneful voice was heard to sing,
His hand no more awaked the silver string.

The comic poet, Pherecrates, introduced music on the stage as a woman with dress and person torn and disfigured. This forlorn creature gives as the cause of her dishevelled appearance the treatment of several musicians amongst whom is Thamyris. "And next Thamyris took it into his head to abuse me by such divisions and flourishes as no one ever thought of before, twisting me a thousand ways in order to produce from four strings the twelve modes." From four strings the twelve modes! This could have been done only upon an instrument with a neck which is proof positive of the existence of the guitar at this period. It also suggests that Thamyris was a modernist, judging from the manner in which his musical ideas were received.

Terpander whose name means "to delight men" was born about 671 B.C., and was a celebrated guitarist and flutist. He taught and composed for the guitar and made some improvements in its construction.

Socrates Takes Lessons

To prove that one is never too old to learn, Socrates studied the guitar in his late years under Damon, the teacher of Pericles. Who knows but that he was serenading the much-maligned Xanthippe when, after she had relieved her overwrought feelings by throwing a bucket of water over him, the great philosopher exclaimed, "After the thunder follows the storm."

Pythagoras did not play the guitar. But, as a result of his scientific treatment of sound, he invented the monochord (single stringed) with a movable bridge or, rather, fret, which enabled future guitar makers to place frets on the fingerboard accurately.

During the Golden Era the guitar was held in high esteem by all Athenians, one of whom was none other than Themistocles, one of the greatest generals that ever lived. In the words of Plutarch, "He (Themistocles) entreated Episcles of Hermione, who had a good hand at the lute and was much sought after by the Athenians, to come and practice at home with him, being ambitious of having people inquire after his house and frequent his company." Plutarch writes that this was before Themistocles became famous.

[Sophocles Papas continues his introductory material.]

The story of the guitar is as fascinating as a Dumas romance. Far more people are now playing this instrument than was the case a few years ago. The concerts of Señor Segovia, at which he has played "everything" from Bach to Debussy, have stirred the enthusiasm of the greatest musicians of the time.

Nero's Prizes

Not only the guitar but music in general was very little cultivated by the early Romans. As Dr. Burney says, "Most mature study of musical instruments would produce only despair and headache." Like other arts, music was introduced into Rome by Greek musicians who were forced to go there if they did not willingly go. Nero is responsible for the first mention of the guitar in Rome, but it is doubtful if Diodorus dared to play his instrument there during the life of Nero.

In A.D. 66 Nero went to Greece and proclaimed himself victor in music at all the Olympic games, and, on returning to Rome, carried with him eighteen hundred prizes which he had extorted from the judges at the musical contests. He also brought with him many eminent Greek musicians whom he had "defeated." Among these was Diodorus, the celebrated guitarist. All these were driven through Rome in the same carriage in which kings who had been vanquished by Roman generals used to be borne in triumph.

That the guitar played no small part in the religious ceremonies of the early Christians, Clemens Alexandrinus and Eusebius prove. "Praise the Lord on the lute, and on the psaltery with ten strings." "When the Christians are met, first they confess their sins to the Lord; secondly, they sing to His name, not only with the voice but upon an instrument with ten strings and upon the cithara." The latter continued in use in the church up to the seventeenth century. In the Pope's chapel, when the falsettos of the Spaniards and sopranos of the eunuchs proved unsatisfactory, women singers were introduced, and Della Valle speaks of Signora Leonora "who sings to her own accompaniment on the lute which she touches in so fanciful and masterly a manner." Prior to this, however, the guitar was flourishing throughout Europe and was much in vogue at the royal courts.

Chaucer was the earliest English writer to mention the lute, and in his "Pardoner's Tale" these lines occur:

Whereas with harpes, lutes and guiternes
They daunce and plaie at dis bothe day and night.

In Shakespeare's works we find frequent reference to music, and the following is his ode to "the rarest musician that his age did behold."

Dowland to them is dear, whose heavenly touch
Upon the lute doth ravish human sense.

John Dowland, the most famous lutenist of the short but brilliant period (1597–1622) of the English school of lutenist song writers, was made Bachelor of Music by the University of Oxford, and for a time was lutenist at the court of Denmark, afterward returning to London in the service of Lord Walden. Later he became lutenist at the court of Charles I. The majority of his works are songs with guitar accompaniment, many of these being extant. He also wrote studies and a method.

Royal Lutenists

The unfortunate child king, Edward VI, in his diary, on July 20, 1550, wrote: "Monsieur le Marechal St. André, the French ambassador, came to me in the morning. He dined with me, heard me play on the lute, saw me ride, came to me to my study, supped with me and so departed to Richmond."

One reason why music, like everything else, made such progress during Elizabeth's reign is that, like all Henry VIII's children, the Queen was a musician herself and her favorite instrument was the lute.

Just about the same period at which we find mention of Signora Leonora as lutenist in the Pope's chapel, the guitar was playing an entirely different part in England at the court of the profligate Charles II. In the Memoirs of Count de Garmont by Hamilton, edited by Sir Walter Scott, we read: "There was a certain foreigner (Francesco Corbetti) at court, famous for the guitar. He had a genius for music, and he was the only man who could make anything of the guitar. His style of playing was so full of grace and tenderness that he could have given harmony to the most discordant instruments. The truth is, nothing was too difficult for this foreigner to play. The King's relish for his compositions had brought the instrument so much into vogue that

every person played on it, well or ill; and you were as sure to see a guitar on a
lady's toilet as rouge or patches. The Duke of York played upon it tolerably
well, and the Earl of Arran like Francesco himself.

All in the Cause of a Saraband

This Francesco had composed a saraband which either charmed or infatu-
ated every person; for the whole "guitarery" at court were trying at it, and
God knows what a universal strumming there was. The Duke of York, pre-
tending not to be perfect in it, desired Lord Arran to play it to him.

Lady Chesterfield had the best guitar in England. The Earl of Arran who
was desirous at playing his best conducted His Royal Highness to his sister's
apartments; she was lodged at court at her father's, the Duke of Ormond, and
this wonderful guitar was lodged there, too. Whether this visit had been pre-
concerted or not I do not pretend to say, but it is certain that they found both
the lady and the guitar at home; they likewise there found Lord Chesterfield
so much surprised at this unexpected visit that it was a considerable time before he thought of rising from his seat to receive them with due respect.

Jealousy, like a malignant vapour, now seized upon his brain; a thousand
suspicions, blacker than ink, took possession of his imagination and were
continually increasing; for, whilst the brother played upon the guitar to the
Duke, the sister ogled and accompanied him with her eyes, as if the coast had
been clear and there had been no enemy to observe them. This saraband was
repeated at least twenty times. The Duke declared it was played to perfection.
Lady Chesterfield found no fault with the composition. But her husband,
who clearly perceived he was the person played upon, thought it a most de-
testable piece.

Corbetti was born in 1612 in Pavia, Italy, and died in Paris in 1682. He
toured all the principal cities of Europe and was guitarist to the Duke of
Hanover and court guitarist to Louis Quatorze of France prior to his
appointment in the same capacity to Charles II. Carlos Schmidl in his
Dizionario Universale dei Musicisti tells us that Robert De Visée, the most
famous of Corbetti's pupils, in his "Livre de Guitarre" which was published
immediately after Corbetti's death included an *Allemande* with the inscription "Tombeau de Monsieur Francisque Corbette" which, by a curious

coincidence, opens with a passage identical with the funeral march from the "Symphony Eroica" of Beethoven.

Some of Corbetti's compositions have been reissued recently by Max Eschig of Paris, but the famous saraband is not included in the new issue, and it may be that Lord Chesterfield destroyed every trace of it. That Corbetti was indeed a great performer is proved by the following epitaph written by Medard, one of his pupils:

Ci-git l'Amphion de nos jours
Francisque, cet homme si rare,
Qui fit parler a la guitarre
Le vrai language des amours.

a free translation of which is:

Here lies the Amphion of our days,
Francis, a man so rare;
With his guitar he sang the lays
Of love, in language fair.

We gather that the following advertisement which appeared in an Irish newspaper shortly after Corbetti's time was a result of the fact that some of the guitarists of that period did not live up to the dignity of the instrument which they played. "We, the undersigned (25) Gentlemen and Ladies of the counties of Claire, Limerick and Tipperary, do hereby certify that Edmond Morgan, dancing and guitar master, has taught in our families for some years past where he behaved with the greatest discretion and sobriety, and acquitted himself with such extraordinary care and skill in his business that it is but justice to comply with his request in recommending him to any family that may want to employ one of his profession."

Matteis—Engraver and Guitarist

Nicola Matteis, born during the latter part of the seventeenth century, was the first music engraver in England, and among the first pieces of music printed were several of his compositions for the guitar. According to the historian, North, "He was a consummate master of the guitar and had so much force upon it as to be able to contend with the harpsichord in concert." (The word "contend" seems to us particularly appropriate in reference to some "pianists" and "guitarists" of today.) Ballard, the first music printer in France, was brother-in-law to the lutenist of Charles IX. Practically all the kings of France maintained lutenists at their courts. Robert De Visée, a pupil of Corbetti, whose compositions are included in my programs,[1] was a guitarist of Louis XIV, at whose court also served as lutenists Corbetti, Lully and Medard.

The Crusades were partly responsible for the guitar and lute movement in Europe, the crusaders upon their return bringing with them many of these instruments. Toward the end of the eighteenth century the guitar received such an impetus that, about the time of the great romanticists, it reached a stage of the most virulent *bacillus citaralis* (guitar fever) as Richard Schmid puts it.

Italy, Spain and Germany have given us the greatest exponents of the instrument, although France, England and the other European countries contributed to some extent also. Many contributors to guitar literature came from the ranks of the great orchestral composers. Why historians have neglected to mention this fact is not known, unless it is that, not being acquainted with the guitar, they deemed it advisable to give brief mention or no mention at all to guitar compositions. Among those who played and wrote for the guitar are Handel, Schnabel, Garcia, Spohr, Hauptman (and his pupils Burgmüller, Cowen and Sullivan), Rossini, Marschner, Donizetti, Verdi, Gade, Denza and Mahler.

Bach as Composer for Guitar

The great Johann Sebastian Bach was one of the earliest masters to succumb to the charms of the lute, for which instrument he played and wrote. He composed several suites which were later transcribed for the piano, violin and cello and are now again published for guitar. Many movements of these suites are played by me in my concerts. Bach also made use of the lute in the *Saint John's Passion* for which he used special tuning.

Luigi Boccherini who, to many, is known only by his charming *Minuet*, was born in Lucca, Italy, but spent most of his time in Madrid where he died.

There he found his knowledge of the guitar very profitable and was patronized by royalty. His works include twelve quintets for two violins, viola, cello and guitar, and nine quintets for two violins, guitar, viola and bass. Of these quintets three are now in print and are of exceptional beauty and interest.

Boccherini was not only a fine guitarist but an excellent cellist and knew how to use both instruments to great advantage. In his quintets the cello has an unusually interesting part owing to the fact that the guitar plays the bass which is generally given to the cello in string quartets. In these works Boccherini employs the guitar very successfully, using all the effects that are characteristic of Spanish music. His *Quintet*, No. 3, was performed for the first time in this country in New York several years ago, Vahdah Olcott Bickford, playing the guitar part and again in Washington, D.C., two years ago, by the Elena de Sayn Quartet, Sophocles Papas playing the guitar.

Had Paganini not played the violin at all, his name would have been immortalized by the guitar, as for a period of three years he abandoned the violin and proved himself as great a guitarist as violinist. A quotation from Schilling in the book *Mandolin and Guitar* by Philip Bone, a nineteenth-century guitar historian, reads: "The celebrated Niccolo Paganini is such a great master on the guitar that even Lipinski (a famous Polish violin virtuoso who had ventured to seek a public contest with Paganini at Placentia in 1818) could barely decide whether he were greater on the violin or the guitar." When Paganini was asked why he gave so much attention to the guitar, he replied, "I love it for its harmony. It is my constant companion in all my travels." Paganini's love for the fretted instruments was born with his genius and, when a little boy, the first instrument that he played was the mandolin.

Paganini's original style of composition for the violin is due to his thorough knowledge of the mandolin and guitar; and those who are well acquainted with these two instruments can recognize their influence on his writings. His works include twelve sonatas for violin and guitar which he played on his tour with Luigi Legnani who was one of the greatest guitarists that Italy produced and who, in addition to playing guitar solos, accompanied the great virtuoso. Paganini also composed trios, quartets and quintets for strings and guitar, solos, studies, and a sonata with violin obbligato.

Weber's Recreation

The great romanticist, Carl Maria von Weber, like most of his contemporaries, played the guitar. Grove says: "He had also acquired considerable skill on the guitar on which he would accompany his own mellow voice in songs, mostly of a humorous character, with inimitable effect. This talent was often of great use to him in society, and he composed many lieder with guitar accompaniment." Eighteen of the songs mentioned are now in print, also a *Divertimento* for guitar and piano, Op. 38, which consists of an *Andante*, *Valse*, *Five Variations* and a *Polacca*, and many solos and duets. Weber loved the guitar so much that he found in it the inspiration for all his operatic melodies.

Too poor to possess a piano, Franz Schubert used the guitar to work on his compositions and accompany his light baritone voice. As a little boy he studied the instrument, and, judging from his writings, was as good a virtuoso as many of the celebrated guitarists of his time. The proud possessor of one of his guitars, Richard Schmid, whose father knew Schubert's brother, Ferdinand, well, edited two volumes of Schubert's original songs with guitar accompaniment, and, in his sketch of the composer's life, quotes Umlauf who said: "In my morning visits, which I usually paid Schubert before office hours, I found him still in bed. I also found him with his guitar already in his hands in full activity. He generally sang to me newly-composed songs to his guitar."

Compositions Influenced

The influence of the guitar on Schubert's compositions is indisputably recognized, especially in his song accompaniments. His immortal serenade marked *à la guitarre* and the notes marked *legato-staccato* prove this further.

One of the most beautiful of his works, a *Quartet in G* for violin or flute, viola, cello and guitar, is particularly interesting as it was not discovered until a hundred and four years after it was written. It was published in 1926 by Drei Masken Verlag of Munich, and in the United States was played for the first time by the Elena de Sayn Quartet at Washington, D.C. This works consists of five movements, *Moderato*, *Minuetto*, *Lento e patetico*, *Zingara* and *Tema con variazioni.* How many variations Schubert intended to write is not known as he completed only two and wrote three measures of the third. However, in order that it might be performed in public, this variation was completed by Dr. Georg Kinsky. A facsimile of the first page, dated February 26, 1814, shows that Schubert originally intended it as a trio.

Commenting on this *Quartet in G* the great Wagnerian authority, Kurt Hetzel, now living in Washington, D.C., said: "*The Quartet in G Major* by Franz Schubert is a masterpiece of no less value than his famous Unfinished Symphony, and I am sure it will be taken into the repertoire of all leading string quartets, as it gives through the inclusion of the guitar a most welcome amplification of the existing tone colors."

Hector Berlioz, "The father of the orchestra," pursued his musical studies on the guitar, that being the only polyphonic instrument which he played. He tells us in his Memoirs that he was born December 11, 1803, and had his first sensation of music at the same time he had that of love, at the age of twelve. Before he had any musical instruction he could play the tambour, an instrument similar to the guitar, and the flageolet. Later he undertook the study of the flute and guitar but had not taken many lessons on the latter when his teacher went to his father and said, "Monsieur, it is impossible for me to continue giving lessons to your son."

"But why? Has he been impolite, or so lazy that you find him hopeless?" asked the father.

"Not at all; but it would be absurd, for he is already as skillful as I am."

Berlioz, Teacher of Guitar

Berlioz became very proficient on the guitar, and, during his adventurous life in Paris, was able to earn money by teaching it. Among his compositions are *Variations for Solo Guitar* and *Little Songs*, settings of Moore's melodies which we are told could rouse his fellow-student, Felix Mendelssohn, out of his moods of despondency. Referring to the evenings spent with his musical companions in the garden portico of the academy at Rome he writes, "my poor guitar and bad voice were pressed into service and, all sitting around a little fountain, we were singing in the moonlight the dreamy melodies of

Freischütz, Oberon, Euryanthe, and so forth, for I must say the musical taste of my classmates was far from low."

The guitar was Berlioz' constant companion and, in his frequent trips to the mountains to disperse his melancholy moods, he went *chassant ou chantant* (hunting or singing); that is, he took with him either his rifle or his guitar on which he improvised melodies on lines from the classic writers. Berlioz, one of the severest of music critics, considered the guitar a most important orchestral instrument, and, in his "Treatise on Instrumentation and Orchestration" devotes several pages to it. One of his guitars which is now in the *Nationale Conservatoire de Musique* in Paris is of double interest as it was previously used by Paganini, his friend and benefactor.

The fascinating power and subtle charm of the guitar can best be illustrated by mentioning the effect that it had on the composer of "Faust," Charles Gounod, the great Frenchman. According to Bone, in the Opera Museum of Paris there is a guitar on which Gounod inscribed "Nemi, 24 Aprile, 1862, in memory of the happy occasion." The incident referred to occurred one evening, when, vacationing by the beautiful lake of Nemi in Italy, he heard a man singing in the distance to the accompaniment of a guitar and was so enraptured by it that he moved in the direction of the music. Upon reaching the singer he spoke to him. In Gounod's words, "I wished I could buy both the singer and the guitar," but, as that was not possible, he did the next best thing, buying the guitar on which he wrote the inscription just given.

Special mention must be made of Franz Gruber whose name was perpetuated by the immortal Christmas song, *Silent Night*, which he composed while an organist at the village of Oberndorf. Bone says, "On Christmas eve of the year 1818, Joseph Mohr, the pastor of Oberndorf, visited the school-master, Gruber, showed him a Christmas hymn he had just written, and requested him to set it to music for two solo voices and chorus with guitar accompaniment. Gruber read the poem and composed the desired parts and accompaniment, returning them the same evening to the clergyman. On Christmas night of the same year, in a small church on the lonely mountainside, this devotional and inspiring hymn was sung for the first time, with its accompaniment of guitar." Gruber was a prolific composer, having written more than a hundred masses and a great number of instrumental pieces, many of which are for guitar.

The Composer's Instrument

The composers who made a life study of the guitar are so numerous that we shall mention only those who stand preëminent in their art.

Although Ferdinando Carulli (1770–1841) does not rank with the greatest of composers, he nevertheless deserves special mention as the first to depart from the old style of suites. He realized the possibilities of the guitar and wrote in what was then a modern style. One of his earliest works, *Overture*, Op. 6, No. 1, for guitar solo, is a complete sonata movement. Later he wrote several sonatas for guitar and piano, in three movements. In style his writings are similar to those of Joseph Haydn. He also wrote the first method for the guitar which is still very popular throughout Europe, numerous studies and other works. Carulli's son, Gustavo, was also a guitarist, but devoted most of his time to teaching voice, harmony and composition, one of his famous pupils being Alexandre Guilmant.

Carulli's style was improved by Matteo Carcassi (1792–1853) who evolved one both more brilliant and more effective. His compositions are numerous, many of them being operatic arias with variations. He also wrote an exhaustive method which is used widely in this country as well as in Europe and is excelled by few that have since been written.

One of the greatest exponents of the guitar was the Italian master, Mauro Giuliani (1780–*circa* 1840).[2] It was his playing that Beethoven heard when he said "The guitar is a miniature orchestra in itself." Like most guitarists of his period, Giuliani was self-taught, and at the age of eighteen we find him an already-famous virtuoso touring Europe. From 1807 to 1821 he resided in Vienna giving concerts and teaching, and was appointed chamber musician and teacher to the archduchess Marie Louise. Many members of the Austrian royal family and nobility studied the guitar with him. Moscheles, Hummel and Diabelli, also excellent guitarists, were close friends of Giuliani with whom they frequently appeared in concert. His works range from easy teaching exercises to the most pretentious types of composition. His style is more brilliant than any of his predecessors and full of the sparkling qualities characteristic of his Italian contemporaries.

Solos with Orchestral Accompaniment

Among Giuliani's major works are several concertos with orchestral accompaniment. The orchestral part of one of these was later transcribed for piano by Hummel who played it with Giuliani in their concerts. Giuliani also wrote several duets for violin or flute and guitar. Of them Bone writes, "In Giuliani's duets for violin or flute and guitar, we find the choicest and rarest compositions for these two instruments ever written, duets which display to every possible advantage the characteristics, capabilities and beauties of both instruments." In these compositions the guitar is not treated as a mere accompanying instrument, but has solo and obbligato passages just as complex as the piano part of a violin concerto and requiring a skillful musician to perform them.

Writer, linguist, poet, violinist and guitarist—such was Zani de Ferranti (1802–1878). At the age of twelve years this genius was not only an accomplished violinist but admired by all Italy for his Latin verse. At sixteen he toured Europe as a violinist and his technic, it is said, was equal to that of Paganini. Later he became private secretary to the Russian prince, C. de Marischkin, during which period he devoted most of his time to studying the guitar and became one of the greatest exponents of that instrument.

It is recorded that Ferranti had a secret method by which he produced sustained tones on the violin, and his playing created a sensation throughout Europe. In the *Parisian Chronicle* of April 9, 1859, appeared the following vivid description: "Between the hands of Ferranti the guitar becomes an orchestra, a military band. If he play the Marseillaise he makes a revolutionary of you; if he sing a love song, there is a seduced woman; if he sing a song of departure, we fly to the frontier."

That this is true of his playing is further proved by the following anecdote. During the performance of a fantasy of martial songs at the concerts which Ferranti gave at the home of Alexandre Dumas in 1855, the great author rose with enthusiasm and exclaimed "Sebastopol will be taken!" Ferranti toured the United States with the violinist, Sivori, and upon his return to Europe was appointed court guitarist to King Leopold of Belgium.

Had Giulio Regondi (1822–1872) chosen the violin as his solo instrument instead of the guitar undoubtedly there would have been two Paganinis as "The infant Paganini" was the unanimous title given him by the critics. He created a sensation wherever he played and at the same time the whole of Europe was wild with excitement over Paganini's marvellous performances on the violin. In many instances the itineraries of Paganini and Regondi were the same, and both were reaping the same laurels, the one at the age of eight while the other had reached middle age.

Bone quotes the criticism of Regondi in a Viennese paper of that day: "As a virtuoso, Regondi is more conspicuous in his mastership of the guitar than were Giuliani, Legnani and others heard here during the season. Regondi's mastership of the guitar is nearly incomprehensible and his playing is full of poetry and sweetness. It is the soul of melody, and he plays the guitar in its purity without any musical tricks. He is an artist whom all musical performers might copy, and even singers and actors, for his art is a natural one. Regondi is the very Paganini of the guitar; under his hand the guitar becomes quite another instrument than we have hitherto known it. He imitates by turn the violin, harp, mandolin and even the piano so naturally that you must look at him to convince yourself of the illusion, for you can hear the *forte* of the piano, the sweet *pianissimo* of the harp combined in its six simple strings."

Regondi's works, technically, might be compared with Paganini's guitar compositions, and at times remind one of Chopin and Mendelssohn.

The Instrument of Spain

Spain, the land of the castanets, mantillas and toreadors, has always played a more important role in the history of the guitar than any other nation. Al though it was introduced there by the Moors and later by the troubadours, it is difficult to believe that the guitar is not the natural offspring of this romantic and music-loving nation.

That the Spaniards have always been lovers of music is proved by the fact that Spain was one of the earliest countries to include music in its university curricula. Don Alfonso, King of Castile, who reigned from 1252 to 1284, endowed a professorship of music in the University of Salamanca. He himself was a composer of note, and William C. Stafford, in his *History of Music* (1830), tells us that one of the manuscripts now exists in the library at Toledo containing his songs with the music written "not only with the points employed by Guido and used in ecclesiastical books, but with the five lines and the clefs."

Stafford, who made extensive travels in Spain, writes: "The Spaniards are singers from nature. They have a fine ear and their songs are full of simplicity and feeling, partaking more of intellect and fancy and of romantic and refined sentiment than of bacchanalian or comic expression. It was been well observed that "The natives of Spain, full of intellect and fancy, dream when other Europeans would reflect, and sing when others would speak. Living but in the fantasies of their ever-active imaginations, Spaniards have always been animated with the love of romance and song. From Pelagius to Mina, from the conquest of Granada to the last moment of their struggle against French domination, they have intoned the suggestions of their patriotism, and equally vocalized the tender themes of love and the bold effusions of public virtue."

There are very few Spaniards who do not play upon the guitar. At Madrid and the other chief cities and towns of Spain, the young men serenade their mistresses by placing themselves under their windows and singing some amorous ditty to their own accompaniment; and in the provinces there is scarcely an artificer who, when his labor is over, does not go to some of the public places and amuse himself with this instrument.

"Take the Andalusian peasant, for instance, who, after a hard day's labor, instead of resorting to the glass or jug for refreshment and relaxation, tunes his guitar and exercises his voice. Night comes on and the song begins. He and his companions-in-toil form a circle....Each of the assembly sings a couplet always to the same air. Sometimes they improvise, and if there be among them any who can sing romances (which is not uncommon), he is listened to with religious silence."

Sor, Master of the Guitar

Three of the 16th century Spanish guitarists whose works are now extant are Luís Milan, Gaspar Sanz and Miguel de Fuenllana. At the end of the 18th century Spain produced not only the greatest guitar composer that has ever lived but one of the greatest of all composers, Fernando Sor (1780–1839), who was undoubtedly a great genius and a prodigy. Fétis tells us that he played his own compositions at the age of five years; a little later he was placed in a monastery at Barcelona to receive a thorough general education and instruction in harmony and composition. There he heard the guitar played by the monks and became so fascinated that he immediately began an assiduous study of it. At the age of sixteen he left the monastery equipped with a technic of the highest order and a profound knowledge of composition and counterpoint. In 1797 he wrote his first opera, "Telemacco," which was performed with great success in Barcelona and later in London. In 1818, during the Peninsular war, he joined the Spanish army and was commissioned as a captain. Later he was compelled to take refuge in France where he met Cherubini and several other great musicians who prevailed upon him to again devote himself to the guitar.

Sor is known as the precursor of the guitar in England where his playing created a furor. As has been stated before, the lute was very popular there even up to his time, but Londoners had never even dreamed of the possibilities of the guitar as revealed by Sor. Philip Bone who made an exhaustive research of the lives of the guitarists tells us that Sor was the first to perform at the London Philharmonic concerts. "He also appeared as soloist at the Society's concerts in the season of 1817 at the Argyle rooms playing his own compositions, a *concertante* for the guitar, and he electrified his audience by the wonderful command he possessed over his instrument." George Hogarth, in his *Memoirs of the Philharmonic Society*, writes, "He astonished the audience by his unrivalled execution."

Sor's works exceed four hundred and are of the highest musical value. Several of these are operatic and orchestral. His guitar compositions include studies, fantasies, thèmes variés and sonatas. His *Variations on a Theme by Mozart* which I frequently play in my concerts is among the finest compositions of the sort ever written, even including those of Beethoven, that great master of the variation form.

An analysis of Sor's sonatas would require too much space. We shall therefore confine ourselves to saying that they are comparable to those of the great German genius. His Opus 15 which must have been written while he was still in the monastery is in sonata form proper but consists of only one movement. In his Op. 22 and Op. 25 he demonstrates his great mastery of form, together with intellectual and emotional depth which has justly won him the title of "The Beethoven of the Guitar."

Likeness to Beethoven's Works

The similarity of Sor's works to those of Beethoven is so marked that it is recognizable even in the smallest of his studies. Most of his works are quite difficult to perform and require a perfectly normal and supple hand. Napoleon Coste, one of the great guitarists of the 19th century and the greatest French exponent of that instrument, was an ardent admirer of Sor and, in a letter to one of his friends, wrote concerning the latter's technic, "Sor had an admirable left hand whose suppleness permitted a reach that it would seem impossible to attain."

It has been said that great artistry is always accompanied by great modesty, and a great artist and composer was Francisco Tárrega (1854–1909) of whom Bone writes: "Of humble origin and ceaselessly engaged in struggles against adverse circumstances he gave to the world an example of genial personality, ardent temperament and of extraordinary intelligence all of which he devoted with fervent spirit to his instrument with the noble idea of raising it to the highest category of art."

Tárrega was a graduate of the Madrid Conservatoire where he won first prize for composition and harmony and where subsequently he was appointed professor of guitar. Although some of his predecessors had seen the possibility of adapting many of the works of the great masters to the guitar, it was left to Tárrega to prove to the world by his supreme artistry and deep insight into the intellectual and emotional value of these works that the guitar is a worthy medium for the interpretation of a Bach fugue, a Beethoven sonata or a Chopin nocturne. Among the compositions which he transcribed are works of almost all the great composers. His original works include studies, miscellaneous pieces and fantasies. Although self-taught I myself have been greatly influenced by the style of this guitarist.

Folk Tune Variations

In all parts of Spain we find the guitar just as we find the castanets, but not all the people are equally musical although every province may be identified by indigenous folk tunes. It is wholly impossible for the people of the United States to realize these geographical distinctions. For instance, in the northeast corner of Spain we find Catalonia, the adjoining province of Aragon. The two groups are so entirely different in their thought, customs and music that one is forced to recognize the racial divergence. It is as though you were to find on the opposite side of the Delaware River instead of two identical races two wholly different peoples.

The immensely varied topography and scenery of Spain, with the tropical beauty of Andalusia and the grim severity of the bleak mountains of the north, had their influence on the Spanish folk tunes of the different provinces. In Andalusia we find some of the most ingratiating melodies ever written, whereas in the north we find tunes of great ruggedness and vigor. This does not mean, however, that we do not find strong and dominant themes in Andalusia.

Many attempts have been made to write down the local folk tunes for the guitar, and some of these have been especially fine; but there is a great deal of variation. This is due to the fact that the people themselves have taken great liberties with the themes. Get a hundred singers together in Andalusia and ask them to sing the same tune in unison and the result would be terrible. Why? Because the very enthusiasm of the singers would make each one insist upon his own particular version or rendering of the melody. You see, every Spaniard is an individualist—a society in himself. He resents directions, control and repression unless it comes from within. He is the freest of souls.

My itinerary has taken me to all the principal cities of Europe, the two Americas and the Orient, and my experiences in these countries are not without their humorous side. Russia and Germany can be named among the countries where the guitar is very much appreciated. When in Russia I saw minute, medium-sized and enormous guitars. Why, I have seen some with seemingly fifty-thousand strings!

When playing at the court of one of the queens in Europe the following rather amusing incident took place. Her Majesty, after having heard me play several pieces, addressed me with, "How nicely you play!" Then after a slight pause to find an adequate comparison, she added, "It is almost like a music box."

"Madame," I replied, "I do not flatter myself that I have yet attained such perfection."

"What modesty sir!" replied the queen graciously.

Modern Composers

Of modern composers for the guitar Ponce deserves special mention as his works are of more elaborate character. His *Sonata Clássica (Hommage à Fernando Sor)* was no doubt inspired by Sor's *Sonata Op. 25*, the structure and general character of which he has very cleverly imitated. This work in its logical development bears a strong resemblance to the style of Beethoven. It also is evidence of Ponce's versatility as a composer, all his other guitar works being written in the modern idiom, some of which are the following: *Thème Varié et Finale, Sonate* (modern), *Tres canciones populares mexicanas* and *Preludio.*

Other composers are Ravel, Stravinsky, Roussel, Samazeuilh, Pierre de Bréville, Raymond Petit, Pedrell, Vittoria, Tansman and Raoul Laparra who has come nearer even than Bizet to capturing the Spanish spirit and romance in his music.

What is the guitar? All that has been said is inadequate to describe its charm.

The immense variety of tone of which it is capable is a matter of constant surprise to the listener. Now we hear piano tones, the cello, the violin; and yet it has its own peculiar quality. It might be said that the guitar is an illusion, a pretense, that holds one by its uncertainty. "It is because of this variety of tone," says G. Jean-Aubrey, the distinguished French critic and essayist, that people, to their profound astonishment, can listen to the guitar for a longer time than to any other instrument played alone—with the exception, perhaps, of the piano. There are those—and I own I am one of them—who cannot listen for long to the harpsichord, even when played by Mme. Wanda Landowska, without experiencing some tediousness of this delicate sound which is charming at first, but is always accompanied by a tiny noise of scrap iron and which keeps an anachronistic character that renders it interesting to one for a moment on account of its strangeness, but does not hold one by its actual vital quality. The harpsichord is an instrument of the past; the guitar is an instrument of the present, which succeeds in preserving the sonority belonging to ancient works without, however, erecting a barrier of several centuries between the listener and the music. The harpsichord has the charm of a bygone thing, amiable and refined; the guitar has that of a thing of today, warm and, one could almost say, fraternal."

Editor's Note: (This article closes this interesting discussion of the Guitar and its music, sections of which have appeared in the last three issues of The Etude.)

1930 *Etude Music Magazine,* Reprinted By Permission of the Publisher, Theodore Presser Company, Bryn Mawr, Pennsylvania 19010. The article appeared in four parts in Vol. XLVIII, Nos. 4, 5, 6, 7, April, May, June, July 1930.

Note from Elisabeth Papas Smith: It is not clear which edition of Charles Burney's *A General History of Music* Papas was using; the book was originally published in three volumes in 1776, 1782, and 1789. The next edition seems to have been in 1935, too late for this article. Nor have I been able to find the other quotations.

APPENDIX F

"Trail Blazers of the Guitar" by Sophocles T. Papas

The editor of *Mastertone* wrote the following preface to the April 1929 installment of the article:

ONE OF THE FINEST

This is the second installment of the article "Trail Blazers of the Guitar" by the widely known teacher, composer and publisher, Sophocles Papas, Washington, D.C. Many *Mastertone* readers have commented upon the first installment as one of the finest and most interesting articles we have ever published. We urge you to read this and the succeeding installments. And for the May (third and last) installment he wrote: This is the third and concluding installment of this splendid and authoritative history of the guitar by Mr. Papas. [The entire three-part article follows.]

When Socrates' wife relieved her overwrought feelings by throwing a bucket of water over him, and the great philosopher exclaimed, "After the thunder follows the storm"—who knows but that he was serenading her on his guitar, for that he played is a historical fact.

Socrates lived so long ago that his history is to us quite ancient, and yet the guitar is so old that its origin was ancient to Socrates himself. Its history is traced as far back as four thousand B.C., and is of aristocratic origin. It was the principal instrument used in the religious ceremonies of the ancient Egyptians, and the performers were revered as high priests. The guitar was probably introduced into Greece some time after the Trojan war, about 1000 B.C., and was no doubt used by the rhapsodists. In the "Hymn to Mercury" which is ascribed to Homer, an instrument is mentioned similar to the guitar, played by Apollo, and we find frequent mention of the "cithara" in the works of the Greek writers, this being the Greek name for the guitar to the present day. It is a well-known fact that Homer sang the Odyssey and the Iliad to the accompaniment of the lute. (The lute differs from the guitar only in shape). Terpander, whose name means "to delight men," is said to have improved this instrument. He also taught it and no doubt was the first to write music for the guitar since this art was known to the ancient Greeks long before his time. Themistocles, one of the greatest generals that has ever lived, and a great lover of honor, held the guitar in high esteem. In the words of Plutarch: "He entreated Episcles of Hermione, who had a good hand at the lute and was much sought after by the Athenians, to come and practice at home with him, being ambitious of having people inquire after his house and frequent his company."

The guitar, in all probability slightly different from the Greek cithara, was introduced by the Moors in Spain and gradually its popularity spread throughout Europe. It varied in different countries, both in shape and tuning. The Spanish method of tuning being the most effective was universally adopted, hence the name "Spanish guitar."

Many of the earliest songs of the Middle Ages were written for the guitar, and, of course, there were also solos. Most of these were written in tablature and were later re-written in modern notation and are now obtainable.

Arnold Schlick, 1512, Francesco Spinaccino, 1507, and Gabriel Battaile, 1611, are three of the earliest guitarists whose music can be obtained at the present day.

No doubt many others wrote music for this instrument at that time but it was not until the latter part of the eighteenth century that it became universally popular through the genius of Ferdinando Carulli, who was the first guitarist to realize the possibilities of the instrument as they are now known to us. He was the first classical guitar composer who departed from the ancient style of suites. His method, which was the first ever written for the guitar, helped to popularize the instrument and is used extensively to this day in Europe. Carulli lived from 1770 to 1841 and wrote over four hundred works, including fantasies, overtures, sonatas, studies, etc. He also wrote many songs with guitar accompaniment and a treatise on harmony as applied to the guitar.

Matteo Carcassi, 1792–1853, who is better known to us through his method, which is widely used in this country, improved Carulli's style and evolved a more brilliant and effective one. He wrote many original *airs varies*, some of which are quite easy and yet very brilliant. He travelled a great deal, giving concerts, and finally settled in Paris, where he died.

Fernando Sor, 1780–1839, was perhaps the greatest Spanish guitarist and undoubtedly the greatest guitar composer that has ever lived, and is justly called "The Beethoven of the Guitar." He played his own compositions at the age of five, and later acquired a thorough knowledge of harmony and counterpoint. His works, which exceed four hundred, are of the highest musical value. One has only to play or hear one of his sonatas to realize his genius and the justness of the comparison with the great German, Ludwig van Beethoven. This composer has to his credit, also, some improvements to the instrument. Sor may more accurately be considered a universal, rather than a national composer, as his compositions are entirely without the characteristics of Spanish music.

Napoleon Coste, 1806–1883, whom it is appropriate to mention here, was a great admirer of Sor, and imitated his polyphonic style of writing very effectively, although his works are easy in comparison with Sor's from a technical point of view. All guitarists are familiar with Sor's works and realize that a supple and perfectly normal hand is necessary to the performance of many of them. Regarding this, Coste wrote to one of his friends "Sor had such an admirable left hand to which its suppleness permitted a reach that seems impossible to attain."

Coste played a seven-stringed guitar, the seventh string being tuned to D, and placed outside the frets. No doubt he was prompted to do this by the fact that Sor wrote many compositions which necessitated tuning the sixth string down to D and he found it more practical to add the extra string. Mertz, whom we mention later, played and wrote for a seven-stringed guitar, also.

Coste made some interesting transcriptions from the tablature writings of the earliest composers as well as some of the classics. Many of these are included in his Opus 52. His Twenty-five Etudes, Opus 38, are indispensable to the guitarist, and most of them are suitable for concert work.

D. Aguado, 1784–1849, was a close friend of Sor, whom he met in Paris. Sor's duet, "The Two Friends," was composed for the purpose of their playing it together. The works of Aguado are of an unusual character and a guitarist's technique is not considered of a high order unless he is able to perform at least some of them. His Andante No. 3 is a good example of his style.

Mauro Giuliani, 1780–?, was a contemporary and rival of Fernando Sor, and a friend of Beethoven. His early life is somewhat obscure but his works speak of his ability as a musician and performer. Among his compositions are many studies, fantasies on Rossini's operas, etc. His writings are very brilliant and some very difficult, owing to the fact that he had an unusual command of his left hand thumb which he used over the frets. He lived in London during the time of Sor and was one of the favorites of his time. He is credited with the invention of the Tertz guitar and wrote a concerto for this instrument with band accompaniment which was later transcribed for the piano. During his stay in England he made transcriptions of many English and Scotch national airs.

Giuliani is the only guitarist known to us who left an heir to his art, for his daughter, Emilia, who later married Guglielmi, a singer, was also a fine guitarist and composer. Her six caprices, Opus 39, however, are the only compositions written by her now in print.

Joseph Kuffner, 1776–1856, wrote more than three hundred compositions, most of them for orchestra and band, which compositions are now forgotten, but his guitar works are still appreciated. With the exception of some operatic fantasies, these are of a pedagogic nature.

Gustave Segner was a Viennese born in 1800, and he came of a family of musicians. He was a member of the Imperial orchestra and professor of the guitar, and also a fine trombone player. His talent for this latter instrument was hereditary, according to Edward Hanslick, but the guitar, for which he wrote a number of compositions, was the instrument of his choice.

Johann Kaspar Mertz, 1806–1856, contributed some invaluable compositions for the guitar which greatly enriched the heritage of classical works for this instrument. He wrote more than four hundred compositions, many of which are very original and brilliant and include several of Schubert's songs arranged as solos in the style of Liszt, fantasies on operatic arias, studies, methods, etc. Shortly before his death he sent his Opus 38 to compete at the international competition for guitar compositions are at Brussels. His work won first prize but he died before hearing the good news.

Luigi Legnani was born ten years after Giuliani and was his rival. Legnani was a friend of Paganini with whom he is said to have collaborated in the latter's guitar compositions. He accompanied Paganini when he abandoned the violin for the mandolin in his concert tours. Legnani is perhaps better known to us through his Thirty-six Caprices, Opus 20. Many of these are suitable for concert use, and all are of the highest technical value. His style, although not entirely original, has many unique points.

Zanti Ferranti taught the guitar at the Brussels Conservatoire for eight years and was retained by King Leopold of Belgium as court performer.

Julio Regondi was a fine performer and considered the greatest of his time. He gave concerts at the age of seven and was hailed as a genius by the critics of Europe.

That the guitar has always been an instrument worthy of serious treatment is proven by the fact that many of the great composers who wrote for orchestra, piano or organ wrote also for the instrument which, perhaps, they loved most intimately. The great Bach wrote several suites for the lute, these later being transcribed for violin and piano solos. Most of these suites are now obtainable for the guitar as well as for the piano and violin, and are well known. Bach also made use of the lute in the Saint John's Passion, in which he used a special tuning. Handel used the guitar in his oratorio, The Resurrection.

Beethoven did not play or write for the guitar but was in close touch with the guitarists of his day, some of whom made transcriptions of his compositions to which he listened with delight and remarked that "the guitar is a miniature orchestra in itself." Sufficient proof that he was a lover of the fretted instruments lies in the fact that he composed for the mandolin.

Anton Diabelli, 1781–1858, better known in this country as a piano pedagogue, was a master of the guitar for which he wrote many studies, sonatas and sonatinas, some with piano accompaniment. He was the publisher of many of Schubert's songs, and was a friend of the great Viennese. This was natural as they were not only musicians but loved the same instrument. Three of Schubert's guitars are now in existence in Vienna, and proof that he was a fine guitarist may be recognized from his quartet written for guitar, flute, violin and violoncello. The guitar part, although not extremely difficult, is rich in every effect of which the instrument is capable, and this could only have been written by one who knew and played it well. This work was played for the first time in this country last year by the Elena de Sayn String Quartet in Washington, D.C., the writer playing the guitar part.

Berlioz, who, in spite of his family's wishes that he become a doctor, "one of the bad lot," as he wrote his father, meaning that he would never be a good doctor—studied harmony and composition on the guitar, as this was the only polyphonic instrument of which he had any knowledge. He also taught this instrument in a girls' school in Paris in order to earn his living when his allowance was cut off by his parents after his refusal to continue his medical studies.

Carl Maria von Weber was also a guitarist and wrote a great deal for it. Some of his songs with guitar accompaniment are still in existence as well as a divertimento for guitar and piano, and other works.

Niccolo Paganini, the "Wizard of the Violin," neglected that instrument for a period of several years and devoted his time to the guitar and mandolin on which instruments he became as great a virtuoso as on the violin. He wrote profusely for the guitar, and his compositions include twelve sonatas for violin and guitar, one for guitar with violin accompaniment, an unusual combination but very effective due to the fact that Paganini was a virtuoso on both these instruments; a number of solos and a quintet for guitar, two violins, viola and violoncello.

Luigi Boccherini, 1740–1805, another great Italian musician, best known to us through his celebrated Minuet, wrote several string quintets, three of which are obtainable. The instrumentation of these is two violins, viola, violoncello and guitar. These quintets are characteristic of his style, the cello parts being of equal importance as the guitar, as Boccherini, who was a fine cellist as well as guitarist, knew how to use both these instruments to great advantage in a string combination. His third quintet in D has been performed twice in this country. One performance was given in New York, Mrs. Bickford playing the guitar, and the other was given in Washington, D.C., by the Elena de Sayn Quintet at the City Club, the writer playing the guitar part. Boccherini also wrote a quintet for guitar, violin, oboe, cello and bass.

Francesco Tárrega, who died several years ago, was one of the greatest guitarists that has ever lived. He made transcriptions of many of the works of practically all the great composers which he interpreted with deep insight. He was one of the first composers to depart from musical superficialities and wrote only what was of intrinsic value. His works embrace more transcriptions than original compositions. His "Capriccio Arabe" which is of typical Spanish character, as are all his compositions, is one of the most beautiful guitar solos ever written.

Ernest Shand, an English guitarist who also died a few years ago, wrote many original compositions which, although not difficult, are very effective. He also wrote fantasies on national airs.

Of the present day European guitarists, Llobet and Segovia are the two outstanding artists. The latter is at present in this country, where he has met with overwhelming success and has been acclaimed as one of the few great artists of any instrument. Heinrich Albert, one of the greatest and most prolific guitar composers, and a pedagogue of note, is now living in Germany and still contributing valuable works for lovers of this instrument.[1]

Page 17 of the March issue of *Mastertone* carried this ad:

Guitarists! Send for our catalog of imported guitar music, including all the Segovia Numbers, carefully compiled by Sophocles T. Papas, twice Guild² soloist. This month's special: Overture in A—Carulli, 50 cents postpaid.

Hawaiian Guitarists! Read this. "I tried the solo parts immediately upon receipt of your book and thought they represented the acme of perfection as regards steel guitar music, but it was after playing the numbers as trios that I fully realized just how sublime the arrangements are." THE FAVORITE COLLECTION OF HAWAIIAN GUITAR SOLOS by Sophocles T. Papas with second and third parts ad. lib. Three parts complete, $1.00.

Tenor Banjoists! Do not fail to get AMERICAN FANTASY by Papas, the best unaccompanied tenor banjo medley ever published. Price 75 cents.
COLUMBIA MUSIC CO., INC., 1221 Connecticut Avenue—Washington, D.C.

Page 17 of the April and May issues of *Mastertone* carried this ad:
Guitarists! You can now have all the Segovia numbers as well as the best works of the great masters which are included in our list of guitar solos selected by Sophocles T. Papas, twice Guild soloist and well-known radio artist. Just write a letter to Mr. Papas, tell him the degree of difficulty of the pieces which you wish. His musicianship and ability to play all these works make him fully competent to assist you in making your selections. Send for catalog. This month's special: Beethoven's Celebrated Minuet.

Hawaiian Guitarists! Every day since the publication of The Favorite Hawaiian Guitar Solos with 2nd and 3rd parts ad. lib. we are receiving new orders and congratulatory letters. One writes as follows: "I tried the solo parts immediately on receipt of your book and thought they represented the acme of perfection as regards steel guitar music, but it was after playing the numbers as trios that I fully realized just how sublime the arrangements are." NUFF SAID. Send your order now, Three parts complete $1.00. Canada $1.20.
COLUMBIA MUSIC CO., 1221 Conn. Ave., Washington, D.C.

Personal Reminiscences

It is difficult to write a biography of one's parent without some biographical information about the author. I hope this appendix fills in some of the gaps.

My first memories of my father and mother together are at the Sedgwick Apartments[1] when I was about four. I remember hiding under the grand piano, the Knabe I still have. I began to study piano with my mother in this apartment, and I can remember how hard it was to reach a major third.

The next residence I remember is the apartment on Macomb Street, across the street from a huge estate, Tregaron, which belonged to Joseph E. Davies, Ambassador to Russia. Our living room was quite long and comfortably held the Knabe grand piano. I do remember my parents arguing when we lived there, especially about food—he came from Greece, she from Wales.

When I was about six I was told that my mother was too ill to take care of me so I was sent to live with a family named Walter, in Falls Church, exactly across from the Falls Church from which the town took its name. Thus began a period of years during which I rarely saw my parents.

Somehow during this time I went on with my piano lessons. My mother apparently was well enough to visit me sometimes, although I don't know how she came out to Virginia. My father used to drive out to visit me, always in a black Ford, sometimes in a new one, which, to his disappointment, I didn't recognize as a new car. It never occurred to me to wonder why I didn't live with my parents or what was wrong with my mother.

After living with the Falls Church people for several years, I was sent to live with my godmother, Katharine Alvord, at 1631 19th Street, N.W., for the year 1936 to 1937. I recall being allowed to go late to school so that I could listen to the coronation of the new King George VI on my birthday in 1937. In the fall I was sent to a Catholic boarding school, Villa Maria Academy, in West Falls Church, and in January 1938 a nun explained to me about the divorce of my father and mother.

At Villa Maria I continued to study piano and play "advanced" pieces in school recitals. I was supposed to return to the school in the fall of 1938, but in July my father and Mercia were married, and in September he asked me if

I wanted to live with him and Mercia in the "new" place on N Street. That sounded like heaven to me: to live in a regular household, with two parents.

My father and Mercia had many disagreements. They had quite different backgrounds: he was a traditional Greek male, she a gal from West Virginia who, while not particularly liberated, had lived on her own and worked until the age of 29. They argued about everything—money, meals, his schedule, and especially me. I was caught in this crossfire and spent a lot of time evading and avoiding, mostly by visiting my girlfriend who lived a block away or by hiding out in my room.

During this time my father wanted me to study the guitar, but I was a ten-year-old and didn't want to practice two instruments, and I never really felt comfortable playing the guitar.[2] During these years Mercia and Daddy separated several times but always reunited.

My own mother lived in a series of rooming houses and was apparently well enough at times to work at clerical jobs. I heard her described as neurasthenic, sometimes as having had a series of nervous breakdowns, and she was occasionally hospitalized. But as a child I never knew exactly what was wrong with her. I tried living with my mother briefly, but she was physically weak and couldn't do all the housework and cooking. And I was young, only 12, and didn't want to do all that work. I told my father tearfully that I didn't want to go back to live with her. I've always wondered how my father explained my position to her and whether she believed him. In general, we all pretended my mother did not exist.

Finally, in the fall of 1942, I went to the Hannah More Academy (HMA) in Reisterstown, Maryland, from which my godmother Katharine Alvord had graduated many years before. HMA was the best thing that had ever happened to me: we had excellent, well-educated teachers, I got out of the combative environment at home, and I found out that I had a mind and that there were interesting things to do with it. I really never lived "at home" again except for necessary visits to the orthodontist and long vacations when I couldn't stay at school or college.

From HMA I went to the University of Pennsylvania where I studied philosophy[3] and graduated with a B.A. in August 1948. All three of my parents came up to my graduation, and a girlfriend entertained "one side" while I spent some time with the "other side." My mother at this time had lost an eye to cancer and had to wear a patch; her eye kept running and she was very self-conscious about her appearance.

In the fall of 1948 my mother was being considered a candidate for a pre-frontal lobotomy to relieve her pain from the cancer which had metastasized. I spoke on the phone with Dr. Watts, or possibly Freeman (the two inventors of this surgery), left Philadelphia for Washington, D.C., to give permission for her surgery, and stayed on. After the surgery she was sent to live in the Home for Incurables on Wisconsin Avenue, and I used to go there to help her eat supper before going to work as a waitress at a nearby Hot Shoppe.[4] She died in May 1949 in St. Elizabeth's Hospital. Then I lived in various places in the Washington area until my stepmother lost a full-term baby in childbirth. I went home to help keep house there for a while, and soon left again, never to return.

During all these years my relationship with my father had grown rockier and rockier. We argued about everything, and when I started working for him at his Columbia School of Music in my early 20s, matters did not improve. I taught music theory, piano, ear training, and sight singing; I also did office work, and his bookkeeper taught me some basic accounting. I finally moved on to work elsewhere.

My relationship with my father improved somewhat during this time, inasmuch as I was no longer living with or working for him, but it was not until I met my husband, Philip H. Smith, Jr., that it really took an upturn. Daddy liked Phil from the start and was also happy, probably relieved, to know that I was to be married—he'd always been worried about this and had introduced me, unsuccessfully, to a number of men *he* considered eligible.

After our wedding in 1953, Phil and I lived near Washington, in Accokeek, Maryland. Daddy and Mercia used to come out to visit and were never critical of us for living in an unfinished house.

After living in Colombia for a year, Phil and I rented a huge, very old six-bedroom house on P Street, a block from Dupont Circle, my old stamping grounds. I began to study the guitar with my father, something I had not done since the age of 10, and soon began to look forward to our weekly meetings. He asked my advice about many arrangements of music for guitar and seemed to respect my opinion. Some of the music I arranged during this period turned up after his death and will be published. The four of them,

Daddy, Mercia, Ted, and David, often visited our family which now included two daughters. Daddy and Mercia were loving grandparents.

My father and I now got along very well: in part I had learned to avoid subjects on which he and I disagreed, and in part I think we both mellowed. In 1961 we moved to Croton-on-Hudson. Daddy and Mercia came up to visit immediately after the birth of our third child. They also came on other visits, and we frequently went to see them on Sleepy Hollow Road and, after 1965, on Wynford Drive.

In 1980 when Mercia was 70 she had a stroke, and by 1983 she and Daddy were really unable to remain in their house. Even their longtime cleaning lady had died! So with my brother Ted's persuasion and help, they moved to the Hermitage, a retirement home in Alexandria, in November 1983. Mercia was happy to make the move, and my father finally adjusted.

The great shock was that Mercia, who was 16 years younger than Sophocles, died first and very suddenly from a couple of massive heart attacks in November 1985. Daddy had to go into the Hermitage nursing wing, euphemistically called Health Care Wing. Without Mercia, he waned dramatically, stopped eating, and died there in his sleep on 26 February 1986.

Although my father and I had a varied relationship, I see many things differently now that I am an adult. I certainly see that he had problems with his wives, which distracted him from his children. Also he was ambitious and wanted to put most of his focus on his career, particularly on those people who could help him in his career. This preoccupation no doubt took away from family time, although as a poorly educated Greek man he probably had little idea of how to spend what would now be called quality time with his wife and children. I am happy that he and I ended up as friends.

APPENDIX H

"Segovia and I" by Sophocles Papas

Soon after [several radio performances in the early 20s] I came to the attention of the then secretary of the Greek Legation, Mr. Christos Diamantopoulos, a handsome and cultured bachelor who liked my music. Through him I met the then military attaché of the Spanish Embassy, Major Vitoriano Casajus [later to become godfather (padrino) to Elisabeth Papas], also a bachelor, who was familiar with the guitar because he had heard his compatriot Andrés Segovia in Spain.

When I told Casajus that Andrés Segovia was about to make his New York debut in Town Hall, he told me that he had a military assignment out west and could not attend the concert, but he gave me a letter of recommendation which I presented to Segovia immediately after the concert. When I realized Segovia did not know English, I spoke to him in French, and he invited me to have coffee with him the next morning at his hotel. Naturally I told him that I was a guitar teacher, and that I was performing on the radio. He seemed glad to know someone who could help his career, especially someone Major Casajus had recommended.

Eventually I was responsible for Segovia giving three concerts in Washington in the early 30s under the auspices of Elena de Sayn....She was familiar with the Russian guitar with its fandango tuning GBDGBD, similar to baroque guitar tuning. I persuaded her to bring him to play under the sponsorship of her Washington Performing Arts Society.[1] I also urged colleagues in other cities to sponsor Segovia concerts. The ones I remember off hand were given in Detroit, Niagara Falls, and Philadelphia.

We met again in Detroit and Philadelphia, thanks to my reliable old Ford, and I never missed one of his New York programs....I learned about the cultivation of right-hand fingernails, which weren't used then.

Later on Segovia played [in Washington] in the Willard Hotel ballroom, then at the Shoreham [Hotel] ballroom. Every performance was a huge success.[2]

"Reflections on the Present State of the Classical Guitar" by Sophocles Papas

This could be the golden age for the classical guitar. The instrument has a distinguished history, an extensive literature, a role on the concert stage. Above all it has its patron saint in Andrés Segovia!

In spite of this, the guitar remains in this country a somewhat exclusive and comparatively unappreciated instrument. (To avoid confusion, let me interject here that throughout this article when I refer to the guitar I mean the classical and not the plectrum guitar.)

Guitar manufacturers and merchants could do a great deal to remedy this deplorable situation if they take the initiative. They would render the artistic world a service at the same time that they enhanced their material profits from the guitar.

Here are some of the areas in which the need for stimulus can be observed by those sensitive to the over-all requirements of the guitar.

First, there is the field of education. The study of the guitar is difficult to pursue in most cities in the United States. There is a shortage of good teachers, a scarcity of opportunity to hear the instrument, and precious few whose knowledge of playing and hearing the guitar doesn't stop abruptly with the strumming of simple chords to accompany simpler songs.

We need to start with the young to remove this barrier of ignorance. Guitar should be introduced into the music curriculum of the public school system. Here let me say that the Boston Music Company has made a beginning for such an addition by publishing a guitar section for its TUNE A DAY series. Inadequate though this may be, since it carries the student such a short way, it is nevertheless a step in the right direction. Whenever a promising student appears, he or she should receive encouragement—and scholarship money should be made available.

Guitar should be made an accredited major in the music departments of all our colleges and universities.

Second, the guitar lacks publicity and cries out for promotion. Annual conventions of music merchants would be an ideal time and place to focus more spotlight on the guitar. A concert featuring a solo guitarist could easily have sufficient musical value to be one of the central attractions. Workshop sessions could be conducted in connection with conventions by men who know the guitar and its music.

Beyond this, publication devoted to events in the musical world should not let the story of the classical guitar lie dormant. Its praises should be sung in editorials and in learned and popular articles. An exchange of ideas through correspondence should be encouraged. Each year I receive letters from many plectrum guitarists who either sense or know for sure that the guitar has riches far beyond what they are tasting—and these letters invariably ask for guidance and instruction. Interest in a worthwhile cause may be difficult to start, but once ignited, the spark rapidly kindles into flame.

Third, there is not enough modern music written for the classical guitar. We need to do more than revive a brilliant past—we need to ensure a promising future. Composers with a particular talent for the guitar should be sought out and encouraged. Special works should be commissioned for the guitar. In this field, the circular theory of development would work in our favor. The more the guitar is played, the more compositions would be written for it; the more modern music for the guitar appeared in print, the more it would be played. This should make the guitar attractive to composers.

Fourth, practical improvements in the guitar are needed. Manufacturers do the guitar a disservice when they fail to produce a satisfactory beginner's instrument at a modest price. Far too many inexpensive guitars sacrifice even accuracy in a foolish attempt to save a fraction of a cent on unworthy strings. Other common faults are improper adjustment of the bridge, the nut, and the frets. Above all, the beginner's instrument should be easy to play. A high-action guitar is an added discouragement to weak, undisciplined fingers. There is time enough to seek perfection of quality in tone and concert volume when the hands have mastered the technique! Manufacturers are penny wise and pound foolish in not realizing that every beginner who is helped over the hump is a potential customer for a good instrument.

I think it possible to develop practical ways to work in these four areas I have outlined. The guitar manufacturers and publishers should form their own organizations within their own music Associations. Then begin by appointing a special committee within its organization to work out specific approaches to the various problems. I myself would welcome correspondence on the subject.

A true crusade for complete acceptance of the guitar must always be led by those of us who love the instrument and long to share it with others.

We must be the evangelists...and an easy kind of evangelism it is, too. For the guitar needs no excuses; no pretenses have to be fostered in its behalf. It needs only to be universally heard and understood to be universally appreciated.[1]

"Scale Practice and Why" by Sophocles Papas

Many ambitious students of the guitar, despite years of study, remain frustrated by a single, basic obstacle: their failure to develop speed in their playing.

Not everyone has this problem. To a very small number of players, velocity comes naturally. The great majority of players, however, will find it necessary to supply, by their own labor, what nature has failed to provide. In this program, nothing is more important than the diligent and systematic study of the scales.

In the preface to his *Diatonic Major and Minor Scales* Segovia says:

> The student who wishes to acquire a firm technique on the guitar should not neglect the patient study of scales. If he practices them two hours a day, he will correct faulty hand positions, gradually increase the strength of the fingers, and prepare the joints for later speed studies. Thanks to the independence and elasticity which the fingers develop through the study of scales, the student will soon acquire a quality which is very difficult to gain later: physical beauty of sound. I say physical, because sonority and its infinite shadings are not the result of stubborn will power but spring from the innate excellence of the spirit.
>
> In order to derive the greatest possible benefit from the following exercises, play them slowly and vigorously at first, more lightly and rapidly later. In one hour of scales may be condensed many hours of arduous exercises which are frequently futile. The practice of scales enables one to solve a greater number of technical problems in a shorter time than the study of any other exercise.

The student would do well to clip this quotation and place it on his music stand as a constant reminder that there is no substitute for the practice of scales; they should occupy one-third of the total time available to him for practice.

Various approaches to scale work should be explored for the sake of a well-rounded technique. The student should practice them using various combinations of right-hand fingers (including the right-hand thumb alone, on all strings), principally apoyando, but using the tirando stroke as well. The thumb should be moved only from the second joint. These exercises should be supplemented, of course, with daily practice of the chromatic scales—in single notes and octaves—and of arpeggios and slurs.

In all this the metronome will prove useful in different ways to different people. Daily practice with the metronome is mainly recommended to the student whose problem is a tendency to accelerate. Others will find that the metronome, used once a week, serves as a helpful and tangible evidence of progress, registering faithfully every gain in velocity and providing not only encouragement but the stimulus for consistent and, if possible, more practice.

APPENDIX K

Sandburg-Papas Correspondence

The first letter was sent to Harbert, Michigan, where Sandburg was then living. The letterfoot says "The Guitar Is a Miniature Orchestra in Itself... Beethoven."

Headquarters, Segovia Society, Inc., for the Advancement of the Classic Guitar, 2000 N Street, N.W., Washington, D.C., September 1, 1945
Dear Mr. Sandburg: I must take this opportunity to once again express the pleasure with which I heard you speak last summer at the Washington Watergate Concert. I always enjoy art in whatever form it may be expressed, but rarely as much as I enjoyed your dramatic Lincoln presentation. I hope that it shall be my pleasure to hear you again soon. In the meantime, I must be satisfied with reading your incomparable poetry.

I also want to gratefully thank you for your offer to help the Segovia Society. I would have written you much sooner as to our progress, but printing is still a long slow process. We have some material at the printers now, but nothing is completed, as yet. I shall, of course, forward the literature as it comes off the press.

At the time of our meeting, you mentioned the fact that you have written several poems about the guitar. As I told you then, it will be a privilege to accept whatever you might choose to contribute. Even before reading those poems which you select, I feel safe in saying that whatever you offer will not only add to our publication, but will actually raise its level. Be assured that your works will be in good company, for such people as the National Geographic's Frederick Simpich, the great Segovia, and Olin Downes have also offered to submit articles.[1]

We hope to publish the first issue of The Guitar some time early next spring. You will be interested to hear the aims we have established. These will be forwarded to you in printed form in the near future. They are: —

1. To foster appreciation of the music of the guitar as revived and revitalized by the modern genius of Andrés Segovia.

2. To establish a magazine devoted to the art of the classic guitar; to organize an annual competition for compositions and performances on the guitar; to originate scholarships for talented guitarists.

3. To extend membership invitations to music lovers and art patrons throughout the country by the formation of Segovia Society Chapters in leading cities.

MEMBERSHIP

1. Donor	$100
2. Cooperating Annual Membership	25
3. Active Annual Membership	5

Another interesting bit of news is the fact that we have dedicated a room (in my school of music) to the Segovia Society. It is newly redecorated and refurnished so as to be fitting and "in atmosphere" for musical meetings of Segovia members. Your American Songbook and album records are among the most popular pastimes of the guests. I certainly hope that you'll be able to stop by at the Segovia Room next time you are in Washington.

Before closing, I must compliment you on the beautiful spread you received in *Life* magazine. To be mentioned in *Life* is honor enough, but to have several pages devoted to you and your wife, as well as your home—and even your goats!—is kudos beyond words. Having been raised in Greece, which is a goat country, I envy your rustic mode of life.

Thanking you for your courtesy and hoping to hear from you soon, I am, Sincerely,

[signed] Sophocles Papas

The next letter also came from the Segovia Society.

September 9, 1946

My dear Mr. Sandburg: We are very grateful for your prompt response in joining our organization, and are proud to have such a distinguished personage as a member.

Your membership card is enclosed; also a copy of the revised By-Laws of the society. These By-Laws will be printed and sent to all members.

Colonel La Farge[2] is already out of the Army and has left Washington for Santa Fe, where he will make his home.

Mr. Segovia is in Montevideo preparing for his next tour. When I mentioned your name to him last winter he was very glad to learn of your interest in our group and told me about the "American Song Bag," which he appreciates. I hope that your paths will cross again in the near future.

We are preparing a Bulletin which we hope to have published this fall. You will receive a copy.

I trust you are enjoying a cool summer.
Sincerely yours,
[signed] Sophocles Papas, Secretary, Segovia Society

Papas's next letter was apparently lost in the mail when Sandburg moved in the late fall of 1945 from Harbert to Connemara, his farm in western North Carolina. The next letter was undated.

[Fall 1945?]
Dear Mr. Sandburg: Some weeks ago I wrote you at the old Michigan address, and I suppose that the letter was not forwarded. So I'm addressing you again and hope that you can oblige us.

We are expecting to get another issue of the Segovia Society bulletin into the press in the near future, and hope that we may have one of your promised "pieces of writing" for publication in it.

We have on hand an article from Mr. Segovia and are gathering other worthwhile material so you can be assured of being in good company. The membership is looking forward to hearing from you as promised in your much appreciated letter to our president Oliver La Farge; and the bulletin editor is hoping that we may have your contribution within the next few weeks so that it can be included in the bulletin issue which will reach the public about the middle of April.

Segovia's concert here last month was a great success and we wish that you might have been with us. The Society is flourishing with a post-war revitalization.

These paragraphs tell you the story and bring you up to the minute on the activities of the Society in Washington. Thank you in advance for whatever material you may see fit to contribute to the next issue of the Segovia Society Bulletin. If you are ever in Washington, and will let me know slightly in advance, that you are coming, the Society will be happy to entertain you as an honored member.

Sincerely,

[signed] Sophocles Papas, Secretary, The Segovia Society of Washington

The following letter was written on Columbia School of Music letterhead: Columbia School of Music, 2000 N Street, N.W. Washington 6, D.C.

July 27, 1955

Dear Mr. Sandburg: The last time we saw each other was several years ago with Andrés Segovia at the Modern Museum of Art in New York. You looked the picture of health then and appeared to be in vigorous health when I saw you on Ed Murrow's program. Mrs. Papas and I enjoyed it very much.

I am enclosing some literature, *The Story of the Spanish Guitar* and a short sketch of Sol Snyder[3] who is planning a full recital early in September to which I will be happy to have you and Mrs. Sandburg as my guests if you could arrange to be in Washington then. Sol has to play before September 14 when he begins college.

With kind personal regards, I am

Yours sincerely,

[signed]Sophocles Papas

Sandburg replied:

May 1, 1958

Brother Papas: You will permit me, I hope to stand and give you salutations. Sometimes the word "Teacher" is one of the finest words in language. In its highest and noblest sense that word goes for you in the work you have done with your pupil Marjorie Braye.[4] Years ago I had a belief that she had aptitudes and instinct about the guitar. And this week I have heard her play that noble instrument. In americanese we can say of her, "she's a natural." I feel gay about you as teacher and her as pupil. So I would pin a rose on you as a great teacher and some nice bashful flower on her as a pupil who has toiled and wrought. I hope to be seeing you in Washington ere the year is out.

Faithfully yours,

[signed] Carl Sandburg

[6 January 1959]

Dear Mercia Papas: Comes along from you and Sophocles the extraordinary and beautiful Segovia album.[5] Let me thank you and say, "Hosannah in the highest!" I hope to be seeing you sometime when in Washington. I can never forget the good results that Sophocles got in teaching Marjorie Braye. She naturally loves the guitar but he brought her along. I want to hear you fellows talk about Segovia who is a hero worthy of the love and admiration lavished on him.

Ever good wishes,

[signed] Carl Sandburg

This reply from Papas as on a revised version of the Columbia letterhead: Columbia Music Company, Publishers-Importers-Jobbers, T/A The Guitar Shop, Sophocles Papas, Dealers in Musical Merchandise, 1816 M Street, N.W., Washington 6, D.C. MEtropolitan 8-1419.[6]

October 9, 1959

Dear Mr. Sandburg: By this time you must have received the John Williams record which I sent you two weeks ago. I hope you like it.

I spent the night with the Brayes on Sept. 13th and was told I missed you by one day.

Marjorie told me that you like the Catalan song I arranged and that you will write words for it. I am delighted with the prospect as I would like to publish it as a song.

With kind regards from both Mrs. Papas and me with the hope that we will see you soon.

Cordially yours,

[signed] Sophocles Papas

SP/ml

August 23, 1960

Dear Carl, I am taking time out from Marjorie's [Braye] to write this brief note. I've been wanting to write you and send you the music and words of the song, "Whiskey Won't Hurt This Baby" which was given to me for you by Mr. Janney of the National Geographic. I will make a clear copy of the words and music over the weekend and mail it to you early next week at the Bel-Air Hotel.[7]

The book that I am sending along with Bill [Braye] is a copy of your "Complete Poems" which I hope you will be kind enough to autograph. I gave the book as a graduation present to the son of Mrs. William O. Douglas[8] because his mother had told me what a great admirer he is of yours. His name is Michael Davidson. I would be grateful if you could inscribe it for me and I know he will be happy and proud. I am also slipping some clippings in the book for you that I think might interest you.

Your work with the new picture with George Stevens sounds very interesting and I know that when I view it I will see evidence of your fine hand. Mercia joins me in sending you our love.

Affectionately,

[signed] Sophocles

This next letter was written on some notepaper my father had made up with the heading, "A ♪ from Sophocles Papas."

September 8, 1960

Dear Carl: I got the message through our regular channel[9] that you inscribed Mike Davidson's book in your usual generous way and I appreciate your doing so. I know that Mike will be very thrilled. Bill[10] has not returned yet.

I am enclosing a song with words and chords which I think you will like. If you wish me to do anything else in connection with it, please let me know.

Affectionately,

[signed] Sophocles

November 24, 1960

Dear Carl: I am writing this letter on Thanksgiving Day. There are so many things I am thankful for-too many to enumerate—but I will mention a few of the most important ones.

I am thankful to God for having given me Mercia, Betty, Teddy and David. I am thankful for our good health. I am thankful to America which gave me the opportunity to enjoy the life I live. I am so very thankful for the friendship of Carl Sandburg, Andrés Segovia, the Brayes, and a host of others.

I am thankful for a Democratic President who I am sure will make this country greater, stronger and an even better place to live.

And now I want to thank you personally for the copy of "Playboy" containing your beautiful poems, and for your new book "Wind Song" sent to David. He received it 2 weeks before publication date.

You will be interested to know that the Guitar Shop is now carrying the Sandburg books on its shelves.

I get weekly reports from Marjorie about your activities, and I am particularly happy to learn the good news about you and Helga.[11]

We are all looking forward to seeing you on your next trip to Washington. Affectionately yours,

[signed] Sophocles

Papas received a prompt reply from Sandburg in response to Papas's note about his grandson.

19 January 1961

Dear Sophocles: Your letter about you and John and me is lovely to have! When I see you I will give you some sweet anecdotes about his earlier years. He tried to say "Grandpa" and it came out "Buppong." Among a few persons that name Buppong clings. Marjorie and Bill always use it. He [John Carl] and his sister and I formed a trio that could sing certain songs; once we went before an audience of United Presbyterians who had a camp near us in Connemara. I gave him and his sister[12] that lute-shaped guitar, a brother to the one that Marje had,[13] and I suppose he fooled with it and became fascinated. You should have him sleep sometime, or at least have a nap, in the bed where Segovia has slept; you can call that corner of your house Saints' Rest.

Please know my heart is soft about what you see with such certainty in my grandson. Love to you and Mercia.

Ever yours,

[signed] Carl

The following is undated but was probably written about March 1961. The letterhead is printed on GEORGE STEVENS PRODUCTIONS letterhead.

FROM: CARL SANDBURG, [March 1961?]

Dear Sophocles:

You have struck some great chords in the personality of John Carl. He has launched out into the world of music beyond the guitar in a very interesting way. One sentence of a letter from him reads, "Using the guitar has greatly increased my knowledge of symphonies and the converse." He follows this with a citation that you might read at anytime when you feel somewhat useless. The sentence goes: "Mr. Papas's teaching is one of the most enlightening experiences I have had and I think he is one of the best and greatest men I know or can hope to meet." And this boy is seldom given to extravagant speech. He has nothing less than deep adoration and gratitude about you.

[signed] Carl

Interview: Remembering Sophocles Papas:
A Conversation with Carlos Barbosa-Lima by Seth Himmelhoch,
27 June 1986

Sophocles Papas was very significant in the development of the guitar in the U.S. in general; he was a kind of pioneer and devoted his life to teaching. He came to the United States in the teens, just before World War I. He was not dedicated to music then, although he had begun to study the guitar. Little by little he became absorbed by music. His first wife was a musician, which probably helped in dedicating his life to music. He taught other instruments in the early 20s: the banjo, ukulele, other stringed instruments. But the guitar was already a favorite and he began gradually to devote more and more time to it.

He was important to the world of the guitar, not only because of his teaching, but because of his association with Segovia which began in the late 20s, from Segovia's 1928 debut in Town Hall. The association was very important, very close; Segovia was a kind of mentor to Papas.

Papas liked people and liked teaching; from the beginning he knew he was not a composer or a performer, but he was good enough to play on the radio; he played accessible pieces to his own possibility. He was also good socially, in relating to people, a great gift because this way he introduced the guitar in certain areas, to people not before exposed to it. It takes someone like him with this natural gift of relating to people. He also had the advantage of speaking several languages, which left him in a good position in the Depression.

He began to get better and better students and the guitar became more popular. By the 1940s Papas was very much established as major teacher. He was known around country and even everyone overseas knew about him. He also knew how to lay the groundwork for promoters and how to open doors for performers. He was interested in anyone who showed any promise as a performer and in different styles of music. His circle of influence in Washington spread to other cities. He was one of the few people who went beyond boundaries of the guitar. He was accepted in other music circles, and was respected by impressarios, record producers, and producers in New York and so on. He was a very generous man, which was important in opening doors. He gave lots of parties and introduced people. I know from my own experience that he always introduced students and other people he was trying to promote. He always introduced people to me; in fact he introduced me to Charlie Byrd. There was always good food around. The guitar and good food seem to go together. His wife [Mercia] was a great cook, and she made Greek dishes although she was herself an American.

I first heard of Papas in Brazil when I was in my teens, from Savio, my teacher, who in turn heard about him through Bonfá. But later I developed a close friendship with the Papas family. I enjoyed his humor, which lasted until nearly the end of his life.

I played in the United States first in 1967, under the sponsorship of the Brazilian Minister of Foreign Affairs. Also Ambassador [Vasco Leitão] da Cunha had heard me in Brazil at a party, and he happened to know Papas and connected us through one of my recordings. Then when I came to play in Washington for the first time, the Ambassador phoned Papas. (The Ambassador happened to speak Greek also, although Papas had excellent English.) Papas called the critics and people to come to the concert. Papas truly made the concert a real event. His reputation was strong so the critics came because they respected Papas. He then opened doors for me even in Europe—through his contacts. He introduced me to other guitar people and to important people. I didn't speak much English, but we managed with a combination of French, Spanish, Italian, and English. He had a European background but became Americanized too, which made a good bridge culturally.[1]

Once he [Papas] told me to phone him after my concert and to come to see him. I made an appointment with him, but I never got there because the person driving me had a flat tire. I thought he would think, oh, just another South American with no sense of time. I had to phone him and with the same mixture of languages made a new appointment with him; he was very understanding. Papas continued to make connections for me and ultimately introduced me to Segovia. The Ambassador of Brazil helped me to get a scholarship to go to Spain to work with Segovia. Papas encouraged me to go there; in fact, he insisted. And I'm glad I went: I won three prizes.

He took a great interest in my career. He knew that I came from a not-wealthy family, and that I needed financial support to make it in music. Papas gave me a kind of extension of family, and I helped him with his publishing company by doing arranging, writing out manuscripts, and so forth. Papas published my Scarlatti transcriptions, which Bob Bialek, head of Discount Records, had produced, and other music of mine, such as the Mignone [Etudes]. He had good instinct about what to publish, what would be successful and he published a balance of artistic and commercially successful works. He was open to other music, and became very interested in Brazilian music.

He began the publishing business himself, back in the 20s, out of necessity because not much guitar music was available. At that time he mainly made arrangements and published the music for students. He began with the easier things, then published from the traditional guitar literature. Then from his teaching experience, he published the technical exercises and later the Segovia scales. The scales are the most popular book he published, and even today it is seen and used everywhere. It came from his association with Segovia.

He helped me by sending out my recordings. But I didn't study with him and in no way did I adopt his style.

I was kind of shy and in fact spoiled when I came to the U.S., but he gave me support and the confidence to keep going. He helped me in my social and thus career relationships, as well as in my business efforts—going to the right places, for example. He told me that you cannot rush things, that "who rushes, stumbles," and thus helped me build my career.

In 1970 he invited me to stay several months at his home, so I wouldn't have to spend money on a hotel.[2] I built a close friendship with him and he gave me the parental protection I had had from my own family in Brazil. I helped him by copying manuscripts and this saved him money. I found it fun to do and it was helpful; also I learned the editing process. I learned lots about the music business from Papas, which I need to know because you have to edit music for the guitar, even Ginastera's work. But I learned lots from him, especially about fingering. Until the year 1972–1973 I was away from Brazil about half of every year. The rate of exchange got worse and worse, so I began teaching at Carnegie-Mellon. This was my first teaching experience, and Papas helped me with the philosophy and psychology of teaching, especially how to get the best from your students. After being on the faculty from 1974–1977, I finally moved to New York in 1980. From the mid-70s I spent lots of time at his house. We took walks and talked philosophically. He had incredible energy and was always creative and still socially active and interested in people. He accepted that his old age was coming.

Now he had some enemies, some of them people who had been helped by him but then turned against him. Ultimately he even had a falling out with Segovia but some very late correspondence indicates that it was patched up.[3]

In 1974 I arranged Papas's first trip to Brazil, to a guitar festival in Porto Alegre. He was on the jury of this international competition. Mercia went too and visited my family in São Paulo and Rio. We also took some side trips, to my country house; he enjoyed the rough roads because, as he said, they were like Greek roads. Later, in the mid-1970s, when Papas began to give up students, he went again to Brazil and simply astounded people with his energy. The Brazilian press gave him incredibly good coverage when he was there. He was received as if he were a secretary of state, but in fact he was a statesman of the guitar. He really was the center of the guitar scene, and not only in Washington.

He lived to be 92. He was a man of great vitality, although he didn't do much exercise—just walked a couple of blocks. But he always had a short nap, like so many Europeans and South Americans. He was privileged to have good health and a healthy attitude to life. He worried just about the necessary things—a good philosophy. He was wise and very young at heart, youthful. At the same time he was very businesslike, therefore successful. He got annoyed with people who didn't behave correctly. He ate anything he wanted. He kept going by his inner being and this collapsed when Mercia died. After Mercia died he was a bit confused but was aware of her death.

Once Charlie Byrd and I made a tribute to him. He was living in the retirement home, but he came to the nightclub and enjoyed it.

In a general sense I think he felt that he had accomplished his mission. He had raised a family: from his first wife he had a daughter, Elisabeth, who is also a musician; her husband is a professor and they live in Canada. From Mercia he had two sons, Theodore and David. Mercia was so generous, dynamic, a remarkable person, and very important in his life. He was a humanitarian. He enjoyed teaching. He made many close friends of his pupils. Many came to take guitar just as a hobby, but wound up being close friends. He had a big bar in his house, he always had fun, people playing, enjoying people and music. The hospitality he and Mercia offered was genuine and generous.

Without his presence I don't think the guitar would have taken off the way it did. The guitar was his vehicle of contribution to mankind.

APPENDIX M

Duarte-Papas Correspondence

11 June 1969
Dear Sophocles, I had a letter from A.S. last week and he said nothing about his eye operation,[1] surprisingly, but seemed more concerned about the baby the cook is expecting. He is studying my Catalan Folk-Song Variations for next season.
Jack

[undated, probably 1970]
Dear Jack, Antonio Carlos Barbosa-Lima was rechristened Carlos Barbosa by Andrés. He is gifted and the latest of Andrés' protégés. Carlos has just completed two records for Westminster. #1 contains "Nine Scarlatti Sonatas" to be published by CMC and #2 has various pieces including your Prelude.
Sophocles

1 April 1970
Dear Sophocles, I read that Andrés and Emilita are expecting issue. This is fantastic—an even more incredible achievement than his continuing concert tours! This will surely subtract years from his age. Emilita has been the best possible thing that could have happened to him—always to be depended upon to do the right thing at the right time!!!
Jack

30 April 1970
Dear Sophocles, We three (including 'The Athenian Duo'[2]) had tea with Andrés and Emilita on Monday and found him in marvellous health and spirits. Emilita flew here to join him, despite being in her ninth month, and they seem to have decided to stay here to have the baby in England.

We had Carlos [Barbosa-Lima] here several times and found him a good player, an outstanding sight-reader (in that he gets to the heart of the music as he reads it—and even plays the fingering!), and a lovely person. He even travelled out here on the underground to see us for 15 minutes on his last day—to say thank you for the hospitality. Most unusual.
Jack

1 June 1970

Dear Jack, Mercia and I were delighted to read in the papers about Andrés' new son. I will write to them in Madrid the end of this week.

I am happy you found Carlos to be a good musician and fine person.
Sophocles

5 June 1970,

Dear Sophocles, We visited Emilita twice in hospital and she seems in good shape, except that latterly she has had some over-lactation (due to Carlos Andrés' laziness in taking his food) with consequent discomfort. They left today for Madrid and were delighted with the medical attention they got here—which was one of the two reasons for having the baby in London. Andrés is in fine form, as interested as ever in everything and everyone. I am writing a suite of three pieces (two of which he has seen) to celebrate the arrival of C.A.S.[3] He has already promised to record them! That is saying something when one remembers they are not even completed yet.
Jack

13 July 1970

Dear Jack, You must have written [to me] before receiving mine re the "Three Songs Without Words." I am anxious to publish them.
Sophocles

31 July 1970

Dear Sophocles, I wrote (now a matter of weeks ago, I think) to say that:
(i) I had no objection at all to your publishing the "Three Songs Without Words" for Carlos Andrés, BUT
(ii) I know well (in this case, perhaps better than you!) how Andrés works with new compositions. He frequently asks for changes to be made, sometimes quite radical and, until this possibility is fully allowed for, I shall not publish the work at all. He made his original 'promise' to record the work before it was even finished and, in his last letter of about a week ago, he renewed that promise—but I know that even then he had not closely studied it. I am now awaiting another, promised, letter following his closer examination of this and another work. When he is finally satisfied, I will publish—but not until then.

(iii) I wrote to him telling him of the proposal that he finger the work (and you would publish it) and also await his response to this. I'm sure he would not finger it and release the fingering until, once again, he is finally satisfied. So, the ball is in his court.

Jack

[undated, probably 1970]

Dear Sophocles, The further copies of 'For My Friends' are not yet to hand but, if they have come by surface mail (as would be logical), this is maybe not surprising. Andrés wrote that he had received a copy from you and says that some of the pieces are 'remarkable nice'! Whilst it is not my place to comment on that aspect of it, I must say the publication itself is 'remarkable nice'! Congratulations.⁴

Jack

15 August 1970

Dear Jack, I too heard from Andrés about the "Three Songs" and he is agreeable to my publishing the work but he added 'when am I going to find time to finger it?' We will see. He is currently preparing works of Carulli, Giuliani and Sor for a new record.

Sophocles

10 April 1971

Dear Sophocles, Andrés was here until today and he and Emilita visited us. He gave the most wonderful concert I have ever heard from him, in the Festival Hall, with four encores and a standing ovation. He has promised to put the "Three Songs Without Words" in his next "normal" record and, with luck, to put it in his programmes next season.

Jack

8 December 1971

Dear Sophocles, Is there any word from Andrés yet about the three Songs Without Words? I have reports that Emilita is expecting another new Segovia—if so, I cannot even visualise when he will retire—he has even stopped talking about it for the first time in many years!

Jack

15 August 1972

Dear Sophocles, I'm sure the bad N.Y. concert (about which I had other reports) was at least in part due to his disturbed state of mind following Emilita's miscarriage.[5]

Jack

3 April 1973

Dear Sophocles, I shall of course be delighted to stay with you.[6] Carlos wrote, in a letter I got today also, that he is also with you—and has often spoken warmly of the times he has been your guest.

Jack

20 May 1973

Dear Sophocles, The homeward trail was a very smooth one and I was back here by 2.00 p.m. on Friday. One hour later Carlos (B-L) arrived for a few minutes to leave a suitcase whilst he is away. He returns on 5 June for a little time.

I want to take this early opportunity to thank you and Mercia for your warm hospitality and kindness. These were qualities I experienced throughout my whole trip but nowhere more than with you, nor was there anywhere where I felt so much at home. It was a heart-warming experience. Beyond that I have high regard for the good and devoted work you have done for the guitar, and equal respect for the success you have had. I imagine there are few in the world who can equal your record. My affectionate regards to Mercia.

Jack

21 August 1973

Dear Jack, As I mentioned before I am semi-retired from the business of teaching and have given up all extraneous activities for health reasons. During the past three years I have suffered slight symptoms of heart disease, which my doctor said could become more pronounced and debilitating unless I stop involving myself in activities which aggravate and cause tensions.[7]

Sophocles

15 July 1974

Dear Sophocles and Mercia, We really enjoyed our visit to your home and the lovely chats. Have you seen Carlos lately? He stayed a few days with us in April. We had a reception for him to meet Jack's pupils and had a very good time and a house-full. The pupils were delighted by his playing. We rate him now in the top flight of players, after Segovia, Bream and Williams, both in temperament, musicality, technique—everything that goes to make an outstanding performer. Jack is recommending his name everywhere he can.
Dorothy Duarte[8]

1 January 1976

Dear Sophocles, Andrés is incredible. He was here in October, gave the worst concert he has ever given in London (bothered by a bad first string—he had to use a second instead) and then, a few days later, gave another just out of London which was, I am told, unbelievably wonderful. He had dinner here and one of my pupils came to play for him—with good success. His views are certainly becoming more "liberal" in relation to early music. My pupil played some Dowland to him, with the 3rd string at F sharp, and a capo at the third fret—this provoked no comment whatsoever—a few years ago it would have done, and no mistake. More, I have a magnificent 11-string guitar, tuned G through G, for playing early music (and nothing else) and I played it for Andrés. Instead of the expected caustic comment, he said "It is very beautiful." Which it is—both in sound and in workmanship.

I didn't remind Andrés of the songs without words—I leave that to you.
Jack

20 April 1977

Dear Jack, I am glad you are busy. We seem to keep busy also with the publications along with the aggravations. I have four pupils also—just to keep my hand in. Actually I missed teaching and should not have retired all at once.

We are now looking forward to the InterAmerican Festival in May. Carlos will play a concerto composed by Mignone and dedicated to him. I am going again to Porto Alegre, Brazil, to judge the competition there (last of June and beginning of July).
Sophocles

31 March 1979
Dear Dorothy, Compared to Sophocles and Segovia he [Duarte, who at this time is about to turn 60] is a youngster. Our government honored Segovia on March 11th at the White House at a lovely reception. Sophocles and I were there. 86 years! And he has been playing in concerts since the age of 12.
Mercia

[undated, fall 1979]
Dear Sophocles and Mercia, Lovely to hear about you and Sophocles being at the White House in honour of Segovia. I agree that both Sophocles and Segovia are truly remarkable for their ages; the fact that they have both loved their work and also younger women has kept them young. I think you have helped Sophocles very much, as has also Emilita helped Segovia. Don't you agree?
Dorothy

3 October 1979
Dear Sophocles and Mercia, Andrés sent a warm telegram of greetings which was read out at the end of the concert [John Duarte 60th Birthday Concert] to great applause.

I hope you are in good health. Jack is very fit and has had a most memorable and moving week.
Dorothy

NOTES

NOTES TO CHAPTER 1

1   The year has sometimes been given as 1894.
2   Greece continued to use the Julian calendar until 1923.
3   Born 17 September 1892.
4   Born 23 May 1897.
5   Born 28 April 1900.
6   Born respectively 28 May 1903 and 11 April 1906.
7   Today I have various cousins in Ioannina and Athens. My father sponsored one of them, his nephew Nicholas, son of Miltiades, who earned a Ph.D. in biochemistry from George Washington University in 1956. He has now retired from his work in research at the Department of Clinical Pathology at the National Institutes of Health near Washington, D.C.
8   "Mass Aggie" became Massachusetts State College in 1931, and the University of Massachusetts in 1947. The campus has always been in Amherst.
9   He must have continued to work hard at his English because I found in his possessions a Greek-English dictionary he bought and inscribed in 1916, from J.I. Williams, Bookseller, 533 Main Street, Worcester, Mass.
10 Probably from his father.
11 During the war, German names and words were especially to be avoided, so that Weiss became White and sauerkraut became "liberty cabbage." See the Dallman interview transcription, p. 116.
12 Boyd's *Directory*.
13 Vournas died at the age of 98 on 31 October 1995.
14 Boyd's *Directory*.
15 I remember my father sending me off to Dr. Pete's at his 18th and I Street office whenever I had a cold.
16 Unidentified.
17 Dallman interview.
18 Dallman interview.
19 In later life my father was ashamed of having been a waiter. And he was horrified when, in 1948, I worked for a while as a waitress at a Hot Shoppe, a Washington restaurant chain.
20 See appendices A and B for his residence and studio addresses.
21 Dallman interview. "Tiptoe through the Tulips" was written in 1929 by Al Dubin and Joe Burke. In later years Tiny Tim made it very popular.
22 *Time*, 2 October 1950.
23 Dallman interview.

24 WJSV later became WTOP.

25 Godfrey, 1903–1983, was an announcer and entertainer on the NBC network in Washington from 1930–1934.

26 1860–1947.

27 1872–1962.

28 Seth Himmelhoch interview with Carlos Barbosa-Lima, 27 June 1986.

29 She lived from 1885–1980 and left a huge collection of guitar music, now catalogued, to California State University at Northridge. My father corresponded with her in May 1975 about the possibility of publishing her arrangements of the Bach Inventions, presumably the Two-Part, for two guitars. See Sharpe in bibliography.

30 Dallman interview.

31 Boyd's *Directory*.

32 The music store put an ad in the directory in 1922: in addition to the company's name, address, and phone (Main 2231), Robinson's advertised: "Music of Every Kind, Musical Instruments, Musical Merchandise, Brunswick Phonographs and Records, Columbia Records and Grafonolas." In a later ad in the early 30s, Robinson's advertises "reproducing/reenacting pianos." Boyd's *Directory*.

33 I have been unable to fully identify some of the music mentioned.

34 The "Air" was dedicated to Mrs. Sydney Gest, who conducted the Junior Etude column in *Etude* magazine; originally published in 1929, this piece is still published by Columbia Music (CO 102).

35 Dedicated to Marian [Alvord], then the newborn daughter of the brother of my godmother, Katharine Alvord, and a close friend of mine in the late 30s.

36 Possibly the German composer Heinrich Albert.

37 On inspection of this Chopin prelude, Columbia Music publication CO 146, I find that only the last chord has five notes.

38 See extracts from interview with Carlos Barbosa-Lima in chapter 7.

39 The buildings of this school are now part of Walter Reed Hospital.

40 Scrapbook.

41 Variant spelling of Ioannina.

42 Those studying with Papas paid $2 per 1/2 hour lesson.

43 Dallman interview.

44 In a house at 42 Moy Road, which I visited a few years ago. Her father was a tobacconist and had a shop on Queen Street, still a main downtown street in Cardiff.

45 Unidentified banjoist.

46 1872–1944.

47 *The Haskin Letter*, 5 July 1928.

48 Unidentified.

49 William Mitchell, 1879–1936, was an early crusader for air power. About 1922 he was given permission to bomb an old ship from the air; the bomb destroyed the ship but somehow the government not only remained unconvinced but court-martialed him

for disobeying some orders. My father said that my mother typed Mitchell's defense for his court-martial.

50 This music club recently celebrated its hundredth anniversary.

51 Unidentified clipping.

52 Dallman interview.

53 Tobias Matthay was a well-known London piano teacher and originator of a method of piano-teaching popular in Britain in the early twentieth century; his name is variously spelled as Matthais, Mattay, and Matthay.

54 It was not until I was doing research for this book that I found out my mother had played the violin.

55 Vol. 3, No. 3.

56 Included in the music being published in connection with this book.

57 His date of birth is uncertain, possibly 1883, but he died in 1967.

58 It looked even more derelict in late 1995: then the front window said "Palm Reader."

59 Spellman has a collection of old and rare guitars in his shop at 1218 Connecticut. See article about Spellman's shop in *The Washington Post Magazine* of 15 September 1991, p. 15.

60 Eveline's English was no doubt better than his at that time (although everyone who knew my father would agree that his English became quite fluent and idiomatic in later life). And of course my mother knew musical terminology as well.

61 Founded in 1908, *Crescendo* was published by H.F. Odell Co., Boston, and existed until 1933, when it combined with *Frets*.

62 Foden resigned in vol. 19, no. 9, March 1927.

63 August 1929.

64 The Willard, built in 1850, was restored in 1976.

65 Scrapbook.

66 A friend of mine writes of the aftermath of Black Tuesday (29 October 1929): "the bread lines, the lost houses, the unemployment, bank closings, failed businesses, bankruptcies, suicides, and the horrendous losses of the well-to-do, especially those who had bought stocks on the margin. 'It is the only time I can remember seeing my father weep.'" Personal correspondence, 2 September 1995.

67 Hoover had proposed such a cut, but FDR ordered the 15-percent cut on 29 March 1933, in the first month of his presidency. See *New York Times* of this date.

68 I still have this fine instrument; it has a marvelous action and is capable of great variations in tone.

69 *Washington Star*, 16 December 1958.

70 After study at the Peabody and in Europe, Eversman had sung German roles at the Metropolitan Opera until they dropped the German repertoire during World War I. *Star*, 5 January 1954.

71 *Star*, 21 June 1942.

72 And apartment mate; they lived for a long time in an apartment building called the Cecil at 1026 15th Street, N.W., which was raised in 1903 and razed in 1958. See the book *Best Addresses* by James M. Goode, published in 1988 in Washington, D.C., by the Smithsonian Institution.

73 Included in the music being published in connection with this book.

74 Scrapbook.

75 No doubt the C Minor, Op. 28, No. 20, and the A Major, Op. 28, No. 7.

76 *Sunday Star* of 13 August 1933.

77 Eversman died on 2 February 1974; *Star*, 4 February 1974.

78 "Sophocles Papas," *Crescendo* (July 1927), p. 30.

79 I can just remember sitting in a darkened movie theater while my mother played the piano for a silent film.

NOTES TO CHAPTER 2

1 *New York Times*, 4 June 1987.

2 The reviews in the New York City newspapers I hunted up are not quite so rhapsodic. Donal Henahan wrote somewhat ambiguously of the "audience who hung on Mr. Segovia's every twang."

3 The Library of Congress was unable to verify this concert or give the date.

4 See review in *Alexandria Gazette*, 13 December 1984.

5 See entire article in appendix H.

6 Dallman interview.

7 Presumably Op. 77. However, Peter Segal told me that Segovia in fact played the last movement of this sonata "pretty much as published." Where he left out many chords was in the beginning of the fourth movement of the Ponce "Sonata Romántica, Hommage to Schubert." Perhaps my father confused the two.

8 Dallman interview.

9 Dallman interview.

10 Dallman interview.

11 She was editor of the "Junior Etude," a column in the *Etude* from 1919 through 1930.

12 This was the article "Trail Blazers of the Guitar" in the March, April, and May 1929 issues of *Mastertone*. See article in appendix F.

13 Dallman interview.

14 This piece by Tárrega is really entitled "Recuerdos de la Alhambra."

15 It is said that Alirio Díaz holds a collection of Segovia programs; it would be interesting to study Segovia's developing repertoire.

16 An obituary for William L. Shirer, the journalist, who died in December 1993, mentioned that in the early 30s Shirer and his Viennese first wife shared a house in Spain with Segovia and his wife. *New York Times*, 30 December 1993.

17 In any case, gut strings presented a challenge to any guitarist. Segovia found that if the room where he was playing was warm, cold, or damp, the gut strings frayed; he had to carry scissors to cut away the wisps. And of course he often had to retune during a piece, a dexterity in itself.

18 For slight variants and more details of this story, see the articles "Guitar Strings before and after Albert Augustine," *Guitar Review*, Vol. 17, 1955, pp. 145–48; *Du Pont Magazine*, March/April 1982, Wilmington, DE 19898; and *New Yorker*, 7 March 1983. Augustine's wife Rose, formerly a teacher of mathematics and physics, has continued with the development of strings since her husband's death in 1967, as well as publication of *Guitar Review*, a guitar quarterly.

19 The do-re-mi-fa-so system of note names.

20 To Herbert Mitgang, the father of one of his pupils and a prominent book critic.

21 And the fifty-year relationship was still a warm one in 1978. See Segovia letter of 23 April 1978. Appendix D consists of the correspondence between Papas and Segovia.

22 *The Guitar: The History, the Music, the Players*, p. 35.

23 *Etude*, 57:610.

24 1888–1974; he died on 6 March, immediately after having had lunch with Segovia.

25 Letter, Alvino Rey to Elisabeth Papas Smith, 31 January 1994.

26 *Washington Star*, 1 November 1964.

27 Washington Performing Arts Society, formerly Hayes Concert Bureau.

28 *Newsweek*, 6:27, 12 October 1935.

29 *Newsweek*, 43:58, 25 January 1954.

30 *Newsweek*, 53:84, 19 January 1959, "Music: They Stay Quiet."

31 Note that this checks with a birth date of 1893; in the past there has been some discussion of his year of birth.

32 *Newsweek*, 107:73, 5 May 1986. Also see Segovia letter of 4 August 1971.

33 Teacher of guitar at the University of Southern California and extraordinary arranger of works for guitar, especially for the Los Angeles Guitar Quartet.

34 *New York Times*, 6 March 1983.

35 See Segovia letter of 4 August 1971. Also see the Duarte-Papas correspondence in appendix M for comments on Barbosa-Lima and also on Segovia.

NOTES TO CHAPTER 3

1 The instrumentation of the group varied from performance to performance.

2 Unidentified clipping of 10 April 1929.

3 Unidentified, but probably some kind of institution to help the poor.

4 A flurry of press coverage centered on Eddie Gilmore's reporting on the USSR, especially an article in *Time* of 22 June 1953. While in Moscow he had married Russian ballerina Tamara Chernashova, but she had not been allowed to leave Russia until this date, i.e., after Stalin's death. Eddie wrote a book about his marriage, *Me and My Russian Wife*, and she in turn wrote *Me and My American Husband*.

5 I remember very clearly when my father, my mother Eveline, and I lived in the apartment building at 3039 Macomb Street, N.W. It was still standing in 1991, although clearly it has been refurbished.

6 *Washington Star,* 3 January 1941; 6 May 1947; 6 October 1967.

7 This building has been torn down and replaced with a modern office building.

8 "Serenata Arabe."

9 Scrapbook.

10 Unidentified.

11 Probably a reference to ensembles directed by Walter Kaye Bauer.

12 Unidentified clipping.

13 *The Haskin Letter,* 3 December 1934.

14 Undated.

15 1901–1988.

16 The Nosegay is still in business but at a new location.

17 Unidentified clipping.

18 Smeck died in New York City in 1993.

19 Unidentified clipping.

20 Undated.

21 Elisabeth Papas Smith; my father always called me Betty.

22 Dallman interview.

23 As of 1991 the building had been converted to an office building, but the flight of marble stairs that used to lead up to the restaurant remains intact.

24 See Segovia letter of 26 January 1937.

25 Undated letter, Marjorie Braye to "Buppong" (Carl Sandburg), probably late 1960. The guitar she owned is one of the Washburn twins.

26 The history of guitar societies in Washington is a tangled web because of splits and schisms.

27 Alvino is still married to Luise, one of the four King sisters who sang popular music in harmony and were almost as popular as the Andrews sisters in the 30s and 40s.

28 Pare Lorentz, Sr., died in 1992.

29 Letter, Alvino Rey to Elisabeth Papas Smith, 31 January 1994.

30 Undated.

31 If you go to The Guitar Shop in Washington and look through the bars into the Spellman collection of guitars, you will see a folding screen with storks on a dark-green background; this screen set the color scheme for the living room of the decorated apartment.

32 Member of a prominent Washington family.

33 Unidentified clipping.

34 The building itself has been torn down, and the corner is now occupied by a motel, Embassy Square Suites.

35 *Star,* undated.

36 This address is very close to the present-day Clarendon Metro station.

37 *The Colonial Call*: "The Voice of Colonial Village," was a small publication put out by a huge apartment complex in Arlington, Virginia, called Colonial Village. It still exists and is near the Court House Metro station in Arlington.

38 His second wife, Paquita Madriguera, was the sister of composer Enrique Madriguera and mother of Beatriz. See Segovia letter of 29 November 1967. Little is known about Segovia's first wife.

39 Dallman interview.

40 *Time*, 29 June 1936.

41 Mercia must have come along sometimes, but Theodore, their first child, was born in December 1940, so she would not have gone on long car trips after the spring of 1940.

42 My father had discovered that, if he drove at a certain speed, he had green lights all the way.

43 A wooden paddle fitted with a rubber ball attached by a rubber string.

NOTES TO CHAPTER 4

1 *Time*, 2 October 1950.

2 *Time*, 5 January 1962.

3 The renowned flamenco guitarist died on 3 March 1993 at the age of 89.

4 New York City, 14 October 1944. Translated from Spanish.

5 See "Explanation of Symbols" in CO 117, for example.

6 *Blue Ridge Herald*, Purcellville, Virginia, Thursday, 24 April 1941.

7 Papas's last name was so often spelled Pappas that he listed himself under both spellings in the phone book.

8 I wonder if the interviewer had mixed up etymology and entomology.

9 *Washington Times-Herald*, v. 10, no. 322, 18 December 1948.

10 June-August issue, 1957.

11 *Guitar News*, July-August 1959, no. 49, pp. 19–20.

12 July-August 1959.

13 July-August 1960. Bistyga later became Mrs. John Marlow.

NOTES TO CHAPTER 5

1 *School Band and Orchestra Musician*, vol. 1, no. 1.

2 *Fretted Instrument News, The Official Organ of the American Guild of Banjoists, Mandolinists and Guitarists*, Providence, RI, vol. 17, no. 6, November-December 1948.

3 This is reminiscent of Schumann, who mutilated a couple of fingers with a device which was designed to increase his reach but did not.

4 Dorothy said in 1992 that the habit was so strongly ingrained that even today she still has the urge to plant her little finger.

5 This was during the time of meat rationing and shortages, and when I was home from school, I was usually the one sent to the store to buy meat. This meant standing in line, but I usually came home with another can of the dreaded Spam.

6 Coelho, a singer and guitarist, was Segovia's longtime companion from Manaus, Brazil. Currently she lives in Rio.

7 Dorothy de Goede, interviewed by Elisabeth Papas Smith, and correspondence, 1992, 1993, 1994.

8 Letter, Marcelle Jones to Elisabeth Papas Smith, 17 March 1993.

9 Papas had been a judge at a competition there in 1963; see chapter 8.

10 1909–1995.

11 Letter, Jim Moran to Marcelle Jones, 13 December 1973.

12 Letter, Jim Moran to Elisabeth Papas Smith, 9 April 1992.

13 Letter, Gregory d'Alessio to Steve Allen, 9 April 1954.

14 D'Alessio spoke with me on the phone twice in 1992. He said that he was not well and therefore did not see people, so I could not go to interview him. His death was announced in the *New York Times* on 18 August 1993. He is survived by his wife of 55 years, Terry.

15 Niven, p. 598.

16 See pictures in the d'Alessio book, especially one of Segovia tuning Sandburg's Washburn.

17 D'Alessio, pp. 53–54.

18 P. 153, d'Alessio; by permission of the author.

19 D'Alessio, pp. 152–53. The Washburn company is still in business making guitars and banjos.

20 Duarte's piece for this contest appears in *Guitar Review* of June 1959; Yoghourtian's, March 1960.

21 His son, John W. Tanno of Riverside, California, wrote, "The guitar is a very fine instrument made by the 'Sobrinos de Domingo Esteso' of Madrid in 1944. I still enjoy playing it from time to time for it is a very responsive guitar with a deep and rich flamenco sound." Letter, John Tanno to Elisabeth Papas Smith, 29 March 1993.

22 D'Alessio, p. 62,.

23 1914–1996.

24 Letter, Jesús Silva to Marcelle Jones, 15 December 1973.

25 CO 322.

26 Letter, Charlie Byrd to Sophocles Papas.

27 Quoted in the *Post*, obituary written by Joseph McLellan, 27 February 1986.

28 Phone conversation, Elisabeth Papas Smith and Charlie Byrd, 17 April 1991.

29 "Profile: Solomon H. Snyder," *Scientific American*, August 91, pp. 29–30, v. 265, no. 2.

30 Letter, Sol Snyder to Elisabeth Papas Smith, 21 May 1990.

31 *New York Times*, 25 May 1993.

32 *Medicine*, Scientific American Special Issue/1993, p. 22.

33 Letter, Sol Snyder to Sophocles Papas, 14 December 1982.

34 *New York Times*, 25 May 1993.

NOTES TO CHAPTER 6

1 She was the editor of CO 147, *Three Dances* by J. Ferrer.

2 In 1991 the College Music Directory listed more than 1,000 schools teaching guitar. Their programs vary widely, from those with only a part-time teacher and a few students to those awarding a Doctor of Musical Arts in Guitar, such as Florida State University in Tallahassee.

3 *Sunday Star*, vol. 3, 1960.

4 Sharpe, pp. 48–49.

5 This appears to be true in the 90s as well. A clue is the position of the left thumb: those who began by playing any form of popular guitar used their thumbs to fret on the low E string, and they usually have a problem holding the thumb in the "classical" support position.

6 In the fall of 1992 John Marlow died suddenly from a heart attack at the age of 52.

7 *Washington Post*, 15 October 1961.

8 In New York City on 27–28 August 1966.

9 Vol. 3, p. 18.

10 See appendix I.

11 This is probably a mixup between the school's certification for veterans and my father's teaching at American University.

12 Sharpe, pp. 48–49.

13 *Evening Star* article by John Fialka, 4 March 1967.

14 Sachiko Berry kindly translated the article.

15 Some of Papas's instruments are now in the Yale Collection.

16 Unidentified.

17 Guitarists still debate about her death whenever the subject comes up. One usually reliable source believes she had an embolism.

18 These are the dense woods of tall trees which Mercia loved so much and where she fed the birds so generously.

19 *Post*, 17 September 1972, D1, p. 10.

20 *Soundboard*, Fall 1993, p. 13.

21 *Soundboard*, Fall 1993, p. 11.

22 *Guitar Player*, vol. 9, no. 2, February 1975, pp. 12, 35, 36, 45.

23 Konstanto is a short form or nickname for Konstantina.

24 The Washington area guitar society continues to change. In early 1993 a new one formed, called the Classical Guitar Society of Washington, D.C., which I thought was the last possible permutation of those words. And then in 1995 I received an announcement from the Washington Guitar Society. This reincarnation appears to be

doing well: during the past year it sponsored several concerts in its John E. Marlow Series, including performances by Manuel Barrueco and Scott Tennant.

25 According to a *Post* article dated 28 April 1978.

26 Both of these works are Columbia Music Company publications. *Canonic Variations*, CO 221, and *Four Preludes*, CO 252.

NOTES TO CHAPTER 7

1 Some relevant material appears in chapter 3.

2 See appendix K for the entire correspondence. The University of Illinois kindly sent me copies of some of the letters.

3 Marjorie Braye and her husband Bill knew the Sandburgs in Michigan, before their move to Flat Rock; she died on 22 July 1967, the same day as Sandburg. I remember her very well from parties at my father's house.

4 According to a Connemara brochure, Sandburg was listening to some Segovia records the afternoon before he died.

5 Undated letter from Marjorie Braye to "Buppong" (Carl Sandburg), probably late 1960. The guitar she owned is one of the Washburn twins.

6 As to Sandburg's sense of humor, "Papas felt that 'his conversation was studded with humor.' North Callahan, *Carl Sandburg: Lincoln of Our Literature*, p. 111.

7 Probably one of the pieces in CO 232.

8 Apparently this did not take place. As far as I know, my father never published any songs with words.

9 Sandburg went to Hollywood in July 1960 to work with George Stevens on "The Greatest Story Ever Told," and again in the summer of 1963.

10 Wife of William O. Douglas, Associate Justice of the Supreme Court from 1939 to 1975.

11 This refers to the reconciliation between Sandburg and his daughter. Their rift and reconciliation are well documented in her book *"Where Love Begins"*.

12 Karen Paula, born 28 June 1943. She must have also studied with Papas.

13 Who also studied with Papas.

14 Letter, John Carl Steichen to Elisabeth Papas Smith, 17 February 1993.

15 *Life and Works*, Callahan, p. 226.

16 The chords are I II6 V7 VI IV♭3 V7 I; Ron Purcell kindly identified the manuscript-hand as Segovia's.

17 See a wonderful picture in d'Alessio's book of Segovia reaching across Sandburg to correct the guitar's tuning.

18 This must have been the above-mentioned progression.

19 Mitgang, pp. 470–71.

20 Letter, Papas to Mitgang, 11 April 1967.

21 Carbon copy of typewritten Sandburg essay, found among Papas papers; source unknown.

22 Sandburg, Helga, pp. 17, 284.

23 Ibid., pp. 284, 286.

24 Sandburg, Helga, pp. 286–90.

25 *Washington Star*, 5 July 1969.

26 Used by permission. See Permissions. The poem first appeared in *Guitar Review*, v. 2, no. 12, 1951. It also appears in d'Alessio, p. 29.

27 Although quoted in d'Alessio's book on page 153, this poem comes originally from the book *The Sandburg Range* published by Harcourt, Brace in 1957.

28 Alice Artzt, interviewed by Elisabeth Papas Smith, March 1991, New York.

29 This is the d'Alessio connection: he was a prominent member of this society.

30 See Segovia letter of 3 January 1938.

31 CO 193.

32 See appendix L for a transcript of the entire interview.

33 Barbosa-Lima must be referring to Papas's translations for the VA during the Depression.

34 Mrs. Duarte not only often took over Jack's voluminous correspondence, but also really organized and ran the Cannington summer schools until the early 1990s.

35 In 1961 polyglot Papas went to Munich to visit Hermann Hauser, the guitarmaker. In his hotel he noticed an ad for a Greek restaurant, so he thought he would take some Greek food to Hauser. He went to the restaurant and said "Good evening" to the waiter in Greek. The waiter said in French, "I don't speak Greek; I'm Italian." Papas said, "OK, we'll speak French or Italian." He looked over the menu printed in German and Greek. When he gave the waiter his order, the waiter called the order in Spanish to the kitchen. "Is the cook Spanish?" asked Papas. "No, he's Greek, but he doesn't know any German and I don't know any Greek." Used by permission of Wayne State University Archives of Labor and Urban Affairs.

36 Except for some short-term study with Segovia, and probably some master classes with other guitarists, Barbosa-Lima studied largely on his own after leaving Brazil and Savio, his teacher there.

37 My brothers and I remember well the room known as "Carlos's room."

38 Letter, Alberto Ginastera to Carlos Barbosa-Lima, 12 May 1976.

39 Columbia publishes several of Duarte's works, and he is still composing, in his 70s.

40 Artzt interview.

41 After my husband and I acquired Columbia Music in 1989, I resumed correspondence with Jack, and we published more of his works.

42 These songs are without words, after Mendelssohn.

43 Actually Daddy was not quite 92 when Mercia died.

44 Letter, Jack Duarte to Elisabeth Papas Smith, 28 November 1989.

45 In a 1990 letter, after I had mentioned that I was writing this biography, Jack wrote to me: "I've always heard that he [Sophocles] helped out Segovia financially in the early years; will that be confirmed or denied?" I have never heard anything like this from any

source, and given my father's married-with-child status in the Depression, I doubt he could have spared any cash support. Nor is there any evidence of this in the Segovia correspondence. He did, of course, help in some ways by hosting Segovia and acting as his chauffeur.

46 Dallman interview.

47 Clare Callahan, interviewed by Elisabeth Papas Smith, 2 December 1993.

48 Possibly Michael Kasha.

49 Junior Village was a home for homeless children from the District of Columbia.

50 *Star*, 5 July 1969, and letter, Alvino Rey to Elisabeth Papas Smith, 31 January 1994.

51 *Post*, 24 May 1977.

NOTES TO CHAPTER 8

1 The first was probably when he and Mercia were living on Calvert Street, in the summer of 1947, when he was nearly 54. He and Mercia went to Santa Fe and Taos, to visit Oliver La Farge. In 1963 Papas went alone to Greece en route to judge a guitar competition in Orense, Spain; this was his first return since leaving about 1914. And in October 1972 he and Mercia went on a guided tour of Greece and Istanbul.

2 They also reveal copious doodling, which skill, in both form and extent, I apparently inherited from my father.

3 Unsigned letter to Elisabeth Papas Smith.

4 However, Papas was harsh with some students (see John Carl Steichen and Helga Sandburg in chapter 7), even hitting their hands sometimes!

5 Irene Rosenfeld, interviewed by Elisabeth Papas Smith, Spring 1990.

6 "Sophocles Papas: 50 Years of Classical Guitar," by Jerry Dallman, *Guitar Player*, February 1975, p.12 ff.

7 Shearer and Papas had a rift of some kind in the 60s, probably when they were both teaching at American University.

8 See Segovia letter of 30 July 1971.

9 *Post*, McLellan's obituary of Papas, 27 February 1986.

10 Later published as CO 300.

11 He is probably referring to CO 197, *Slur Exercises and Chromatic Octaves*, published in 1970.

12 Letter, Jim Skinger to Elisabeth Papas Smith, 26 June 1992.

13 See article on scales in appendix J.

14 Unsigned letter to Papas, second page and signature missing.

15 Letter, Kevin F. Kersten to Sophocles Papas, 12 February 1973.

16 Letter, Kersten to Elisabeth Papas Smith, 2 May 1991.

17 Letter, Lloyd Ultan to Sophocles Papas, 28 November 1967.

18 This is certainly an unusual combination of instruments, but he must have been trying to include my pianist-mother.

19 This includes Stephen Foster tunes, Christmas carols, and *My Bonnie Lies over the Ocean.*

20 Which includes *Maytime Waltz, Santa Lucia, Robin Adair, Annie Laurie, Aloha Oe, Drink to Me Only with Thine Eyes, Traumerei, Song of the Volga Boatman,* and *Swanee River,* with dedications mostly to students, including Walter Howe, a longtime student and a very good banjo player.

21 Which includes *Long, Long Ago, Merry Widow Waltz, My Bonnie, Aloha Oe, O Sole Mio, The Last Rose of Summer, Silent Night, Cielito Lindo,* and *The Minstrel Boy,* with dedications to students, including the family ophthalmologist Dr. G. V. Simpson, whom I well remember.

22 Undated.

23 CO 127.

24 CO 197.

25 Since 1988 the company has tried to increase the number of chamber works for guitar as well as duos, trios, and quartets. Papas never published any chamber music after the first banjo works.

26 CO 170a and b.

27 For Papas's own account of one competition, see his article, "Report of the International Competition," which appeared in *Frets,* December 1961.

28 "Bulletin of the Society of the Classical Guitar," Winter 65, v. 18, no. 3, p. 15, 409 East 50th Street, New York 22, N.Y.; now defunct.

29 *Washington Star,* Sunday Magazine, 5 March 1967.

30 *Washington Post,* obituary, 27 February 1986.

31 Translation courtesy of Philip H. Smith, Jr.

32 Article by Elinor Lee, 15 December 1953.

NOTES TO CHAPTER 9

1 Pp. 469–70.

2 Translation from the Italian.

3 Letter, Solomon Snyder to Elisabeth Papas Smith, 21 May 1990.

4 Ted has a Ph.D. in mathematics and works for a small company in Virginia, near Washington. David is a professional photographer who works for a large company in San Francisco and also does a fair bit of free-lance work.

5 27 February 1986.

6 *Washington Post,* 8 June 1986.

7 *Washington Post,* "The Papas Protégés: Washington Guitar Quintet's Debut Dedication" by Richard Harrington, n.d., probably June 1986.

8 *Post,* 6 June 86, article entitled "Wood Vibrations: Celebrating the Music of the Guitar and Harpsichord," by Joseph McLellan.

9 *Washington Post,* Limelight, "The Guitar Times Five," Sunday, 6 January 1991, p. G3.

10 Charles McCardell, review of Washington Guitar Quintet in Performing Arts, *Washington Post*, 15 January 1991.

11 *Guitar Review*, no. 65, pp. 24–25.

12 *Soundboard*, Winter 1985–86, vol. 12, no. 4, cover, pp. 353–54.

13 Courtesy Wayne State University.

14 During this party Sandburg announced that "Marjorie Braye, Chicago virtuoso of the guitar," would play. She was a Papas pupil and old friend of the Sandburgs. She began to play a simple study but broke off saying, "I'm not used to the guitar—my fingernails are broken—my hand is sore."

15 Phone conversation, 18 March 1991.

16 *Post*, "On the Town," Friday, 15 January 1993.

NOTES TO APPENDIX B

1 In the 1922 directory, Robinson's Music Store has a display ad on p. 192: Phone Main 2231, Music of Every Kind, Musical Instruments, Musical Merchandise, Brunswick Phonographs and Records, Columbia Records and Grafonolas; Robinson's in an early 30s ad advertises "Reproducing/Reenacting Pianos."

NOTES TO APPENDIX C

1 In another version of this recipe, he specifies that the spaghetti is to be served on dinner plates, covered but not mixed with the sauce and heavily sprinkled with grated Greek cheese. This is from an earlier undated newspaper clipping.

NOTES TO APPENDIX D

1 On the back of this letter is a list in my father's handwriting:
   stool
   music
   guitar
   strings

2 Elisabeth Constantina Papas.

3 Theodore Thomas Papas, born 30 December 1940.

4 The Carnation Contented Hour was an NBC radio program featuring Percy Faith's Orchestra. It began in 1931 and was sponsored by the Carnation Milk Co. whose ads referred to 'contented cows.'

5 See chapter 2 for more information on strings.

6 Herrlee Glessner Creel was a renowned professor of Chinese. He studied guitar with Daddy, probably when stationed in Washington during World War II; he was interested in using the guitar for therapy and wrote an article entitled "Guitar Therapy."

7 Gaston Doumergue, 1863–1937, was President of France from 1924–1931 and Premier in 1934.

8 I believe Mercia lost a full-term baby in February.

9 She was pregnant with David Stephen Papas at this time.

10 I believe he is referring to Charlie Byrd.

11 Elisabeth Papas Smith's first child was born on 31 August 1954.

12 A Vanderbilt.

13 The daughter of Segovia and Paquita died in her early 30s of pneumonia. Segovia said that this was the greatest tragedy of his life.

14 This was probably one of Segovia's eye operations.

15 The race riots after the assassination of Martin Luther King.

16 Hotel in Washington, D.C., still there, on Connecticut Avenue between L and M Streets.

17 Jack Duarte asked me about these pieces in 1990. I wrote to a few people, but they never turned up.

18 Segovia's article, originally entitled "La Guitarra y Yo," was published as a series in the early issues of *Guitar Review* in both English and Spanish; issues 4, 6, 7, 8, 10, and 13, 1948.

19 But we never arrived: the weather was icy, we slithered off the road into the median, managed to get back on the road safely, took the next exit, and returned to Waterloo for a stiff drink!

20 CO 197.

21 These two pieces are together in print in CO 210.

22 Hurok died suddenly of a heart attack just after Segovia had had lunch with him.

23 See CO 213, "Diferencias sobre un Tema" by J. Muñoz Molleda.

NOTES TO APPENDIX E

1 At times Papas appears to be quoting Segovia, but the quotations marks in the four-part article are inconsistent. I have in general been faithful to the original but have made some corrections in the spelling of proper names.

2 Giuliani's dates are variously given as 1780 or 1781 to 1828 or 1840.

NOTES TO APPENDIX F

1 *Mastertone*, A Fretted Instrument Monthly for Player, Teacher and Dealer, March, April, May 1928, Reprinted by courtesy of the Gibson Musical Instruments Company.

2 Probably the American Guild of Banjoists, Mandolinists, and Guitarists.

NOTES TO APPENDIX G

1 For references to residences and studios, see appendices A and B respectively.
2 After some study with him when I was in my 30s, I have taken it up again since 1990.
3 I started out as a music major but changed to philosophy (aesthetics) as a form of adolescent rebellion: I can't major in music! Both my parents are musicians!
4 My father, who by this time had a fine reputation in the music business, was horrified that I was working as a waitress, although of course in early days he had worked as a waiter.

NOTES TO APPENDIX H

1 See review in *Alexandria Gazette*, Thursday, 13 December 1984.
2 *Guitar Player*, February 1975, vol. 9, no. 2, p. 12, cont. on pp. 35, 36, 45, based on Dallman tapes.

NOTES TO APPENDIX I

1 Reprinted from *Accordion and Guitar World*, Bedford Hills, N.Y., n.d., possibly 1964.

NOTES TO APPENDIX K

1 There is no evidence that Simpich or Downes or Sandburg ever submitted any material.
2 He refers to Oliver La Farge, 1901–1963, author of *Laughing Boy* and other books, who was president of the Segovia Society at this time. See also Segovia letters of 5 April and 18 May 1946, and 29 January 1947.
3 See chapter 5.
4 Marjorie Braye and her husband Bill knew the Sandburgs in Michigan, before their move to Flat Rock; she died 22 July 67, the same day as Sandburg. I remember her very well from parties at my father's house.
5 According to a Connemara brochure, Sandburg was listening to some Segovia records the afternoon before he died.
6 Papas moved to 1816 M in 1956. See appendix B for his studio addresses.
7 Sandburg went to Hollywood in July 1960 to work with George Stevens on "The Greatest Story Ever Told," and again in the summer of 1963.
8 Wife of Associate Justice William O. Douglas of the Supreme Court, from 1939 to 1975.
9 Presumably Marjorie Braye when she took her lesson.
10 Unidentified.
11 This refers to the reconciliation between Sandburg and his daughter. Their rift and reconciliation are well documented in her book *"Where Love Begins"*.

12 Karen Paula.

13 This must be one of the so-called Washburn twins. See d'Alessio material in chapter 5.

NOTES TO APPENDIX L

1 See note 35 to chapter 7.

2 My brothers and I remember well the room known as "Carlos's room."

3 See the Segovia correspondence in appendix D.

NOTES TO APPENDIX M

1 Segovia had problems with his eyes for years, hence the thick glasses. I believe he once had a detached retina caused by bumping into a doorway when sleeping in yet another hotel.

2 A new guitar duo Duarte considered as good as the Lagoya-Presti pair.

3 Carlos Andrés Segovia, the new baby.

4 See CO 183.

5 Apparently she had more than one miscarriage.

6 Duarte was about to come to Washington to conduct master classes at Catholic University.

7 Papas's cardiologist did not allow him to fly to Waterloo, Ontario, for my graduation piano recital on 1 April 1973, but Mercia came.

8 Mrs. Duarte not only often took over Jack's voluminous correspondence, but also really organized and ran the Cannington summer schools until the early 1990s.

BIBLIOGRAPHY

Bobri, Vladimir. *The Segovia Technique*, New York: Macmillan, 1972.

Boyd's *District of Columbia Directory*, R. L. Polk & Co., 911 G St., N.W., also 902 F St., N.W., depending on the date of the volume. This is a fascinating series, available at the Historical Society of Washington, 1307 New Hampshire Ave., and the Martin Luther King Library in Washington. Early volumes contain such notes, in the street-by-street section, as "paved" or "paved with brick."

Buxton, Frank and Bill Owen. *The Big Broadcast: 1920–1950*, Flare/Avon/Viking: New York, 1972.

Callahan, North. *Carl Sandburg: His Life and Works*, University Park and London: Penn State University Press, 1987.

------. *Carl Sandburg: Lincoln of Our Literature*, New York: New York University Press, 1970.

d'Alessio, Gregory. *Old Troubadour: Carl Sandburg with His Guitar Friends*, New York: Walker & Co., 1987.

Dallman, Jerry, interviewer; no. RSS reel/7 13177: Sophocles Papas interview. Sound recording. 4 reels. With book (125 pp.) *Guitar Teaching in the United States: The Life and Work of Sophocles Papas*, based upon interviews with Mr. Papas; published by the Washington Guitar Society, P.O. Box 19512, Washington, D.C., 20036, supported by a grant from NEA, copyright 1978, Washington Guitar Society. The tapes and book are held at the Library of Congress in the Performing Arts Division.

Himmelhoch, Seth, interviewer. Taped interview with Carlos Barbosa-Lima, 27 June 1986.

Kozinn, Allan, et al. *The Guitar: The History, the Music, the Players*, New York: Wm. Morrow & Co., Inc., 1984.

Mitgang, Herbert, ed.. *The Letters of Carl Sandburg*, New York: Harcourt, Brace & World, Inc., 1968. This is not a complete collection of his letters, but it was especially useful for its chronology. Margaret Sandburg told me in 1992 that she and the Sandburg archivist at the University of Illinois are working on a complete collection of Sandburg letters.

New Grove Dictionary of American Music; Vol 3, L–Q, ed. by H. Wiley Hitchcock and Stanley Sadie; Sophocles Papas on pp. 469–70. London: Macmillan Press Ltd., 1986. Tom Heck, who wrote the Papas entry, is a guitarist, archivist, and librarian.

Niven, Penelope. *Carl Sandburg: A Biography*, New York: Chas. Scribner's Sons, 1991.

Sandburg, Helga. *"Where Love Begins"*, New York: Donald I. Fine, Inc., 1989. This book, whose title comes from a Sandburg poem that begins, "There is a place where love begins," tells of the reunion of father and daughter.

Sharpe, A. P. *The Story of the Spanish Guitar*, London: Clifford Essex Music Co., Ltd., 1963. This book, originally published in 1954, was out of print in 1991.

PERIODICALS CONSULTED

Note: I consulted many periodicals in researching this book. The older ones, many of which are out of print, are held in various libraries in North America. Some periodicals consulted were *Accordion and Guitar World*; *Banjo, Mandolin and Guitar*, a British publication; *Crescendo*; *Etude Music Magazine*; *FM Guide*; *Frets*, later to become *Fretts!*, and still later *Music Studio News*; *Fretted Instrument News*; *Guitarists*; *Guitar News*; *Guitar Player*; *Guitar Review*; *Mastertone*, a Gibson publication; *Newsweek*; *New Yorker*; *School Band and Orchestra Musician*, later to become *School Musician*; *Scientific American*; *Soundboard*; and *Time*.

NAME INDEX